INFO-FOBIA

How to Survive
in an Information Society

by

MATTHEW LESKO

Editor: Kurt Samson

Research: Mercedes Sundeen; Mary Ann Martello

Production: Stevan and Beth Meserve

Illustrations: Martha Murphy

Cover Design: Lester Zaiontz

Cover Photo: Gary Landsman

Suit: Monogram It All, Inc.

Title: Doris Mattingly

INFO-FOBIA — HOW TO SURVIVE IN AN INFORMATION SOCIETY
Copyright © 1996 by Matthew Lesko. All rights reserved. Printed in the
United States of America. Published by Information USA, Inc., P.O. Box E,
Kensington, MD 20895; 301-924-0556. Web site: http:\\www.lesko.com.

FIRST EDITION

Library of Congress Cataloging-in-Publication Date

Lesko, Matthew

Info-Fobia — How to Survive in an Information Society

ISBN 1-878346-38-5

Other books written by Matthew Lesko:

Getting Yours: The Complete Guide to Government Money

How to Get Free Tax Help

Information USA

The Computer Data and Database Source Book

The Maternity Sourcebook

Lesko's New Tech Sourcebook

The Investor's Information Sourcebook

The Federal Data Base Finder

The State Database Finder

Government Giveaways for Entrepreneurs III

Lesko's InfoPower III

The Great American Gripe Book

What To Do When You Can't Afford Health Care

1001 Free Goodies and Cheapies

Free Stuff for Seniors

Everything You Need to Run a Business At Home

Free Health Care

Free Legal Help

Table Of Contents

**What's Good And Bad About Computers
and The Internet?** (cont'd)

What's Wrong With Libraries, the Media and High Priced Experts?

The Best Information Is Free

Using Your Telephone To Find Free Experts

Using Your Telephone To Find Free Experts (cont'd)

America's Top 20 Most Frequently Asked Questions

375 Organizations That Will Do Research For You For Free

Animals and Agriculture

Business and Industry

Consumer and Housing

Energy and the Environment

Health

National and World Affairs

Other

Statistics

Introduction

You don't have to be a 20 year-old computer geek to be on the winning side of the information revolution. Some people will get through it nicely without ever owning a computer. The hype of the Internet is just that - hype. For most people, the technology is not there yet. Neither is the available information. The media is creating this wave, but for most, it's making more information problems than it's solving.

Afraid of getting left behind by the Information Superhighway? Guess what? It's not a highway, it's still a jogging path, barely a dirt road. Rest easy, there's still time.

But you shouldn't wait too long - there's too much good information out there if you know where to look. Doctors can be treating you with out-of-date information. Lawyers can be charging you for legal advice you can get for free. More information has been created since 1930 than in the entire history of the world up to that point in time, yet most of us still can't find accurate information to make an informed decision.

The diagnosis is that you and most other Americans are suffering from a bad case of INFORMATION ANXIETY.

We live in the 1990s, with information and research skills developed in the 1940s. Ask any student where to get information and they'll probably point towards the nearest library. That's the same thing I learned 40 years ago. When was the last time you used the library to solve an information problem?

As adults, we're now taught other myths about problem-solving - told to pay high-priced medical, legal and financial experts - or encouraged to purchase an expensive computer and get on the Internet. But high-tech answers require information that is - and always has been - available elsewhere.

If you don't have the money, or are baffled by high-tech mumbo-jumbo, you have a problem-solving tool that is quicker than the Internet, better than the World Wide Web, cheaper than a hard drive and easier to use than a VCR. It's called the telephone. Yet most of us use the phone only to talk to family and friends - and to yell at solicitors. We've never been trained to use the phone as an information tool - but those solicitors have, you bet.

This book will explain a number of tools to help you survive in the information society - things that I have found true in over 20 years of information gathering. You'll learn what's good and bad about each one and when to use them - and when not to use them. Some you'll never even need.

There's no need to suffer from INFO-FOBIA or to be embarrassed about it. We live in the wonderful country, where anyone, whether you're H. Ross Perot or a street cleaner, can get the best information in the world - and most of it for free. This book is not about computers or the Internet, it is about knowing where to turn for the best data. On any subject under the sun.

I believe that the only thing that stops us from doing what we want in life is a lack of accurate information. In this society, this is as unnecessary as buying a cow a hat. This is an INFORMATION SURVIVAL MANUAL. Use it well and it will guide you through the minefields of new technology without a scrape. You are now armed with the best information money cannot buy.

Coping with the Information Explosion

2.

1973 Was the Beginning of the Information Explosion

Some people say the information age began with the first digital computers in the 1940s, or with the advent of commercial television in the 1950s. I don't believe this. No matter how important these developments were, I think the information explosion really started with the oil crisis in 1973. A group of small countries halfway around the world, whose combined economies represented under 10 percent of our own, increased the price of oil by 400 percent and brought this mighty country to its knees.

Before this, most individuals and organizations believed that in order to make good decisions, all the information they needed was either inside their communities, inside their organizations, or inside themselves. That something else - something out of our control and short of war - could have such a drastic effect on both our economy and our lives was the trigger that started a real information explosion. Individuals no longer only had to worry about simply doing a good job. Unfriendly takeovers and corporate downsizing meant you might have a new boss in the morning, or find yourself out on the street two days short of retirement.

Companies in the 1950s and 1960s only had to worry about what was going on within their organization -

sales, inventory, and quality control. Today, old markets disappear
in a heartbeat while new ones
emerge overnight. New technology or even a new piece of legisla-
tion can change the way we do things. A stroke of the
pen or a news report can put a company out of business or make your job obsolete in less time than it takes
ink to dry.

The year 1973 was also a watershed year for our economy and our standard of living. From 1870 to 1973,
the country's Gross Domestic Product (that's all the
stuff this country makes) grew at an average rate of 3.4
percent. From 1973 to 1993, this rate fell to 2.3 percent. This means that before 1973, we were experienc-
ing a growth rate that was 50 percent higher than it is
now. If we had continued at the 3.4 percent rate, the
average family would have at least $5,500 more each
year to spend, and there would have been enough extra money in the economy to buy every homeowner in
American a new house. But since 1973, eight out of
every ten workers have seen their wages fall by an average of 15 percent.

Don't get me confused with Ross Perot. I'm not going
to pull out a bunch of charts to show just how this happened. I'm only saying that after 1973, something very
fundamental changed - and the need for information
has accelerated ever since.

The world became a lot more complex, starting in
1973. To survive, we have to learn an entirely new set

of skills for collecting and processing information for making intelligent decisions.
We can't put it off any longer. We can no
longer solve information problems with research skills that were developed in the
1940s and 1950s. Welcome to the future.

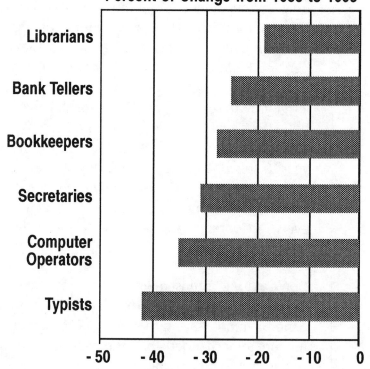

Info Jobs that are Shrinking
Percent of Change from 1983 to 1995

Source: Bureau of Labor Statistics

3. Runaway Change and the Information Explosion

If the 1973 oil crisis kick-started our need for better information on a global scale, the increase in the rate of change itself has helped fuel The Information Explosion. Things are changing faster than ever before, and the best indication of this is the products we develop to help us keep up. Like the chicken or the egg, sometimes it's hard to figure out which came - the change or the products.

Did Federal Express happen because we needed documents quicker to make decisions faster? Or do we now make decisions quicker because Federal Express can deliver overnight? I believe Federal Express was inevitable. Our society is changing so fast that we need information more quickly, simply in order to compete. If we wait two or three days for the regular mail, documents could be out of date by the time we get them. And then came fax machines because Federal Express wasn't fast enough.

What about cellular telephones and beepers? When did telephone calls become so important that you needed a car phone or had to be answered in a plane or at your daughter's soccer game? Phone calls used to wait until you got back to the office unless there was an emergency, but now everything seems to be an emergency - and everyone's got a car phone. If calls aren't answered

immediately, a business situation can change. Deals fall through and careers are jeopardized, simply because of those pig-tail antennae on every car. In less than ten years, we are expected to be reachable at any given moment - even 32,000 feet up.

Change has become a freight train without any brakes. It's not waiting for anyone, and any worker who can't or won't learn to adapt will be left behind. Much of what works in business today probably won't work in the near future. Skills you need today will be obsolete tomorrow. If you understand how something works, you're going to need a refresher course before you know it. People who don't deal well with change will inevitably be hurt, just like those workers who believed they could earn a decent living working in a factory with only a high school education. Those jobs are gone and they're not coming back, and I believe many of the so-called "Angry White Males" in this country resist change and new technology. Instead of adapting when factory jobs began disappearing, they got mad at the system for failing them. In fact, they failed to change.

We've all heard that "the only thing that will remain constant in our society is change." It's become a cliche. But every cliche carries a hard nugget of truth. As the pace of change accelerates, you need to know where to find the best information and how to get it fast. That's what this book is all about.

4. The Growth of Information

More information has been generated in the last 30 years than in the preceding 5,000 years, and the total amount of printed information doubles every eight years. These are the best figures we have. Believe it or not, information increased at a snail's pace between the time we crawled out of caves and we jumped on the moon. But today, with computers in many homes and research institutions everywhere you look, new information is being generated faster than we can record it. It's almost like we're making up for lost time.

Consider this example. Chemical Abstracts is a company that tracks advances in chemical science. It took 31 years, from 1907 to 1937, for the company to collect its first million articles on new advances in chemistry. The next million articles took 18 years to compile. Today, it collects a million articles every 1.7 years.

Information is coming at us at an alarming rate. I recently received an e-mail message that illustrates how far we've come, and how fast. It told me that *Wired* magazine computed that 1.6 billion 3.5 inch floppy diskettes were made in 1990 — and 4.5 billion were produced in 1994. In just four years, the amount of stored information would fill 21 billion books. And even if these floppies are only half-full, or only a third, they still contain more information than any library on earth.

Just 50 years ago, there were only a handful of television channels and several dozen large-circulation magazines. With cable, we now have hundreds of stations, and the number of magazines is in the thousands, and growing.

Along came the Internet. A group called Network Wizards reports that the number of computers with information that you can tap into has increased from 1.3 million in January 1993 to 9.4 million in January 1996 — just three years later.

With such growth, you'd think that getting good information for making decisions has become easier. Instead, it has become more complicated. And that's what fuels our anxiety about all this new information technology — there's simply too much.

Some have said, "Data, data everywhere, but not a thought to think." As the amount of our information increases at an unprecedented rate, it starts to drive the cart, and not the other way around. The truth is, no one's at the wheel, and that can get scary. You need a map and an owner's manual, which is what this book is all about.

What follows are statistics and quotes that show how fast we are moving into a society driven by this torrent of information. Throughout this book, I present charts and graphs that underscore the phenomenon of how fast information sources are increasing — not to scare you, but to arm you. I want to increase your awareness of how much information is out there, and how

best to cope with all of it. But above all, I want to teach you just how to navigate in a flood.

The information you need is there, and it is better than ever. But finding it takes practice, patience, and a good map.

About as many homes now have personal computers as dishwashers.

Source: Odyssey, San Francisco, Ca. and
U.S. Statistical Abstract

Approximately 60% of all U.S. workers are "knowledge workers" — people whose jobs depend on the information they generate and receive over our information infrastructure. As we create new jobs, eight out of ten are in information-intensive sectors of our economy. And these new jobs are well-paying jobs for financial analysts, computer programmers, and other educated workers.

Source: Vice President Al Gore

The number of technical workers in America has grown 300% since 1950.

Source: U.S. Department of Labor

The Library of Congress holds more than 88 million items and receives 31,000 more items each day.

Source: Legal Research Center

Approximately 40% of all the computers used in business are in the United States.

Source: "On the Edge of the Digital Age,"
Minneapolis Star Tribune

In the 1950s, 33% of the U.S. labor force worked in manufacturing. By the 1990s, that number dropped to 17%.
Source: "On the Edge of the Digital Age,"
Minneapolis Star Tribune

U.S. Steel employed 120,000 men and women in 1980. Now it has 20,000 and they're producing more steel than 120,000 did. By the year 2025, there will be no factory workers.
Source: Jeremy Rifkin, author of "The End of Work"

5. The Information Was There before the Computers

A few months back I was doing a talk show, talking about all the information sources that are available for the price of a telephone call. I was going on and on, like I usually do, when all of a sudden the host stopped me in mid-sentence and asked, "Do you mean that all this information was there before computers and the Internet?" I was shocked at the question, but later realized how much it said about what we understand about information and, more importantly, what we don't. It was a great question. Having been in the information business for more than 20 years, I guess I've lost sight of some basics that are important to those just getting interested. So the answer to the question is YES, YES, YES. Except in very special cases, computers don't create information or expertise, they just make it easier to manage or access.

6. The Answers Are Easy, It's the Questions that Are Hard

It's The Questions, Stupid - That's what I'd nail on the wall if I were running a presidential campaign. President Clinton's, 'It's The Economy, Stupid,' sign that hung on the wall of his campaign headquarters may have struck a resounding chord in his first campaign, but whether it's the economy or a common enemy, the hardest part of decision-making has always been asking the right questions, not pointing fingers.

With our breakneck new technology, we now have access to the best information in the world. Yet we continue making ignorant decisions because we're not asking the right questions. There are answers available - you just have to know who to contact and what to ask.

As a nation, we wrestle with big questions. How Can I Become a Millionaire? How Can I Have a Perfect Marriage? Why Am I Unhappy? How Do We Make Our Streets Safe?

Such questions have answers, but they are all very complex. It's much easier to simply throw up our hands and give up. Why? Because there is no one answer - and because we don't know the right questions to ask.

Instead of asking 'How Can I Become a Millionaire,' we should ask for information on which industries have the greatest potential in the next ten years. Instead of 'How Can I Have a Perfect Marriage,' we can easily get information on the major factors that lead to divorce, the psychological impact of children on a relationship and how to cope with the changes, even how to become more caring lovers in order to keep passion alive in our marriages.

Instead of wringing our hands and asking, 'How Do We Make Our Streets Safe?' we need to ask how and where to get information on reducing street crime. There's plenty available - heck, with one phone call you can get a listing of the ten most effective programs that have reduced inner-city crime around the country. All of this data is available, almost automatically, if you know the right questions to ask.

"Data, Data Everywhere, But No One Stops To Think."

This should be the motto for our new, information-based society. Because I write books on finding information, I know that most people understand that the answers are out there, somewhere. But they don't know where to look, or the right questions to ask. I constantly struggle with trying to understand exactly what people really want to know when they ask me questions about finding information. Why do they want to know this? I ask myself, and it helps fine-tune their ques-

tion for me. But this is their homework, not mine. Instead of asking broad, vague, or fuzzy questions - spend time beforehand narrowing your question down as best you can.

I believe there is enough information to create a reference book on just about any subject under the sun. And because I know where to find the data, thinking up the titles would be the hardest part. I can fill in the pages between covers easily enough - it's really just a numbers game. With all the information at our fingertips, it's just a matter of figuring out exactly what we want to know, the right questions to ask, and then making enough telephone calls to locate the best sources. You need to be specific; you need to think first.

7. How to Win the Information Game

To win in this economy, you either need to get information before your competitors or collect better data. Yet most of us act like sheep. We wait for a story to be published in *Time Magazine*, *The Washington Post* or CBS News and then, along with the rest of the flock, we make our decisions. Have you ever seen a motivated sheep that wasn't being chased by a wolf? Or a successful one?

If you read about a promising young company in the news, you'll be waiting in line to buy the stock. And it will be at a higher price than it was the day before. The real winners bought stock long before the story ran because they were way ahead of the media. The information was there before the story appeared, and the smart investors knew it. Relying on reporters for investment tips makes about as much sense as relying on your grandmother's advice about cold remedies.

But just because something appears in the media doesn't mean you're out of the game. If you know where to look, you can still outrun the competition by getting more timely and accurate information from free sources. Also, how often do news reports get all the facts straight? Just read the Corrections column in tomorrow's paper. For more details on why you shouldn't rely on the media for quality information, read chapter 25, "The Media Is Superficial."

8. 80% of Your Information in 20% of Your Time

After many years of successfully locating information and experts that few knew existed, I've come to realize that you can get about 80 percent of the information you seek by dedicating just 20 percent of your time to the search.

And I've learned that much of business follows this 80/20 rule.

Twenty percent of the companies in any given industry will be responsible for 80 percent of all sales. Twenty percent of players on a team will score 80 percent of the points. Information works the same way. No matter how much information you need, it will take you just 20 percent of your time to get 80 percent of the information you need. And the remaining 20 percent will take you four times as long as the first 80 percent. It's almost physics.

I don't know why this happens, but I see it all the time. Whether I'm working on a book, or trying to find out the best options for people looking for long-term health care, I keep running into this 80/20 rule. The phenomenon might be explained by the fact that there is so much information available. It has become pretty easy for most professionals - whether they are doctors, lawyers, investment advisors or journalists - to

do a quick on-line information search and collect enough facts to be armed and dangerous. But if you really want answers, you have to dig further.

Our society runs information, and it comes at us in shotgun blasts fired by these professionals who are armed with just 20 percent of the information - it's not only reckless, it's dangerous. We all want our problems boiled down to a two minute sound-bite so we can feel we're making informed decisions. But no decision, especially the difficult ones, can be made with just two minutes of information. With this kind of thinking we'd still be living in caves. Good decisions take understanding and subject knowledge. Fortunately, both are at our fingertips today. For thousands of years, we have relied on "experts" to guide us through life - doctors, lawyers and teachers. But with personal computers, we can become our own experts. We are the information revolution.

There's a learning curve in gathering information. You can gather a ton of data in a short period of time, and this may be what you want - a ton of data. But as you spend hours sifting through this information, you will discover what I have - that spending a little time to focus your search, and being willing to dig - will yield much better results in far less time.

9. Is the Search Worth It?

Our information society has created so many facts and experts that you could spend every hour of every day just getting information on how to live your life, and have no time left to live it. There's enough information out there that you could spend several days just researching the best toilet paper to buy. But who cares, as long as the roll isn't empty? If you're looking for the exact time, you can call the U.S. Naval Observatory. The observatory's atomic clock is pretty accurate. It will give you the time down to nanoseconds. But who cares? Your wristwatch works, right? It's close enough.

The price of living in an information-rich society is time, and you have to carefully weigh the value of any information you seek against the amount of time it takes you to locate it. It certainly isn't worth it to spend half a day trying to get information on the best toilet paper. But it can be worth a day, a week, a month or even a year getting information on the best career path to chose, the best investments to make, or the best expert if you have an illness or disease.

Life involves choices. First, choosing the right problems to work on, then the proper strategy to solve them. The amount of available information on most any problem is almost without limits and it's increasing at a breakneck pace. None of us can do more than simply

try to keep up. Your time is valuable and limited, so choose your problems wisely.

Full Text Articles Available Online

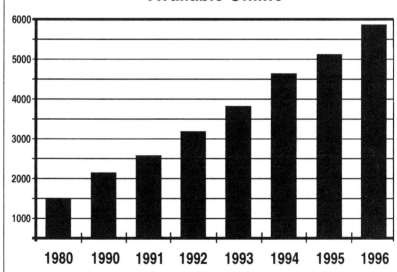

Source: Bibliodata, Needham, MA

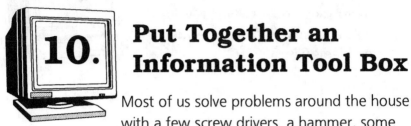

10. Put Together an Information Tool Box

Most of us solve problems around the house with a few screw drivers, a hammer, some nails and a couple of rusty pliers. But when we have big problems, we hire a plumber, a carpenter or some other trade expert who knows what they're doing. Then there are other people who are ready for any home fix-up that comes along. They have a 100-piece socket wrench set, power saws, all the tools.

Gathering information is pretty much the same. There are some people who solve most of their decision-making problems using the media, books, or by asking their family, friends and neighbors. They only call in professionals when they have a complicated problem. Then there are others with computers, fax machines, Internet access and every other new info-gadget that comes along. These people love getting information and enjoy playing with all the latest tools. And they usually get better information, faster.

Let's take this analogy a little further. Years ago, when we were a frontier society, we had to be self-reliant. If a wheel broke, you had to know how to fix it. We built new cities and towns, built our own houses, made our own clothes and grew our own food. But now our society has developed past this point. These skills are no longer required of the average person.

Those who develop these skills do so because they either like to fix things or they need to earn a living with their hands.

Today we need people who are good at fixing things, but we also need information to survive. We no longer have to know how to build a house, but we do need to know how to choose the best careers, or learn the latest treatment for a disease - and this requires gathering accurate information. There are many tools to get this information - some good, some bad. Some are free and others expensive. If you have a lot of money, you can buy the best information in the world.

Some wealthy people paid to have fine houses built for them on the frontier. But back then, most American didn't have that kind of money so they did it themselves. The same holds true in today's information society - most Americans don't have money to buy the information they need, so they have to learn how to get it themselves. And that's why I'm here.

Here's a basic checklist for a great information toolbox:

1)   The telephone.

2)   The government.

3)   The library.

4)   Books and periodicals.

5) Computers.

6) Paid experts.

7) Free experts.

8) The Internet.

9) The media.

This book will tell you what's good and bad about each of these tools, and when you should use each of them. It will also show you how to get information that's even better than what you might get if you had all the money in the world. But unlike the railroad tycoons and mining millionaires of the last century, you don't need a lot of money to get what you want. This book shows you how to get the best information in the world - for free.

What's Good and Bad about Computers and the Internet?

11. Should You Buy a Computer?

From all the ads and stories you see in the media, you would think every house in America has gone high-tech - with at least one personal computer. This Information Revolution has many of us scared. Woe be unto the computer illiterate worker in decades ahead, we're told over and over again. It's estimated that half of the computers in the world are in the US, but compared with the number of televisions, the number seems like small potatoes - and couch potatoes at that. In early 1996, only 35% of US households had computers, compared with 93% with TVs. Still it was a huge jump from 1990, when just 14% of households had a PC. Sure it's growing fast, but before you write yourself off as a techno-holdout, or worry yourself sleepless for not owning a home computer, first ask yourself if you even need one.

If you don't write much, don't handle a lot of data, and don't need to communicate with other computers or users in website chat-boxes, then save your money. These are the three basic functions of computers - it's all they do. Before spending two grand or more for a PC, think about what you want to accomplish in life, and whether a computer will help you achieve your goal. If your needs fall outside of these three categories, think twice - and keep your money in the bank.

How much do you write? Investing in a personal computer probably isn't worthwhile if you only write a few letters each year. But if you are in charge of your club's newsletter - or you want to impress your boss with perfect memos or correspondence from home - then by all means make your life easier with a PC.

If you have students in the house, you almost have to have a computer at home, provided you can afford one. These days, kids are competing against other students who either own or have access to a computer, from the first grade onward. Any student without one is at a considerable disadvantage when it comes to papers, reports and information searches.

Thinking about testing the high-tech waters by first trying one of those fancy electric typewriter/work station/word processors? Forget it. Kick in a few extra dollars and buy a cheap computer instead, even a used one. A computer that's one or two years is old good enough if you are only using it for word processing.

Do you handle a lot of data? What's a lot? More than 25 checks a month or more than 200 names on a mailing list is, and a computer will make your life much easier. But is it worthwhile spending $1,500 or more on a new computer just to process 25 checks a month? Probably not. But if you also write a lot of letters or have a mailing list of more than 500 or 1,000 names - or if you write 50 checks a month - it's time to step into the twentieth century and buy your first computer.

Do you need to retrieve information from other computers? If you don't even have a computer yet, you probably don't know what kind of information is out there, let alone what it might be worth to you.

On-line services - communicating with other computers - is the fastest growing sector of the computer business. The industry has already figured out most of the problems associated with word processing and processing data, and it's very easy to learn. But effectively using on-line services is a different story because the market is growing and changing so rapidly. Whatever you learn about using on-line services today, in a few months you're going to have to learn something new. Still there's a bright side. Like any technology, the longer you wait to get started, the easier these services are likely to be to learn because the industry is working hard to iron out all the bugs.

Going on-line may not be your main reason for buying a computer today, but it probably will be in the future. How would you like to pay all your bills electronically? Or review your bank balance in the middle of the night to see if an important check has cleared? How about being able to get an instant fact sheet on any drug you are taking, or being able to talk to an expert to see why your roses aren't blooming as well as they did last year? Would you like to tour the Louvre in Paris or even the North Pole, without leaving home? I've done all of these things recently, but have they changed my life enough to substantiate the cost of a new computer? That's debatable. None of these services are as easy as simple word processing or data manipulation - and using them can get expensive. Ask anyone who has become infatuated with the electronic autobahn, if you can get them away from the screen for a minute.

As the number of ways you can use computers grows, their price continues to fall, and using them keeps getting easier, sooner or later you'll probably want one. But every day you wait increases the quality and quantity of what will be available once you finally take the plunge. So when in doubt wait, but stay tuned.

12. Should You Be on the Internet?

We are rapidly becoming a nation of webheads and Internet users, yet many people are just as afraid of going on-line as they are of getting left in the dust. As with any new technology that promises so much, it's important to keep a close eye on its capabilities - and your own needs - before making a decision about whether or not to buy in.

The bottom line is that if you're cost conscious and suffer from even a slight case of techno-phobia, you should put off hooking up, at least for now. But if you like computers and are fascinated by their possibilities, that's reason enough to join the cybervillage. If you already have a computer and children in school, homework alone is a powerful argument in favor of logging on. And if you're listening to all the Internet hype and worrying that the world is passing you by on the information autobahn, don't fret - it isn't, yet.

Just one year ago, it was extremely complicated for the average person to log onto the Internet and get anything useful out of it. But that was then, and this is now. The Internet has come a long way in one short year, and every day it's getting easier and easier to use. But it can still be a bumpy ride and very frustrating if you're looking for specific information.

There is a lot of good stuff on the Net - and I mean a lot - but you have to ask yourself if the information is

useful and whether is's worth your time, money and effort to find it? If you log onto the Internet, you can take a walking tour of Paris funded by that city's great museum, The Louvre. Or you can find out the adverse side effects of almost any prescription drug or download scenic photographs of Iceland, brought to you by the Icelandic Tourist Board.

A walking tour of Paris is interesting, even fun. And it can even be very useful if you are planning a trip to Paris. But how many of us are planning a visit? Learning adverse side effects of medications can also be very valuable, even life-saving. You can make a single phone call and get the same information from the Department of Health and Human Services, and a telephone is technology you already know how to use. Scenic photos of Iceland helped my 11-year-old with a world studies project, but it took over an hour and a half to get the photos printed out correctly. We probably could have gotten the pictures faster at the local library.

If you are looking for unique or specific information, the Internet is probably not the best source. Most of what you need might be on the Internet, but it is also already available in a form that does not require a computer. If you're looking for an easier way to get this information, the Internet probably isn't there yet. But it's getting closer.

One way to look at your Internet decision is by putting it into the context of something else. Some people

spend thousands of dollars on an encyclopedia for their children - and only use them
a few times a year. In this case, go on-line
instead. Some people kick vending machines when they don't work. If you do,
THIS NET'S NOT FOR YOU. Then again, it probably will
be someday. But if you're patient, computer literate,
have the time to learn how to navigate the net to find
out what's there and what isn't - and also have an extra $20 or $30 a month to burn, then it's time to join
the on-line army.

What's the Net Worth?

There are two basic types of information on the Internet; sources run by commercial organizations and those operated by government, non-profits or other special interest groups. Before computers, anyone with a copying machine was a publisher. Now, anyone with $60 can have their own web page that will be instantly indexed and accessible to an estimated 20 million web users. The 20 million figure, one of the more common estimates, is probably wrong. Who knows? But it is big. Unfortunately, this low entrance fee is likely to create billions of bytes of information that is unqualified and of poor quality. We've opened the gates, but who's fact checking?

Commercial information sources on the Net do offer some useful information, but most of them are trying to sell you something. I have a web page (http://www.lesko.com), and it has plenty of good information, but most of what I put there is to encourage people to buy my books. The most useful information on the Net comes from government sources, nonprofit organizations and special interest groups. It's an inexpensive way for groups to get their message out or, in the case of the government, it satisfies the law that requires information collected by tax dollars be made public. Government Net sites cover a broad range of subjects. You can track legislation, look for a job or even apply for money.

14. CyberSex and the Virtual Amusement Park

A word of warning: The Internet Can Be Addictive. There are people with on-line dependency problems, Netheads who can't break the habit. They spend hours each day on-line, and sooner or later, it gets expensive. There are even recovery groups for them.

Like a huge bookstore or a great museum, it's easy to wander around for hours on the Internet, getting lost as you bounce from topic to topic. Then forgetting what you were looking for in the first place. It can be fascinating and also very time consuming. But the Net also offers participants the opportunity to meet others in cyberspace. It is not unusual to develop a relationship on-line, to chat regularly with the same person or persons and, with time, maybe fall in love. Some people even have sex on-line, although I, for one, would love to see their offspring.

On the Net, or on other commercial on-line services like America Online or CompuServe, you can log into ongoing discussion groups that are more like singles bars than science clubs. You pull up your cyberchair and join in the fun, adding your ten cents' worth to the overall chatter. When you find someone who seems interesting, you can talk to them, on-line, away from the group. And then nature takes its course.

There are some people who find this abhorrent, yet many others have developed serious relationships after meeting on-line. It's better than the personals ads in

most newspapers. I've read that even Rush Limbaugh meet his current wife this way, and Tom Clancy - the best selling author - left his wife and family for someone that he met on-line. Go figure. I recently met a woman on an airplane who told me she was returning home to Los Angeles after a very romantic weekend in Cleveland with someone she met on-line. Two weeks from now, she told me, he's leaving Cleveland and moving to LA to be near him.

Although many people believe computers will depersonalize us, it also allows us to reach out to others without the embarrassment and nervousness of a blind date. Richard Farson, in a book called "Management of the Absurd", says, "throughout history, some of the most profound political discussions and the greatest love affairs have been conducted by people writing to each other."

Like it or not, computers and on-line services are bringing back writing as a means of personal expression, something we lost with the telephone. It's becoming an entirely new art form. The truth is, we already live in a culture that has become de-personalized. We drive alone in our cars and complain about how hard it is to meet anyone special. Not anymore.

In addition to the dating aspect, the Internet can be a great source of amusement - far more entertaining than television - but nowhere as rewarding as a walk with your loved ones, or baking cookies with your kids. If you can't make up your mind about going on-line and don't want to stroll virtual sidewalks in Paris or chat up a cyberlover, my advice is to wait. It's only going to get easier, cheaper and better to use.

15. A Computer for the Kids?

If you have children in school and can afford a computer, buy one. It's a library, tutor, playground and babysitter, all rolled into one. By second grade most kids start writing reports, and a computer will help them get projects done more quickly and thoroughly, while features such as spelling and grammar checking, and cut and paste editing, will make their reports look like they were prepared by a professional.

Also, by the time your kids reach the workplace, computers will be part of almost every job - be it forest ranger, chemist or auto mechanic. One of the main reasons computers are not more prevalent in the workplace today is because most senior management predates the Baby Boom. They didn't have computers then and they don't need them now, they'll argue - on their way out the door.

The recent explosion in on-line services is also helpful for kids of any age. My 10-year-old son recently went on-line and downloaded pictures of the three different kinds of columns used in ancient Roman architecture. My 14-year-old recently dialed into the NASA computer to complete a report on how space-age technology has been transferred into consumer applications, like Teflon.

Although much of the current on-line information is still full of cyberhype and may not be worth the trouble, the entire system is changing rapidly. Services are quickly becoming easier to use and the information they offer is becoming more and more valuable for students of any age.

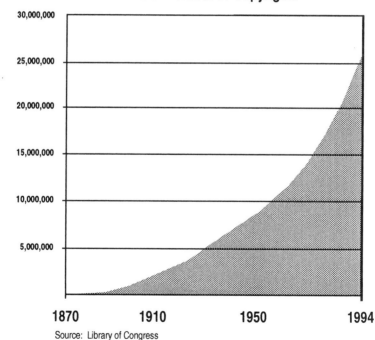

Growth of Printed Material
Total Number of Copyrights

30,000,000	
25,000,000	
20,000,000	
15,000,000	
10,000,000	
5,000,000	

1870   1910   1950   1994

Source: Library of Congress

16.

Your Kids Won't Do It Without You

When you purchase your first computer, chances are your children won't use it for word processing or on-line research - not unless you help them. They will quickly learn all the games by themselves, but you need to show them how to really use their new toy. You need to sit there and show them how, step by step. And you'll learn a few things too.

17. The Joy of Home-based Learning

One of the greatest pleasures I've had with my children is using the computer as a learning tool.

Every since they were three years old, we have used computers together. There is wonderful software available to help you teach your child to read, learn phonics, math or almost anything else. There is plenty of educational software for kids up to about 10 years old, but after that there are fewer titles.

Think of educational software as having a number of personal tutors at home. Educational experts developed these programs so that together you can go step-by-step through each learning process. What better time one-on-one is there than helping your own children learn? And now you don't have to be a teacher to do it.

Your kids can certainly succeed in life without a computer at home. But if you want to help them compete later in life, buy or borrow one, or send them to a friend's house to use theirs.

If your child doesn't have the basic skills of reading, writing and math, concentrate on these first - with or without a computer. If a child doesn't have these basics, they will only use the computer as a video arcade and the computer will be using the child, instead of the child learning to use the computer.

How to Go On-line

Don't complicate your life on-line. If you want to ride the information waves, choose something easy at first. Try it for a while and if you don't like it, you can easily change. If you try to learn all of the available on-line options to the Internet right off the bat, you'll go crazy. There are hundreds of options, and the biggest problem is that in six months, most will have changed. It's moving that fast.

The two basic ways to get on the Internet are to go directly through an Internet Provider or through one of the commercial services, like CompuServe, America Online, Prodigy or Microsoft. You're talking $20 to $30 dollars a month. Some of the smaller Internet providers now offer prices as low as $12 a month if you pay up front for a year or two. A beginner should use a sophisticated service to insure you get the proper support and software to make your first experience as easy as possible.

I would start by going through one of the big commercial providers, and I would choose either CompuServe or America Online. Prodigy, the third provider, seems to have an uncertain future and does not appear to be as helpful. Microsoft is new and worth watching - they say they signed up one million subscribers in their first seven months of business.

The basic difference between America Online and CompuServe is that CompuServe has better database

capabilities, allowing you to search published magazines, newspapers, and books. It's like having a vast library at your fingertips. There are extra charges for using these databases, but they are worth it for professional use or for serious students with some extra cash. If literature databases are not of much interest, America Online might be your best bet because they have one of the simplest E-mail address. Mine would be lesko@aol.com. On CompuServe it would be a whole bunch of numbers that I'll never remember and neither will anyone else. But as I'm writing this, CompuServe just announced a new service called WOW. If I join WOW, my E-mail address will be lesko@wow.com. Now that's a pretty neat address.

The other option is using an Internet access provider. These are companies that specialize in getting people on the Internet, but they don't offer special services of their own like literature databases or an on-line encyclopedia. For a beginner who wants to make the process easy, using a commercial database is a much simpler way to start surfing the Net.

Remember, prices, features and services continue to change, and any specifics I could give will be out of date by the time you read this. Choose CompuServe or America Online and give it a whirl, you can always cancel. Or do some research and start with the list below of the more popular commercial database services and Internet access providers.

Commercial On-Line Databases that also Provide Access to the Internet

- CompuServe
- America Online
- Prodigy
- Microsoft

Major Internet Access Providers

- American Information Systems
- Global Vision, Inc.
- Internet Access Co.
- New York Net
- Netcom

19. Why Computers Are Harmful to the Information Explosion

Computers have caused as many problems as they have solved, yet we couldn't have had an information revolution without them. In order to survive these days, you have to know what computers can do well. But to succeed, you have to understand their limitations.

Besides doing computations extremely fast (hence the name COMPUTErs), their major asset is handling large amounts of data. Without them, we would have been unable to manage the explosion in new information over the last 30 to 50 years. But computers can't make decisions based on quality. They can store mountains of magazine articles and scientific studies, but they can't tell you which one is better than the others, or which data is more accurate - they can't discriminate.

So managing the information explosion has changed from dealing with quantity - which computers have pretty much solved - to dealing with quality, a problem they've made more difficult. Believe me, whether you're surfing the Internet or accessing on-line databases, you're often going to wind up with a bigger headache than the one you started with.

When I grew up in the 50's, if you wrote a book or published an article in a magazine, you practically walked on water. The process was very selective, and what was

published was mostly quality stuff by great writers and reporters. Today, anyone with a copier can become a publisher, and where there used to be a limited number of magazines available at the corner news-stand, we now have thousands - some good, some bad, some ugly. Remember how easy it was to find something to watch when there were only three television stations? Now we channel surf because there are so many options - so much information. And much of it is being channeled into computer databases. We've become information hoarders, like those old guys living with sixty years' worth of newspapers stuffed into a three-bedroom apartment.

Not long ago, a computer search on almost any subject would turn up a handful of articles. But today an online search can uncover thousands of sources, and this is where the headache begins. You get a thick printout at the library or the weighty results of your search on the Internet, and then what? How do you tell a good source from a bad source when there's too many of either? Easy - pick up the phone. As I said in Chapter 30, "The Telephone Is Your Key To The Information Highway", the answers are seldom more than a few digits away when it comes to locating an expert, and your telephone is the key to the information highway.

In minutes, you should be able to find someone who can narrow your search down to a handful of really important articles or sources. Once you learn how to find free experts, you'll discover many of them have al-

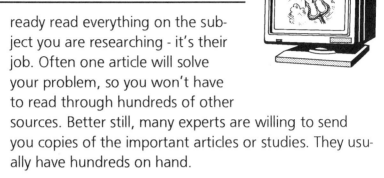

ready read everything on the subject you are researching - it's their job. Often one article will solve your problem, so you won't have to read through hundreds of other sources. Better still, many experts are willing to send you copies of the important articles or studies. They usually have hundreds on hand.

Most important of all, these experts usually know what new developments are just around the corner. They know what will be in the databases tomorrow, because they are working on the reports today - crunching numbers and making charts. Get them talking and you can get a head start, cut straight through to the bottom line, and save a lot of time. All you need is a telephone. It's technology you already know how to use.

20. Who Needs a Fax Machine?

Fax machines are everywhere. Some people even have them in their cars. But do you need one? First, are we talking about a fax for your home or office? If it's for your office, you should have one already. It's hard to imagine any business, large or small - or even someone working freelance from home - operating without one. Sending documents, invoices or proposals by fax is cheaper than mail and faster than Federal Express. This means that you can procrastinate even longer without guilt.

Having a fax at home is still considered a luxury, kind of like microwave ovens 20 years ago. They're fun gadgets. You can fax recipes to your friends and your kids can get forgotten homework faxed by friends - when they suddenly remember an assignment at 9:00 at night.

One major consideration when buying a fax is that it takes two to tango. Owning one doesn't make much sense unless the people you want to communicate with also have one. Most businesses have them, so they make sense in your professional life. But most households don't - at least not yet - so you might want to ask around to see who does. Survey friends, family members, and anyone else on your list. If they are aren't already fax-wired, why buy one yourself?

Should I buy a fax machine before buying a home computer?
No. You'll find a computer much more valuable than a fax. So buy the computer first.

If I buy a computer with a built in fax, will both be good enough? Unless you are a sophisticated computer user, probably not. These systems only allow you to fax what is already in the computer. So if you want to fax an interesting article to your uncle Fred, you first have to get it into your computer. And that requires another piece of hardware called a scanner, that will cost a lot more than a separate fax machine.

Does this mean I shouldn't get a fax in my computer? Just the opposite. The built-in fax gizmo in a computer is part of something call a fax/modem, and you need one to dial into the Internet and other on-line databases. So make sure a fax/modem is included. The neatest thing about having a built-in fax is that you can write a letter and fax it to someone straight off the computer. You'll never have to see a piece of paper, a stamp or a postman with an attitude.

21. It's Smart to Be a High-Tech Holdout

Here's a little secret about breakthrough technology. The longer you wait to buy the latest info-gadget or service, the cheaper it will become and the easier to use. This has been true of computers and other information products, just as it once was true with automobiles.

When automobiles were first introduced, they were very expensive and seemed extremely complicated for people who relied on horse power to get around town. Plus there were few roads - like having a computer with no software - and they were slower than the average horse. Still, people were dying to be the first one on the block with a Model T. They believed the salesman's promise that this new wonder would solve their problems, even though it was all sizzle and very little steak. Had the early car salesmen told the truth - that the horse was faster, easier and cheaper than the automobile - we'd still be in the saddle.

But things gradually changed. As more and more cars were sold, they became cheaper and easier to use, and then came the roads. Talk about putting the cart before the horse!

Personal computers evolved the same way. When they were first introduced in the early 1980's, they were very expensive and complicated for users, plus there were no roads - no software. I remember one sales

pitch at the time - you could keep all of your recipes on the computer. This seemed ridiculous. Why would anyone spend $5,000 (that's what they cost back then) just to keep recipes handy? Or they said you could balance your checkbook using your new personal computer, an even dumber argument. The complicated software you needed to balance a checkbook back then took far longer than doing it by hand. And even if you were checkbook challenged and never balanced yours, you certainly were not going to turn over a new leaf and start doing it by computer.

If they didn't rope you in with these brilliant features, they would play to your fears. Your children would never get to college unless you had a computer in your home, they said, sounding just like encyclopedia salesman. The truth is that many college graduates never had an encyclopedia at home. I know we didn't.

It took about 10 years for computers to catch up with the early sales pitches, but they eventually did. Now you can buy a computer that is 100 times better than the first models for just $1,500. Today it may not be a bad place to keep your recipes. Software like Quicken has finally made balancing your checkbook by computer easier than by hand. Finally, the fear factor may hold true. Because so many homes now have computers, kids need access to a PC in order to have the competitive edge they'll need to get into a good college.

The on-line information business has followed the same cycle.

The longer you wait, the cheaper new technology becomes. Hand held calculators once cost hundreds of dollars, yet now they give them away on cereal boxes. Just a few years ago, it took hundreds of dollars just to get a car phone installed, yet now they practically give them away if you buy time on a telephone network. Not the product, mind you, the service.

Remember that the manufacturer's goal is to get more and more people to use their product. To accomplish this, they are constantly working on new ways the make their product less expensive, more versatile, and easier to use. So when in doubt, it's smarter to wait for the technology to come to you.

22. Can You Make Money on the Internet?

Everyone wants to get rich quick, but the only people I've found who are making any money on the Internet are those who are helping others get access. A few people somewhere are making a little money - like a flower shop I used to read about in Michigan, or a small book store that sells mostly American pornographic titles to foreign customers.

Actually, all the hype about making money on the Internet sounds just like the pitches made during the California Gold Rush in the mid 1800s. You heard a few anecdotes about people who struck it rich, but the people who made a killing were those selling picks, shovels and overalls. Today, the pick and shovel salesmen are those companies who help others establish an identity on the Net.

As the technology develops, I'm sure more and more people will figure how to make money on-line. But for now, it's better to sit back and watch.

What's Wrong with Libraries, the Media and High-Priced Experts?

23. Books Are Out of Date

I remember when my first book became a New York Times bestseller. I made some money - not a whole lot - but I helped some people. Yet every one of them could have gotten more up-to-date information if they had only known where to look. In short, the book was out of date as soon as it hit the stands.

The book was titled "Getting Yours" and it described over 1000 money programs the government offers to help people start a business, buy a house, go to college, etc. There are too many to count, but I found that most people don't even know the money's there. I wrote a best seller, but I'm no literary genius. In fact, I almost flunked a writing course in college (You may have figured this out already from reading this book). But my first best seller did just that - it sold. And you know what? I didn't write it, I simply copied information from *The Catalog of Federal Domestic Assistance*, a book published each year by U.S. Government Printing Office (GPO). You can find it in most public libraries.

The reason I was able to copy the information was simple - nothing in the government can be copyrighted - it already belongs to all of us. Anyone can take government information and resell it. Believe me, I've been doing it for more than 20 years - and so have hundreds of other publishers, consultants and experts. I

simply bought this huge book from the GPO and literally cut and pasted all of the information into my book, added an introduction, and sent it off to my publisher - then Viking/Penguin in New York. Viking/Penguin then spent close to a year editing the book, which puzzled me. The government had just spent millions of dollars editing the book, and these New Yorkers wanted to do it all over again. I think it's called reinventing the wheel.

About a year later the book finally hit the bookstores, and I was on TV trying to sell it. People saw me on the tube, liked what they heard, and went out to buy a copy. Before I knew it, my book showed up on the New York Times best seller list - but by that time, a lot of the information was out-of-date and incomplete. If my readers had only known where to look (*The Catalog of Federal Domestic Assistance* - published each year by U.S. Government Printing Office), they could have found more information that was at least a year more current, and with much more detail than what I passed along in my book. I only used about 10 percent of the material. So why did people buy my book? I guess because the author of *The Catalog of Federal Domestic Assistance* doesn't do talk shows.

The problem with high-volume publishing is that by the time a resource book hits the street, it's usually out of date. Traditional publishing is fine for fiction, or books about history or literature. But if you need current information to make well-informed decisions, most are obsolete by the time you get them. If you want to invest in the stock market, you aren't going to get much guid-

ance by reading a book, right? The market changes every minute. Not surprisingly, this is also true of most important life decisions, such as health, careers, law, etc.

I always warn my readers that much of the information in my books is already out of date, no one can keep current. Still, I've always felt my books are about sources not answers, and the sources are still there even if the answers have changed. *The Catalog of Federal Domestic Assistance* is published every year, so it is one of the best sources of information on government money. The Arthritis Information Clearinghouse has the latest information on arthritis treatment and research, so why buy a book that was published over a year ago? If it was published a year ago, the information is at least two years old - probably older.

The same is true for magazine articles. While they may not take a year to appear, most articles have been in the publishing loop for at least six months. And if the article has to do with scientific research, say treating a disease, the delay between the end of a study and the time it appears in a medical journal - and is then widely reported in the press - can often exceed two or more years. So if you're reading about breast cancer in *Cosmopolitan Magazine*, it's probably yesterday's news. If you really want the latest findings, call the National Institutes of Health or the Cancer Information Center Breast Cancer Hotline.

Books aren't going to disappear, but they're rapidly becoming less valuable as tools for making decisions. Technology is moving fast, and we have to move fast to keep up with the changes. Even if books do one day become purely recreational, there will always be experts who are willing to share what they know with you, and they'll be working way ahead of the publishing curve.

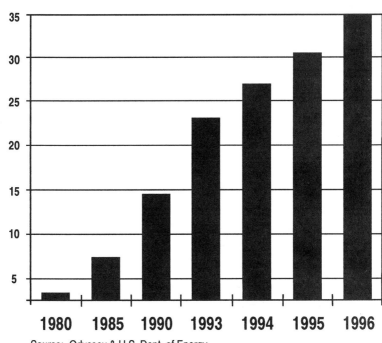

Percent of Households with Computers

Source: Odyssey & U.S. Dept. of Energy

24. Why the Library is a Bad Place to Get Information

If information is so vital, why aren't libraries the most important building in our communities? Or why aren't there long lines out front of the library every day? Here's one reason. A few years ago, my 10-year-old son wanted to get some information about volcanoes. He said, "Come on Dad, let's go to the library." With that kind of enthusiasm, what could I do? I said, "Let's go."

But when we got there, the librarian showed us an encyclopedia and my son looked up volcanoes and got some information. But I stood there thinking, "Wow, I'm 50 years old, and when I was ten they were using the exact same encyclopedia - in 40 years we've gone nowhere."

So I grabbed my kid, ran out of the library and went home. First we called the official Volcano Information Clearinghouse, a government office in Colorado. They were terrific, and within the week they had sent us a poster of the eruption of Mount St. Helens, along with a computerized printout of all 50 active volcanoes in the world and their current status.

This was fun research - and my son learned an important lesson about gathering information: It's not boring! What we received was more up-to-date, and cer-

tainly more exciting, than that dusty old library encyclopedia.

Librarians are held captive by their own expertise. Like lawyers - who see a legal solution to everything - many librarians look only to books for answers. But in this age of information overload, the best answers are rarely in books anymore. Instead, they are more likely to be tucked away in some unpublished report or in some expert's head. Librarians aren't trained to pursue these non-traditional sources of information. They've invested their time learning about books. Many libraries are now investing in computers and databases, and librarians are taking classes to become more on-line literate, but knowing how to use a computer to search the networks remains just a small part of understanding the information puzzle.

Published material seldom solves the kinds of information problems the average citizen faces today. People want to know about the best investments, where the best jobs are, how to get a small business loan, or what is the latest news about treating arthritis. Answers to these questions are changing every day, and books - because of the time it takes for them to be edited and printed - are usually out of date before they hit the streets. To survive in an information society, people need to know about what's happening today and what's about to happen tomorrow, not yesterday or last year.

Libraries have a rich history of archival skills, and most libraries try to apply these same skills to solving today's

information problems. They can't. Today's information problems require a different set of skills, and even a special kind of personality, to solve. Archival skills usually are best suited to someone who is typically quiet and enjoys working analytically with inanimate objects like books, card catalogs, yes, even computers.

But to get the best information, you also need people skills. You have to use people - not books - to find almost 80 percent of the information that is not on the bookshelf or in the computer. Libraries are not yet prepared to invest in acquiring these new skills, to train workers in tracking information or investing in telephones and long distance lines.

Another problem at the library is packaging. When a customer comes into the library with a problem, they are typically given a book or a computer printout that might have the answer they're looking for. But these computer printouts can become a bigger nightmare than the original problem. The person walks in with one question and gets 400 potential sources of information to sift through - and these may not even have the answer. People want answers, not more problems, more work. If libraries want to help, they must package their answers more carefully.

Don't get me wrong - I don't hate libraries. I'm just frustrated that of all institutions, they have yet to enter the information age. They may think that having a computer puts them on the cutting edge of research, but it's just taking up shelf space if they don't know how to use it to help others. I believe the library

should be the most important building in an informed democracy, but they just need to work a lot harder.

What's good about libraries? Their literature and archival functions are integral to our society, and I hope we never give up wanting to read good books or learning about history. But even with their limitations, libraries can also play an important role in locating the most up-to-date information. They are loaded with books listing information sources. For instance, if you need the names and addresses of the largest tea cup manufacturers, the library may not be the best place to look. But they do have a book called *Gales Encyclopedia of Associations* that will give you the name and address of the Tea Cup Manufacturers Association who in turn can tell you how to get such a list.

So even if a library can't give you the exact answer you need to an information problem, a library, through it's investment in expensive source books, can sure help point you in the right direction.

25. The Media Is Superficial or How to Use the News

Like cars and computers, the media causes as many problems as it solves in our information society. You've seen the commercials that say, 'More people get their news from ABC News than from any other source'. The problem is that most people take the news at face value and are unaware of just how limited the news media really is. Most of information we see is just a sketch of the real story, and much of it is old news at that. Better and more accurate information always is available, but you have to know where to look.

What the average person doesn't realize is that reporter on TV probably read a two-page press release on the subject, and boiled it down to a one minute soundbite. The media has tailored itself to an audience with a short attention span because we've become so busy. It's as if the entire country has developed attention deficit disorder, and much of the media now believes in this McNews Lite approach. Unfortunately, this results in as much misinformation as it does information.

If you see a news report on problems with silicone breast implants, you never get enough information to make an informed decision about their actual safety. Can you call the reporter for more information? Why bother. The reporter doesn't know any more than what was in the press release, and by now they've moved on to other stories. Can you call your doctor? Not unless you want to pay for an office consultation. They aren't going to explain it on the phone, but even if they do, it's unlikely they've heard the news or read the study. They're too busy treating patients.

So where do you turn for the real story? If it's about breast implants, you call the Food and Drug Administration's breast implant hotline. They'll send you a copy of the actual study. You can read it and call back with any questions, or go over it with your doctor.

Most people don't realize the superficiality of the media, or how to use the news. It is a tool - a headline service identifying subjects that we might want to know more about. But to get more information, you have to know where to call.

Read a story in the paper about something you know a lot about, your community or the place where you work. You will probably find most information in the first paragraph is correct, but after that you will almost always find mistakes and inaccuracies.

Journalists are not experts on the subjects they write about. Their expertise is in being able to relate to us what they have learned in a very short amount of time. We all fight the clock, and journalists have very tight deadlines. They may spend a couple of hours doing a story on credit card fraud, and the next couple of hours writing about Bosnia. Their reports are overviews and provide general information, but not the whole story.

If you really want information about Bosnia, why rely on someone who has spent a half a day, or at most, a week, studying the situation? Instead, you can call an expert in the government who has spent years studying Bosnia. They'll talk your ears off for free, and you'll soon know far more than any journalist working the story. So how do you locate an expert on Bosnia, breast implants, or almost any other subject imaginable? Read Chapter 31, "How to Find a Free Expert on Any Topic".

There's no law that says the media must report the truth, but we believe they wouldn't print it if it wasn't true, right? Don't bet the farm on it. The media is manipulated by thousands of public relations firms around the country who send out tons of press releases every day. Up to 70 percent of what is reported is the result of a press release, and I'm as guilty as the next person of playing the media game. I spend a lot of time trying to get my books mentioned by the media, and when they are, what you hear is information that I provided them. I'm not biased, I'm practical. But like most people, businesses or professional organizations that send out news releases, I too have an agenda. Mine is to sell books.

If you see a news report on the remarkable growth of the frozen yogurt market, you can be sure the story originated from a press release issued by the frozen yogurt manufacturers association. They want to brag about their industry and attract new investment money. If the story gets you excited about opening up a frozen yogurt shop, first double check the information. For all you know, the yogurt boom is over and you should open a microbrewery instead. Again, you can get this information for free by contacting a government yogurt expert, as I show you in Chapter 31 "How to Find a Free Expert on Any Topic."

The media has become central in our society, and everyone with a product or new idea to sell has learned how to use it. We are reaching the point where "The Only Honest Thing on TV Is the Home Shopping Network." Why? Because most talk shows, and even newscasts, are built around people selling something while pretending they are not. Infomercials pretend to be talk shows when they are in fact commercials. But programs like the Home Shopping Network are at least honest enough to be up front about their mission - to sell, sell, sell.

26. Why Doctors and Lawyers Are Wrong

I pity professionals these days. It's impossible for them to keep up with the latest changes in their field. The answers are changing almost by the hour. You've seen the headlines. A new treatment for Alzheimer's disease one week is found to have toxic side effects the next, coffee is bad for you, then it's good for you, there's a new interpretation of sexual harassment, and so on and so on. Doctors and lawyers spend most of their time treating patients or working with clients. They can't even keep up with the latest developments in their own legal or medical specialty, let alone with more general changes in their chosen field. Still most of us believe that doctors and lawyers have all the answers. In fact, if they do give you a straight answer, it's only a guess - but they don't tell you that, do they?

So not only are professionals expensive, much of their expertise is outdated. But it doesn't take a high-priced doctor or lawyer to get good medical or legal information. If you know where to call, you can get better, more timely and more accurate information than you can from your doctor, lawyer, financial consultant or whoever else charges you a lot of money for their expertise. And you can get this information for free.

For instance, your boss makes a pass at you at the Christmas party and you wonder if you can file a sexual harassment complaint or not. You don't have

to spend $200 an hour for some lawyer to look into it. Because the laws are constantly changing and being reinterpreted by the courts, lawyers will be running up the clock researching the current law. Instead, you can call an 800 number at the Equal Employment Opportunity Commission and talk to what they call an officer of the day. These people will listen to your story and tell you if they think you have a potential case. If you do, they'll even sue your boss and get you money. So why hire someone for $200 per hour to learn the law when you can make a toll-free call and talk to someone who actually wrote the law, and they're free?

This also holds true for keeping up with the latest advances in medicine. Some years ago I had back problems that persisted for about 10 years. My doctor would tell me things like, 'Lesko, your back pain isn't so bad. Everyone's got some back pain. Come back when it gets really bad, then we'll operate.'

I didn't like this grin-and-bear-it approach. Being in the research business, I decided it sounded like a job for INFO-MAN. Armed with just a telephone, I decided to find my own cure. First I called around the National Institutes of Health and found one expert who had been studying back pain for over 25 years, and handed out millions of dollars each year to back pain researchers all over the world. Surely he would have an answer if one existed, I told myself.

This expert doctor was wonderful. He explained that many of the back problems in our society are caused by

the way we live. We're stressed out, wound up, full of tension, he explained. We sit on our rumps all day and seldom exercise, despite the jogging machines and treadmills in the basement. He told me the results of studies that hadn't even been published yet, information he had because his office was funding the project.

He also told me something my doctor hadn't, that the YMCA had a back pain course with a 75 percent success rate. So I took the course at my local YMCA, and within a few weeks my back pain was gone. I was healed and I did it all with free information.

So why not get better information than your doctor? Why cross your fingers and hope they're reading the medical journals each week, when you can make a few phone calls and find out what will be.in the *New England Journal of Medicine* next month, or even next year.

And this holds true not only for doctors and lawyers, but for most other professionals. Investment advisors, management consultants, real estate brokers - even teachers - find it almost impossible to keep up with the latest information, yet they charge big money.

You don't have to hire a high-priced expert. With a little patience and a telephone, the chances are you can get better information, and get it for free.

27. You Can't Trust a Professional

Professionals are important, right? We believe they have all the answers. But in our information society, you have to be very careful with what they say. Why? Because the same experience that makes them an expert also helps them appear right when they are dead wrong. I'm an expert in my field, information. With 20 years of experience, I'm very practiced at making myself look good, and could even lie and get away with it, if I wanted to. After 10 years of talk shows, I've probably been asked almost every question that could possibly make me look bad.

"Lesko, you're telling people how to get things free from the government. Isn't that promoting welfare and encouraging bad habits?" I've actually been asked this.

I know such questions have some merit. But when you have only three minutes of television time to prove your point, you can't waste time discussing the grey areas. So I've developed great answers that make me look good. There's a lot of free information out there. That's my message - that's the bottom line.

If I don't have a good answer, I'll go home and spend a few hours developing one. Another talk show host is going to ask me the same thing, I know.

I've also learned how easy it is to lie on TV. None of the hosts, producers, researchers or anyone else is going to know my subject as well as I do - I've spent years at it!

And as a result, I can easily fudge numbers, stretch statistics, or downright lie to prove a point. No one has the time to get the data to prove me wrong. But I don't, because I don't need to stretch. The information really is there, and smart people are getting rich using government info-sources.

Former President Ronald Reagan held White House Press conferences where he spouted off completely incorrect facts and figures, and even told stories that only took place on the Silver Screen. Yet people believed him. Doctors, lawyers, politicians - all professionals - have to develop quick answers, even if they aren't necessarily true. They're survival skills. But you have to know this, and be very careful when looking for answers.

For example, if your doctor recommends cataract surgery, how can you argue? Your doctor has already reached the decision that you should have the operation. But instead of taking your doctor's word, wouldn't it be better to know the most current medical facts, as they relate to you? With just one phone call you can reach the National Eye Institute, part of the National Institutes of Health. They will send you a free study that shows that 33 percent of all cataract surgery did not have to be done. So instead of trying to debate with your doctor and dodging jargon, you can simply bring in the study. Ask your doctor why you're different from the people in the report who had the surgery, yet didn't need it. With this you're going to accomplish two things. First, your doctor is going to think harder about whether the surgery is right

for you. But more importantly, your doctor is going to start looking for more information - and not just about cataracts, either.

The best way to use professionals is to know the facts, or let them know that you know where to get them. Otherwise, many of them will use your ignorance. That's why we so many people are unhappy with doctors, lawyers, politicians and other professionals - they pretend to have all the information. We normal people couldn't possibly understand it all, they tell us. But we can!

"Just do as I say, and everything will be all right," professionals tell us, and we accept it.

The average consumer has no idea where to go to get the information they need to really use the advice of a professional. Our response is, "Just solve the problem - but if you screw up - I'm going to sue."

We all can take more responsibility for our own lives, and getting professionals to work more effectively can help. Instead of feeling like we're working for them, let's make them do their jobs. We're the ones paying their bills, so let's gather enough information to take them to task. The days are gone when their "expert" advice is above reproach. Show me a professional with a pat answer and I'll find an expert with the real facts in just a few phone calls. And you can do it too.

The Best Information Is Free

28. The Government Is the World's Largest Source of Information

Our government is an information power-house, the largest source of information and experts in the world. And all of it is available to you for free, or at very little cost. Only Uncle Sam can afford to give so much information away. The government now represents more than 35% of our entire economy, and most of what it does is produce information and expertise. It certainly doesn't make anything; I've never seen smoke stacks in Washington.

There is a story in the next section about potato expert Charlie Porter. Who else but the government would pay someone $60,000 a year to study potatoes? But Porter's expertise is just the tip of the iceberg at the Department of Agriculture - let alone in all other federal agencies. There's solar energy experts at the Department of Energy and back pain specialists at the National Institutes of Health. It's barbecue utensils at the Department of Commerce and underwear at the U.S. Trade Commission, copper and gold experts at the Department of Interior and travel specialists at the Department of State. Information on investments? Call the Department of Treasury.

Did you know the government has a huge amount of information on pets, from anacondas to zebras - at the Animal Welfare Information Clearinghouse? Or

that you can find out who your
neighbor owes money to by contacting your state office of the
Uniform Commercial Code? The
best hearing aids? Contact the Na-
tional Institute of Standards and Technology. Looking
for a date? In most states, the Division of Motor Vehicles can even get you the names and addresses of all
rich, single men over 6 feet tall that live in your zip code.

There is probably not one facet of your life, not one
question or problem, that can't be answered by Uncle
Sam. The problem is that other people are getting rich
selling you the same information, while others have an
agenda and are giving out biased data. You can get it
better, faster and often free, if you go straight to the
source.

The *Wall Street Journal* can tell you how the economy
is doing, but you can get the information yourself - a
day earlier - simply by calling the Department of Commerce. *U.S. News and World Report* can tell you where
the good jobs are, but the Department of Labor will tell
you the fastest growing jobs <u>in your city</u>. You can
waste money having a lawyer research a particular law,
or call someone in the government who actually wrote
it - and they're free. Do you really want to trust a com-
mission-hungry real estate agent who swears a neighborhood is safe? Call your state Department of Justice
and get the truth without spending a dime. Or what
about your stock broker's suggestion that you buy a
hundred shares of Megabionics? We often forget that
most stock brokers are just salesmen. They don't know

biotechnology from bologna. Instead, you can call one of a dozen government biotechnology experts and learn about promising research and medical advances that will soon make many people wealthy, information that won't appear in the *Wall Street Journal* for months, maybe even years. It's called getting ahead of the information curve, and it's the smartest way to invest.

Let's compare government information to that produced in the private sector. Each year, about 50,000 new books are published by the private sector. These are all the books that are available in libraries, bookstores or by mail order. But just one government office, the National Technical Information Service, alone publishes about 100,000 titles each year. That's twice as much as all the commercial publishers combined, and studies show that they only publish about 80 percent of what they could. We're not talking Pueblo, Colorado here.

Why even the Internet is here because of the government. The Internet was started by the Department of Defense and to this day is still subsidized by your tax dollars.

The quality of government information is also usually better than what you find published in the private sector. If you buy a book in the bookstore, it is usually represents a year or two of work by the author. But if you get a report or study from the government, it could easily represent hundreds of man-years of work.

The problem with government information is that most of it has not been gathered to help individuals solve problems. Instead, it is collected to help policy decisions or because a law says it must be. For example, the Bureau of the Census is now spending about $3 billion to count all the noses and toilets in this country. They are not only counting all the people in a house, but even the number of rooms, toilets, garages and almost everything else in the house. Why? Because the Constitution says we have to count how many people we have in order to know how many congressmen and women each state should have.

As a result, we get a $3 billion market study that companies like Proctor and Gamble use to determine the market for toothpaste or laundry detergent. Or that Citicorp uses to determine where to put up the next bank. These big companies could not afford to collect this kind of information themselves, so they get it free from Washington and make billion-dollar decisions based on it.

So why doesn't the average citizen use this information? Because they don't know, it's there. If they did, they could use it to determine the best neighborhoods to live in, or where to open up a jewelry store, a dental practice or auto repair shop. That's free marketing information that would cost you thousands if you hired a professional.

The irony is that the government spends billions of dollars on information, but virtually nothing to let people know it's there.

That's why it takes a little work. But if you take the time to learn how to use the system, you'll have access to best information on earth. It's not easy. Information is like any other resource, you have to know where to dig and how to use a shovel.

We live in the greatest democracy in the world. Whether you live on Park Avenue or a park bench, you have access to more free information today than ever before in history. In a democracy, we own the government. And since we've paid for it, let's get our money's worth.

29. A Million Non-Profit Groups Are Willing to Help

Trade associations, special interest groups, unions, and service clubs are a great source of information on special topics. It seems that any time 10 people of a shared interest get together, they start a group, a club or an organization. They mingle with like minds and share information. Because of this, they are an integral part of the Information Revolution, and a great place to look for specialized data. They collect data, develop expertise, poll their members and interview each other, creating a valuable storehouse of information that they are usually willing, even eager, to share with the outside world.

The Internal Revenue Service identifies about one million of these groups and you can get their addresses from them, but a much better place to start is with the *Encyclopedia of Associations* published by Gale Research Inc. in Detroit, Michigan. Most libraries have copies, so start there. The directory includes the name of each group, its address and phone number, its officers and a brief description of what they are all about.

If you want a snapshot of our culture, take a look at the organizations in this directory. There are groups dedicated to Barbie dolls, bullfighting, even green olives. You can find the Bobsledding and Tobogganing Federation, the Hearing Dog Resource center, the Toy

Train Collectors Association, or the Arthritis Foundation. The index alone is an eye-opener, but the information you can get from these groups — and most deal with far more serious matters — can be priceless and far more timely than what you can get from other sources.

This book is available in most any library, and when you look into it you'll see that if you are interested in green olives you can contact the Green Olive Trade Association, or if you are an ex-bullfighting aficionado you can contact the International Council Against Bullfighting. There are also groups called Parents of Murdered Children, the Institute for Educating Secretaries, the Horizontal Earth Borers Association, and even a Toilet Seat Manufacturers Association that is now defunct. What is that telling us about our society?

Using Your Telephone to Find Free Experts

30. The Telephone Is Your Key to the Information Highway

The more information that is pumped into our society, the more we have to rely on experts to help us wade through it. Sure you can turn on your computer and go on-line to look up a topic. But the fallout from the information explosion will drive you up the wall. You're likely to get thousands of sources, articles or even books on most any topic. How do you sort through it; where are the answers?

There's a simple way of solving information overload. You pick up your telephone and make a few calls. I know that I keep repeating this, but it's true. I've found that with seven telephone calls, on average, you can find a free expert on almost any topic. This is a person who has read everything listed on-line, has an opinion of which articles are worthwhile, and which aren't. They know the crackpots and the researchers who are breaking new ground - it's their business. Off the top of their head, they can tell you which articles to read to answer your questions. And because they are experts, they can also tell you what studies are in the works; what will appear in the literature next month, or on-line next year.

That's the greatest part of the information explosion, it sidetracks a lot of your competitions. While they're searching on-line, you can have the best of both

worlds - by using computers as a compliment, not a replacement, for the phone. We don't need to go back to school, or learn some new techno-mumbo jumbo, to ride this information highway. We've been using the phone for years.

Growth of Technical Information
Total Articles Published on Chemicals

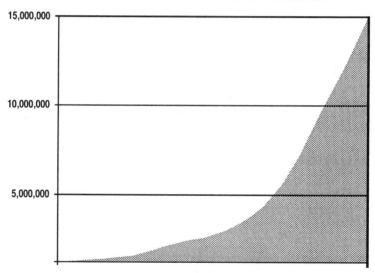

Source: Chemical Abstracts Service

How to Find a Free
Expert on Any Topic

If you have never tried to find a free expert before, it may seem difficult. But if you think about it, most of us have done it, even if the experts we found weren't the best ones. If you were worried about needing cataract surgery, you probably called Aunt Margaret who had cataract surgery last year. In your eyes, Aunt Margaret was your closest expert - about your eyes. And when you called her, the problem wasn't getting her to talk about the surgery, it was getting her off the phone. Real experts are just like Aunt Margaret, they love to talk about what they know.

You can find a real expert the same way you found Aunt Margaret. Think of someone who HAS to know something about what you're looking for, and eliminate anyone in business who sells such information. The problem is that most of us would think we had to call a practicing eye surgeon for expert advice on cataract surgery. But what we really need is better information, to make sure what the eye surgeon says is true and up-to-date. Impossible? Not at all. In fact it's easy once you know where to look.

Let's take the cataract example. Most free experts are in one of two places: the government or nonprofit or-

ganizations. And if you don't think this is a big enough pool of experts, you're wrong. The government now represents about 37% of our entire Gross National Product, and there are more than one million nonprofit organizations and associations registered with the Internal Revenue Service. Between the two, you can find an expert on just about anything.

Why do these two groups offer so much free information? The answer's easy with regards to associations. We're a nation that loves to organize and form groups. If you get ten people interested in the same topic, they'll start an association to swap ideas and to tell others about what they know. Why the government has so many free experts is a bit more complex, and you'll need to read Chapter 28, "The Government Is the World's Largest Source of Free Expertise" to get a clear picture.

So where should you start first? I'd start with the government, because they're more likely to have better information, and more of it. You can go to the library and look through a book called the *U.S. Government Manual*, or through other directories of Federal Government services. My book, *Lesko's Info-Power III*, pinpoints offices that study the subjects you need information about. If it's cataracts, you'll find an office at the National Institutes of Health.

But it can be even easier. If you don't want to go all the way down to the library and wade through thick manu-

als, you can call several government offices and they'll do the work for you over the phone.

These include:

1) Federal Information Centers: These offices were set up by Congress to help taxpayers cut through government red tape to find which office can best help them use the government. See page 369 for the Federal Information Center telephone number.

2) Information Clearinghouses: These services are often funded in part by government grants, and they exist solely to guide consumers toward information and experts both inside and outside the federal government. See page 159, "375 Organizations That Will Do Research for You for Free" for an office that can help you.

3) Congressional Offices: Your elected officials - Representative's and Senator's - have people on their staff that will help you find the right government office with the expertise you need. They have a local district office where you live or you can call the Capitol Hill Switchboard at 800-972-3524 and talk to their Washington office.

Associations are easy to locate. There is a book in almost every public library called *Gales Encyclopedia of Associations*. It's enormous, several volumes, but it's well indexed and easy to use. You can use it to find as-

sociations with experts on almost any subject - from aardvarks to zippers.

One other source might may be helpful - trade magazines and newsletters. This country is loaded with little known magazines and newsletters that cover very specific areas of interest to subscribers. Unlike *Time* or *Newsweek*, the writers of these trade magazines and newsletters cover specific topics and develop very special expertise. There are magazines for cigar smokers and newsletters for left-handed people. To find the experts who write for these magazines, you'll have to go to the library, but there are excellent books that index all of these publications and a good reference librarian can easily find them for you.

32. The Care and Feeding of Experts

There is no magic in how to get what you want from an expert. Simply treat them the way you would want to be treated yourself. This can be easy to forget when you're frustrated after making dozens of telephone. But it is important to remember. Your frustration level is bound to escalate as you search for information.

- You get put on hold for what seems like hours.

- No one you talk to understands your question or seems to think you're off your rocker.

- After getting transferred and trying other numbers, you wind up talking with the same person twice.

What's important is not to lose your composure. Keep in mind that it will take an average of seven phone calls to find the person who can help. Otherwise, by the time you reach the expert you'll be angry and frustrated and that attitude will come across over the phone and the expert will end the conversation ASAP. Remember these expert wants to share what they know, but not with someone with a bad attitude. You need to make them want to help.

Getting information from computers, libraries or books requires a different set of skills than those needed for dealing with experts. You have to develop telephone

skills and interviewing techniques that will make experts want to talk to you. Remember when dealing with both public and private sector experts, they get the same paycheck whether they give you two weeks worth of priceless information and guidance - or just two minutes. They will decide whether you'll get what you want, and on what terms, or whether you sound unworthy of their expertise.

Here are a few pointers. These guidelines sound like basic common sense, but they are very easy to forget by the time you get to that sixth or seventh phone call.

1)   Introduce Yourself Cheerfully

The way you open the conversation will set the tone for the entire interview. Your greeting and initial comment should be cordial and cheerful. They should give the feeling that this is not going to be just another telephone call, but a pleasant interlude in their day.

2)   Be Open and Candid

You should be as candid as possible with your source since you are asking the same of him. If you are evasive or deceitful in explaining your needs or motives, your source often will sense this and be reluctant to help. If there are certain facts you cannot reveal, due to client confidentiality or some other factor, explain this. Most people will understand.

3) **Be Optimistic**

Throughout the entire conversation, you should exude a sense of confidence. If you call and say "You probably aren't the right person" or "You don't have any information, do you?" it makes it easy for the person to say "You're right, I can't help you." A positive attitude will encourage your source to stretch his mind to see what information might help you.

4) **Be Humble and Courteous**

You can be optimistic and still be humble. Remember the old adage that you can catch more flies with honey than you can with vinegar. People in general, and experts in particular, love to tell others what they know as long as their position of authority is not questioned or threatened. In fact, if they are made to feel like an expert by the way you treat them, chances are that they will give you more information than they originally intended.

5) **Be Concise**

State your problem simply. A long-winded explanation may bore your contact and reduce your chances for getting a thorough response. Write it down first.

6) **Don't Be a "Gimme"**

People who say "give me this" or "give me that," seldom succeed is getting the information the need. Demanding information shows little consideration for the other person's time or feelings about a subject. Al-

ways ask politely for information or a particular document that you're interested in.

7) Be Complimentary

This goes hand in hand with being humble. A well placed compliment about your source's expertise or insight about a particular topic will serve you well. In searching for information in large organizations, you are apt to talk to many of your source's colleagues, so it wouldn't hurt to convey the respect that each expert deserves. For example, "Everyone said you're the best person to talk to." It is reassuring for anyone to know they have the respect of their peers.

8) Be Conversational

Avoid spending the entire time talking about the information you need. Briefly mention a few irrelevant topics such as the weather, the Washington Redskins, or the latest political campaign, but stay away from controversial topics. If an expert lives someplace that you've visited, always tell them how much you loved that area, or better yet, mention a specific feature - such as a state park or neighborhood. The more social you are without being too chatty, the more likely that your source will open up to you and deliver the goods.

9) Return the Favor

It often helps to share with your source information or even gossip you have picked up elsewhere. However, be certain not to betray the trust of either your client or another source. If you do not have any relevant informa-

tion to share at the moment, it is still a good idea to call back when you are further along in your research when do have some information of value to offer.

10) **Send Thank You Notes**

A short note, typed or handwritten, will help ensure that your source will be just as cooperative if you need more help in the future.

Growth of Info Workers
Percent of Total Work Force

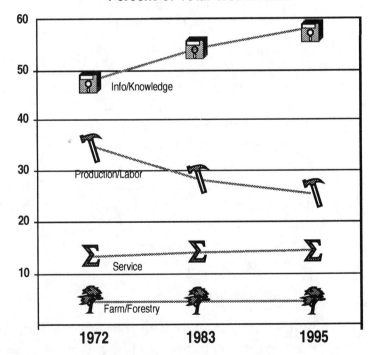

Source: Bureau of Labor Statistics

33. How I Found Mr. Potato: Charlie Porter

The techniques for locating an expert can also be illustrated by a classic story from the days when I was struggling to start my first information brokerage company in 1975.

At the time, my business amounted to just a desk and telephone crowded into the bedroom of my apartment. As so often happens in a fledgling enterprise, my first client was a friend. His problem was this: "I've got to have the latest information on the basic supply and demand of Maine potatoes within 24 hours."

My friend represented a syndicate of commodity investors that invested millions of dollars in Maine potatoes and, when he called, the potatoes were selling at double their normal price. He needed to know why. I knew absolutely nothing about potatoes, other than that they taste better with sour cream and chives, but I thought I knew where to find out more. I agreed that I would be paid only if I succeeded in getting the information, something I no longer do, as you might well understand.

Luck With the First Telephone Call

The first call I made was to the general information office at the U.S. Department of Agriculture. I asked to speak to an expert on potatoes, and the operator referred me to Mr. Charlie Porter. I remember wondering

if Mr. Porter was the man who handled crank calls, but the operator assured me that he was an agriculture economist, the agency's potato expert. I called Mr. Porter and explained how I was a struggling entrepreneur who knew nothing about potatoes, but needed his help in answering a client's urgent request. Graciously, he gave me much of the information I needed and said he would be happy to talk at greater length, either over the phone or in person at his office. I decided to meet this potato expert face to face.

Getting Out of Charlie Porter's Office

For almost three hours the following morning, the Federal government's potato expert explained, in minute detail, the supply and demand for Maine potatoes. Charlie Porter showed me computer printouts that showed how the price had doubled in recent weeks. For any subject that arose during our conversation, Charlie had immediate access to a reference source. Rows of books covering every conceivable aspect of the potato market lined his office. A ticker tape of the latest daily prices for potatoes all over the country lay across his desk.

Here in Charlie's office was everything anyone might ever want to know about potatoes. The problem was not in getting enough information, but how to gracefully leave so that I could relay this information to my client. Once Charlie started talking, it was hard for him to stop. It seemed that Charlie Porter had spent his professional career studying the supply and demand

for potatoes and someone with a genuine need finally had sought his expertise.

One Potato....Two Potato....

When I finally had to tell Charlie that I really had to leave, he pointed across the hall in the direction of a potato statistician whose primary responsibility was to produce a monthly report showing potato production and consumption in the United States. From this statistician, I learned all the categories of potatoes tallied by the government. I found the U.S. Department of Agriculture counts every potato chip sold each month, even how many Pringles are consumed versus say, Lay's Potato Chips. The statistician even offered to place me on the mailing list to receive all this free monthly potato data, but I had a deadline to meet.

34. A Case Study: Jelly Beans

Back in the 1980s when my business was gathering information for large Fortune 500 clients, we were asked to determine the size of the market for jelly beans. Ronald Reagan was eating jellies in the White House, and our client was considering entering the market. But first they wanted to know how many jelly beans were sold each year, who sold them, and to whom. A simple enough question today - now that the jelly bean market has exploded and gone gourmet, with candy shops specializing in hundreds of flavors. But back then, the Easter Bunny was the biggest customer.

What follows is a set-by-step description of how we finally located this information for our client. In your personal life you'll probably never need information on jelly beans. But there will be times you'll have to seek out other difficult information, and the skills and techniques presented here can easily be transferred to other problems, like finding a the best treatment for an illness or a new career.

Opening Round

We already knew that our client had contacted major market research firms and did some literature searches on candies, but they had come up with practically no useful information. Again, our search began because

Ronald Reagan was President and jelly beans had become the candy of choice among several very high government officials.

1) Our first call was to the U.S. Department of Commerce to see if the government had a jelly bean expert. It did. We were referred to Cornelius Kenny, who knew the confectionery industry like the back of his hand. Mr. Kenny was out that day, we were told, but he would call us back when he returned to the office.

2) A search of Gale's *Encyclopedia of Associations* identified four relevant trade associations. However, upon contacting them we were told they only provided market information to their members, and we didn't feel like joining.

3) The White House seemed like another good bet. There had been a lot of publicity about Reagan's fondness for jelly beans, but the Public Affairs office at 1600 Pennsylvania Avenue admitted that they had no statistical information on the industry. They did, however, tell us about a lifesize water buffalo constructed of jelly beans, and even and portraits of the President. They suggested we contact several lobbying organizations that specialized in representing the confectionery industry, but calls to these groups proved, well, juicy-fruit-less.

4)   We next called the U.S. Bureau of the Census, and found John Streeter, an analyst who monitored the "panned" candy industry. He told us:

- jelly beans have never been counted and there would be no way to get the answer;

- the non-chocolate panned candy category within the Bureau's Annual Confectionery Survey contains jelly beans;

- the seasonal category of non-chocolate panned candies, according to his estimates, contains 90% jelly beans because most jelly beans are sold during Easter and that jelly beans are about the only non-chocolate panned manufactured candy sold on a seasonal basis;

- $37,804,000 worth of non-chocolate panned candy was shipped by U.S. manufacturers in 1984, which represents about 48,354,000 pounds; the figures for total non-chocolate panned candy for 1984 totaled $251,525,000 and 237,308,000 pounds; and

- government regulations prohibited him from revealing the names of jelly bean manufacturers, but he did refer us to two trade associations he thought might help.

So this analyst at the Census Bureau, who tried to discourage us with warnings that no such figure for the jelly bean market existed, actually gave us a ton of good information and some useful leads.

Armed and Dangerous With a Little Information

At this point, we had a market estimate from one government expert based on the Census data. It may have sounded like we'd found our answer, but taking it to our client would have been premature, even irresponsible. The main drawback was that the estimate reflected only one person's opinion, and although he was an expert, he was not a true industry observer. We needed to talk to someone actually in the business of selling jelly beans, to help us interpret the figures.

The Census expert referred us to one of the trade associations we had already contacted. However, when we called back saying that Mr. Streeter at the Census Bureau suggested we call them, the association promptly responded with a list of the 25 major jelly bean manufacturers. This is an example of how using the name of a government expert can get you in the door and get you the information you're looking for. When we phoned several manufacturers, they laughed. Jelly beans had never been counted, they told us, and their advice was to give up.

At this point Mr. Kenny, the confectionery expert at the U.S. Department of Commerce called us back and he, too, said that the market had never been measured. However, he did hazard a guess that the jelly bean market could be roughly 50 percent of the total Census figure for non-chocolate panned candy.

A separate call to a private research group which does trend analysis by surveying grocery stores shared its estimate that 90 percent of all jelly beans are sold at Easter.

Easier to Be a Critic Than a Source

Our lack of success with a few manufacturers caused us to change tactics. Instead of asking them to estimate the size of the jelly bean market, we began asking them what they thought of the figures we had already received from the industry analysts at the Commerce Department and the Census Bureau. We also decided to try to find someone who actually filled out the Census survey, and get a reaction to the bureau's figures.

We next spoke with the owner of Herbert Candies, a small company that included jelly beans in its product line. He gave us his 1984 jelly bean production and cost statistics, told us he filled out the Census report, and readily explained what he thought the Census statistics meant in terms of jelly bean production and cost. Furthermore, using his calculator, he helped us arrive at national figures for 1984. He also told us which companies manufactured 80 percent of the jelly beans in the U.S.

Now, armed with actual figures for 1984 jelly bean production, average cost per pound, average number of jelly beans in a pound, and the percentage of jelly beans produced during Easter, we resumed calling manufacturers — this time to get their opinion of our figures. This was the real turning point in dealing with the manufacturers. Because everyone in the industry

knew that there were no exact numbers on the size of the jelly bean market, as professionals, they had been afraid to give us a figure because anyone might challenge it. However, because they were experts in the business, they were not afraid to criticize someone else's information. Reactions from insiders were just what we needed to help hone a good working number. The manufacturers were able to tell us why our figures were good or not and they gave us sound reasons why the numbers should be adjusted. "Based on our sales figures your numbers sound a little low," they told us. Or, "Not all manufacturers report to the Bureau of the Census, so that figure may be low."

To show how this tactic prompted many manufacturers to be candid about both the industry and their sales in particular, here are some highlights of our conversations with nine companies. What is presented below may seem to be too detailed, but after reviewing their responses, you'll see that it proves our point about how open business executives can be about their company, given the chance to play it safe.

1) Owner, Herbert Candies (small manufacturer and retailer).

- 90 percent of jelly beans are sold at Easter;

- 60 percent of Census non-chocolate candy data in the "seasonal" category data are jelly beans;

- the average cost of jelly beans is $1 per pound;

- when President Reagan first got into office, the jelly bean market shot up 150 percent, but it soon fell back to its prior rate;

- four companies have 80 percent of the market, with E.J. Brach controlling the largest share at 40 percent, Brock Candy the second largest, followed by Herman Goelitz and Maillard; and,

- Herbert Candies sold 30,000 pounds of jelly beans in the last year, 90 percent at Easter; 10,000 were gourmet beans at $3.20 per pound and 20,000 were regular jelly beans at $2.80 per pound.

2) Marketing Department, Nabisco Confectionery.

- suggested we call SAMI, a private market research firm;

- estimated 90 percent of jelly beans are sold at Easter; and,

- confirmed that E.J. Brach had 40 percent of the market.

3) Vice President of Marketing and Sales, Herman Goelitz (producer of "Bellies," Ronald Reagan's favorite).

- between 35 percent and 50 percent of his jelly beans are sold at Easter;

- $1.00 per pound could be the average retail price;

- a retailer can purchase jelly beans wholesale at $.60 per pound; and,

- the retail price ranges between $1.25 and $5 per pound.

4) General Manager, Burnell's Fine Candy (manufacturer of hanging bag jelly beans).

- 75 percent of jelly beans are sold at Easter;

- $.60 to $.75 per pound is average manufacturer's price;

- $1.59 is the average retail price; and,

- 75 percent of Census seasonal category candy is probably jelly beans.

5) Senior VP of Marketing and Sales, E.J. Brach (largest manufacturer)

- produces 24 million jelly beans annually at an average price of $.86 per pound;

- there are approximately 100 beans per pound;

- Brach's selling price is about industry average

- they have about 50 percent of the market; and,

- 90 percent of the seasonal market at Easter sounded too high.

6) Product Manager of Marketing Department, Brock Candy (second largest manufacturer).

- 85 percent to 95 percent of all jelly beans are sold at Easter;

- average price paid by retailers is $.59 to $.99 per pound;

- there are 130 to 140 jelly beans in a pound;

- E.J. Brach has 40 percent to 50 percent of the jelly bean business — 32 to 45 million jelly beans sold in a year sounds correct given Brock's production figures, but the figure is probably on the high side;

- Brock Candy is number 2 in the industry; and,

- there are only a handful of jelly bean manufacturers and basing total production on E.J. Brach's sales figures would be a good way to reach an overall industry total.

7) Traffic Manager, Powell Confectionery (medium size producer).

- 75 percent of all jelly beans are sold at Easter, judging by Powell's sales;

- average retail price $.75 to $.80 per pound and the average manufacturer's price is $.65 to $.70 per pound;

- 35 to 45 million jelly beans per year sounded "reasonable"; and,

- it seems fair to double E.J. Brach production figures to get the total market, because it has about a 50 percent share.

8) President, Ferrara Panned Candy (largest panned candy producer).

- familiar with Census data and believes that jelly beans represent about 75 percent to 80 percent of seasonal sales; 80 percent to 90 percent of all jelly beans are sold at Easter;

- 32 to 45 million pounds per year seemed a bit low; and,

- E.J. Brach has 50 percent of the packaged jelly bean market, but less than half of the bulk jelly bean market

9) New Product Development Manager, Farley Candy.

- familiar with Census data and believes that the numbers are understated because not all companies report their figures; and,

- an industry estimate of 32 to 50 million pounds per year seemed low.

So much for all those who discouraged us from even trying to count all the jelly beans! The data we gathered with these telephone conversations provided more information than our Fortune 500 client ever expected.

Deciding on an Estimate

As you can see from the interviews outlined above, traffic managers all the way up to company presidents were willing to give us their best estimate of the size of

the market, and even divulge their own company's sales figures.

After talking with government and business experts, we estimated total annual sales in the 45 to 50 million pound range. It may not be that obvious from just reading the highlights of our interviews, but that consensus became apparent after talking with about a dozen people associated with the industry.

Information Is a People Business

It is amazing what company executives and government experts are willing to tell you if you approach them the right way. You can find the answer to any question (or at least a good estimate) as long as you make a lot of phone calls and treat each person on the other in a friendly, appreciative way.

The biggest difference between those who succeed in their information quest, and those who fail, boils down to whether or not they believe the information exists. If you persist in thinking the information can be found, nine times out of ten you will get what you need.

35. Your Neighbors Are Nitwits

I'm amazed at how many people ask their neighbors for expert opinions on important personal problems. You might as well ask their dog! I've been at neighborhood parties and heard people ask neighbors for advice on everything from miracle weight loss diets to surgery for hemorrhoids. Remember, I live just outside of Washington, D.C., and could walk the entire party to the National Institutes of Health. It's just down the street! But in the shadow of the greatest medical mindbank in the world, where millions are spent studying diets and hemorrhoids, my neighbors are asking each other for medical tips. Instead of calling the best experts in the world.

We do this because of the comfort factor. We know George had an operation for his problem, and his wife looks half her age. So we ask them. Medical experts? Not by a long shot.

36. Why Would an Expert Talk to Me?

Why would an expert want to talk to you? Because they're only human. Any interest in what interests them adds meaning to their work. Their research is often lonely, shared with only a handful of colleagues. When someone from outside calls, it's like a pat on the back, an acknowledgement that what they're doing is worthwhile. Nine times out of ten, an expert will talk.

Of course, there are limits. If you need information about the President of the United States, you're just can't call the White House and chat with the honcho in the Oval Office. But you will be able to talk to a staff person who will willingly send you more information about the Commander in Chief than you'll probably ever need. Or you can call the National Archives and speak with experts who spend entire careers studying the Presidency.

It works the same way in the private sector. If you are looking for information on Microsoft, you won't have much luck calling Bill Gates' office in Redmond, Washington and asking for him personally - although it never hurts to try. Instead, you can call experts in the state government, the federal government, trade associations, and the trade press. These people will probably be more than willing to share what they know about the computer giant. You just have to ask.

While it's human nature for most people to want to help someone else, the key to how much quality information you get depends on how well you treat these people. We'll cover that topic later. Remember, most experts are mid-level government workers who spend their entire career studying some subject. Few people even know they exist, so they're flattered by your attention and feel it is their duty to help you. I learned this with my first information business, when I found potato expert, Charlie Porter. Mr. Porter was an expert in Maine Potatoes who worked at the U.S. Department of Agriculture, and he helped me make money on one of the first research projects I'd ever done. You can read all about him in Chapter 33, "How I Found Mr. Potato: Charlie Porter."

37. Starting Places For Finding a Free Expert

Perhaps the greatest thing about locating a free expert to help you with any problem is that you don't even have to do the work yourself. Many agencies and organizations will track down an expert for you - for free. Listed below are places to turn to when don't know where to go.

1) Free Information Clearinghouses

See page 159, "375 Organizations That Will Do Research for You for Free." This listing of 375 organizations will help you finding free experts on almost any subject. All you need is a phone. Call a clearinghouse that deals with your question, or might. Be nice. Even if your question is not in their area of expertise, they often can recommend another clearinghouse that can help. Remember that these people are paid to help you with your information problem for FREE.

2) Encyclopedia of Associations

I've written close to 60 reference books, and this the only one I wish I'd written. It describes organizations representing every business, trade and interest in the country - be it fraternal, cultural, educational or even humorous. Yes, you can find out how to join Baldies of America or the Posthumous J. Edgar Hoover fan club.

Face it, we're a country of joiners. If there are ten people in this country interested in the same subject, they will start a club or association, and sooner or later they'll end up in Gales. There are more than 20,000 listings on everything from The American Association of Aardvark Aficionados to the Zinc Development Association. So where to you go for information on aardvarks or asteroids? Ask the experts. They'll chew it around and give you more information in five minutes than you would get in a month searching at the library. The book is published by Gale Research Inc., in Detroit Michigan, and is available in most libraries, but don't buy it until you've used it a few times - it's expensive. Updated every year, the cost at the time of publication of this book was $450.

3) Your Local Library

Although I say a lot of bad things about libraries, I love them. If you read closely, what I say is that libraries have trouble getting you the best answers in today's fast changing society. But they're great for pointing you in the right direction, in identifying where you can look for answers. A library, or a good reference librarian, can show you dozens of great books that list sources of information on any subject. You can find directories that list everything from abortionists to zoologists, from companies that buy toy ideas to literary agents that will review a rough draft of your novel. Visit the library and make a list of names and telephone numbers, then go home and start running up a phone bill.

The library also has the best indexes, both computerized and manual, of books, articles and other printed documents that you can search to find experts to call. If someone wrote a book or article on the topic last year, or even ten years ago, they are probably still keeping up on the subject and will be able to give you the information you need or tell you where to get it.

Most public libraries will also do free research for you by phone - but don't tell anyone. When I had a research company, I charged business clients up to $100 an hour to do what the local library was doing for free.

4) The U.S. Government Manual

This book describes all the government departments and agencies. If you don't have one of my big directories of government information sources, this is the next best thing. It costs about $33 and is available from the U.S. Superintendent of Documents, Government Printing Office, Washington, DC 20402; 202-512-1800. It's a great place to start if you're trying to find out who in the government might have the information you need. The best part about this book is that it describes what every department and agency in the government does. From this mission statement, it is easy to pinpoint which office might handle your area of concern. The book is also available in any public library.

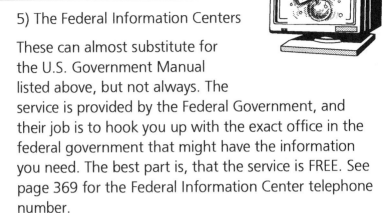

5) The Federal Information Centers

These can almost substitute for the U.S. Government Manual listed above, but not always. The service is provided by the Federal Government, and their job is to hook you up with the exact office in the federal government that might have the information you need. The best part is, that the service is FREE. See page 369 for the Federal Information Center telephone number.

6) State Information Operator

This source may not work for as many problems as the Federal Government or the *Encyclopedia of Associations*, but it is an important tool. Once you get familiar with state government offices, you will understand they are priceless. They can help you get money to start a business or fix up your home, give you free legal help to fight your insurance company or your bank, provide free help for your sick pet or free videos on retirement planning. Who would have thought it? Call your state capitol information operator and talk sweet. This is the key. See page 370 for a listing of state capitol operators.

7) See also Chapter 39, "Cruising for Experts on the Internet."

38. What to Do When an Expert Doesn't Give You an Answer

The most important thing about looking for information is that as long you have a source, there is still hope that you will get your answer. That means that as long as you have a source, you're still in the game, because once you run out of sources the game is over. So what you should try to get from a source that can't give you any answers is to try to get them to give you another source. You contacted this source because she was at least a lot closer to the answer than you are, so her guess on who might be helpful to you will be a lot better than yours. And it will keep you in the old ball game.

39. Cruising For Experts on the Internet

E-mail Is the ATM machine of the Information Revolution.

For many years, it's been possible to go on-line and search literature-based databases to find experts who have written books or articles on specific topics. These databases have always been expensive and pretty time-consuming, so they haven't been used much by the average consumer. But the Internet is different.

Today it is very easy and inexpensive to search for experts using the World Wide Web and other search engines like Gopher and Veronica. The Net is not as easy to use as the commercial databases, but it is getting easier every day and it offers far greater potential than what's contained in the literature-based databases.

I was recently surfing the Web for one of my boys, trying to get information on the origins of silicone. On the US Geological Survey Web Page, we found a section called "Ask-A-Geologist." We left a message and within two days we had our answer E-mailed back to us. Of course we could have used the telephone, but it was 10 o'clock at night and besides, the Web was cheaper and I didn't have to be face-to-face over the telephone.

Using E-mail instead of the telephone for contacting experts is especially useful for people who are shy or uncomfortable talking on the telephone, and those who

hate playing phone tag. I don't believe E-mail is as good as the telephone for quizzing an expert, but it does get the job done. Like ATM banking, you can solve needs without talking directly to a human being.

E-mail is also helpful if you are trying to contact very important people. I spend a lot of time trying to contact high-powered media people, and it has become very hard to get them by phone. They get hundreds of calls each day and need to be very selective, for times sake, on whom they call back. Ten years ago, when faxes first became popular in offices, it was easier to get the attention to busy people by sending a fax. At that time they received few faxes, and when they did, it usually got their attention because it was still unique. But in just ten years, faxes have become just as common as the telephone and busy people have become as selective about reading and responding to fax material as they are with taking or returning telephone calls.

E-mail is like fax machines were ten years ago. It's still new - even to very busy people - and has a much greater chance of being noticed. Yet with the spread of personal computers, you can't relay on this advantage much longer. I'm afraid E-mail is destined to become old news, too, but you can bet something new will be there to take its place at the forefront of attention-getting communications technology.

40. Forums, News Groups and Chat Rooms

To me, computers offer us two great opportunities. One is their ability to handle large amounts of data, which we have already discussed, and the other is their ability to share information faster than more traditional forms of communication. Although we don't often consider computers as helping to ease our suffering - usually just the opposite. But consider the following case in point.

Suppose there is a young veterinarian in Iowa whose first client is a three legged dog. Not only has she never seen a three legged dog before, but she didn't learn anything about them in Vet school. So what does she do? Does she turn the patient away? She may be the only Vet in town, and the dog's owner, probably a little kid, is going to cry all the way home.

In the past, the vet could visit the library or wait for The Journal of Veterinary Medicine to publish an article on treating three legged dogs. Maybe she would be forced to wait for the annual conference of Veterinary Medicine in Las Vegas and hope they have a speaker on the subject. Or maybe be lucky enough to run into someone at the conference who has treated three legged dogs in the past.

Computers have eliminated this problem. Through news groups, forums and chat rooms, this young veterinarian can quickly find an on-line community of veterinarians who help each other. By posing her question on-line,

she could probably get an answer overnight from some wise old veterinarian who has treated dozens of three legged dogs during his long practice.

Today, this young veterinarian doesn't have to struggle with problems, waiting to get answers at the annual convention. She can now be part of a convention every night. If the answer is out there, on-line technology allows her to find it quickly. By getting her question answered almost immediately, she can make other kids happy by helping their sick pets. Or she can work on getting an answer to a problem no one has solved yet. As our problems are solved faster and human resources are used more efficiently, the quality of our lives will also improve at a faster pace. And I think everyone understands that the quick rate of change that is now occurring in our society is not likely to slow, but to speed up.

This is not Buck Rogers kind of stuff. I've personally used it myself. A few months ago my 13 year old needed some help with an algebra problem, but I couldn't help - it's been a long time since I studied algebra. So we logged onto CompuServe and hooked into a Forum for math teachers. Forums on CompuServe are where like-minded people share their common interests. There are files you can download, as well as places to leave questions for experts. But the portion of the service that we used allowed us to talk to anyone else currently browsing in the forum. You can get the names of the people who are currently there, and personally ask anyone a question. The question ap-

pears on their computer screen and if they're real people - as opposed to someone's three legged dog who accidentally turned on the family computer, you'll usually get a response in no time. We did, and soon had the answer we needed.

Similar services are available on most all commercial on-line services. This feature has also brought us infamous on-line dating services, not to mention pornography and cybersex. I read that Rush Limbaugh met his current wife on-line, and that Tom Clancy, the famous writer, left his wife of many years to hook up with someone he met on the information superhighway. Yes, there's more than intellectual issues that can be resolved on-line.

The Internet is the motherload of interactive on-line communication. There are literally thousands of News Groups there where you can leave messages or simply keep up on the latest developments on almost any topic. If you're looking for a job, there are groups that will help you write a better resume. Others list actual jobs anywhere in the world. Or you can keep up on your favorite sport, like bicycle racing, and learn things like the best routes for cycling through Tucson, or why shaving your legs will help make you faster. You can also join support groups for almost any disease, be it obesity or cancer. Or, on a lighter side, join a group plotting the demise of Barney the purple dinosaur.

41. Coping with Misinformation

The techniques learned in this book should help you stay clear of most of the bad information floating around out there, but everyone gets fooled sometimes. You will have to learn how to deal with misinformation, often so-called good information sources. Below are a few examples of misinformation and how you can best deal with them.

Problem #1: Don't Get Lost in Jargon

Researchers often must deal in areas of expertise where they do not have complete command of the industry jargon. Sometimes it is easy to believe that you have found the exact information you needed, only to find out later that you missed the mark considerably. If you have to do a job quickly, it is easy to believe that you know more than you really do, or to fail to ask for a complete explanation of jargon. This usually happened because one, you don't want to sound like an idiot, and two, you don't want to waste the expert's time, or your own. But this face-saving/overly time-conscious attitude often backfires, and can cause embarrassment as well as skewed results.

Here is a true story from a U.S. Department of Agriculture expert that illustrates this point.

One day this government researcher received a call from an assistant to the President, a White House hot

shot who acted pretty impressed with himself. He told the USDA expert that he was in a meeting with the President and the head of the Meat Packers Association and needed to know - immediately - how many cows were being raised in the United States. The livestock expert asked if that was exactly what the staffer meant, and the aide impatiently said it was. So the USDA bureaucrat gave him the figure.

However, within minutes, the White House aide called back in a huff, and said that the president of the Meat Packers Association had laughed at the figure, and claimed it underestimated by half the number of cows. The assistant then realized his mistake. He needed the number of cattle, not cows. The expert had only given him the number for females.

The aide's problem was with semantics, as well as industry jargon. He was probably a city slicker who never knew the difference between cows and cattle, but similar mistakes can happen to anyone. For example, if you want to know the market for computers, be specific. Are you talking about free standing office units or central processing units, laptops or home computers?

Solution #1: Act a Little Dumb

To prevent this type of embarrassment, you have to find an expert with whom you can ask dumb questions. You have to be comfortable. You will get the most help if you act very humble and explain how little you know about a subject. If you request information with the arrogance of a White House staffer, you are likely to get

it all wrong - just the facts you ask for and nothing more. However, if you call up an expert and say something like, "Oh God, can you please help me? I don't really know much about this, but my boss needs to know how many cows there are in the country." With more than a hint of indecision in your voice, and honestly admitting you don't know much about the field, the expert is more likely to ask you some key questions that will ensure that you get the right figures. He may even enjoy giving you the information that you need - be it cattle or cows. And they won't resent your phone call.

Problem #2: Double-Check Published Figures

This is a more serious problem than the difficulties with industry jargon. Mastering terminology just requires a little homework. But overcoming a deep-seated belief that information must be accurate if it is available from a computer, in published sources, or from the government, can be like changing your religion. It took me years, as well as dozens of professional embarrassments, to overcome this problem.

Just because a figure appears in print does not make it gospel. Remember the saying, "Figures don't lie, but liars can figure." Keep this in mind when you read anything in print, even if it comes out of a computer. Always check the facts. A good illustration of this has to do with Census Bureau information.

A few years ago we were doing a market study on stereo speakers, and discovered that the figures the U.S.

Bureau of the Census had for this market were off by over 50 percent. No one in the industry complained to the government because the market was relatively small and the manufacturers couldn't be bothered. But most of the companies knew the figure was incorrect, and none of them relied on the Census figures. Another case involves a Fortune 500 company. It told us that for more than five years, it had been filling out the U.S. Census form under the wrong Standard Industrial Code (SIC), so none of the data was being accurately tabulated into the overall industry tally. Mind you, this firm was the second largest manufacturer in that industry.

The number crunchers at the Census Bureau and other agencies and organizations are not always interested in the meaning behind the numbers they report. Much of their work is simply taking a number from block A, adding it to the number in block B, and placing the result in block C. Verifying where the numbers come from is not their job.

Published sources can be an even bigger problem. Many of us believe that we read in magazines and newspapers, or hear on television or radio. It must be true, we assume. The reporters have to check this stuff out first. Nonsense! Anyone and their brother can be interviewed by a magazine or newspaper, and usually what they say will get printed or quoted on the air - provided it's not too outrageous. But often you are more likely to get into print if what you're saying **is** outrageous. After all, most news stories are just accounts of

what someone said as interpreted by a journalist, and almost everyone loves to see their name in print.

The more general the media, the less accurate its reporting is likely to be about a particular industry. An article in an ice cream industry trade magazine is more likely to be accurate than a similar story in the *New York Times*. The trade journal will have reporters who cover ice cream for a living, and they will flush out bad data as a matter of course. The newspaper, on the other hand, maybe does one ice cream story a year, and will print almost anything it hears. So just because someone is quoted in an article does not mean the information is accurate.

I have experienced this firsthand. When I'm on nationwide book promotion tours, interviewed by newspaper reporters, or appear on radio and television talk shows, I can say almost anything, and it will be printed or broadcast without being fact checked. I give countless facts and figures based on my own research - remember, I'm trying to sell books - and seldom will I be questioned or seriously challenged about the authenticity of my data. I don't know if it is laziness, apathy, or just lack of time that allows so much unchallenged information to be presented as fact by the media. Once I have even blatantly lied to a reporter who thought he was a clone of CBS' Mike Wallace of *60 Minutes*. Before I started doing media interviews, I assumed that any good reporter would find holes in my figures and would expose me as some kind of fraud. I didn't know for sure how they would do it, but my own inse-

curity prompted me to prepare for
the worst. But I found most reporters spend little or no time studying
the topic before they an interview,
and if you become annoyed or angry - like I did with the
Mike Wallace wannabe - you can seriously scramble
their integrity with an exaggerated fact or half-truth
that they will never verify.

Solution #2: Find Another Industry Expert

Whether a figure comes from the Census Bureau, a
trade magazine or from a television program, your best
bet for determining whether the number is accurate is
to track down an industry expert and ask for a comment on the figure. What you want is their biased opinion about its accuracy. If the expert believes the figure
is correct, but can't explain why, it's time to find another expert.

Problem #3: Trust an Expert's Best Guess

This seems to contradict what I just said, but stick with
me and you'll see the difference. There are many times
when you cannot start with published or printed data.
All you can do is pick the brains of experts within a
given industry. This means that the facts and figures
will be those experts' best guess. Often this is the only
way to get the information you need - it's soft data and
often full of holes - but it's still the best available.

After spending hours trying to find a friendly expert to
share their opinion on industry or economic facts and
figures, you certainly don't want to make an antagonis-

tic remark about the accuracy of the data. Whenever possible, check for confirmation from other sources.

Solution #3: Ask Harder Questions.

The best way to judge whether a source is knowledge-able about the fact or figure they have quoted is to ask how they arrived at that number. Such a question will likely initiate one of the following responses:

"I don't know. It's the best I can think of."

- A response like this will be a clue that the expert may not know what he is talking about and you should continue your search.

"This is the figure I read from an industry association study."

- This should lead you to verify that such a study was conducted and to attempt to interview people involved with the report and its findings.

"The industry figure is XX because our sales are half that, and we are number 2 in the industry."

- This is probably one of the best types of answers you can get. Any time an industry expert gives you a figure based on something he is positive about, you can almost take it to the bank. The best you can do after this is to find other industry analysts and ask them to comment on that figure.

Misinformation can result in decision-making disasters. But by following the simple techniques described

above you can avoid many of the
mistakes that so often result in
false or biased data. Then you'll be
a long way down the road to mak-
ing good decisions - based on the best information available.

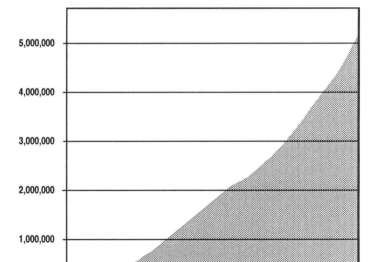

Growth of Inventions
Total Invention Patents

Source: U.S. Patent & Trademark Office

America's Top 20 Most Frequently Asked Questions

42. Lesko's FAQs

I've been in the information business for more than 20 years and have answered thousands, if not tens of thousands, of information requests. Either for a fee - when I was a consultant - or for free, as a guest on thousands of radio and television talk shows. Listed below are my top 20 most frequently asked questions. For those of you who are not on-line, " FAQ" is computer jargon for Frequently Asked Questions.

1. Where Do I Find Money and Help to Start a Business?

Not only is this the most popular question I get asked, I recently saw a list of questions most often asked of the top encyclopedia companies, and it was at the top of their list too. I've devoted entire books to this question but the best starting places are as follows:

Your Local Small Business Development Center

These are not U.S. Small Business Administration offices, but state offices that get federal support. They are great starting places because they can provide almost any kind of help to get your business going. In addition, they do it all for free or for a very small fee. They can help you prepare a business plan or provide you with legal, marketing, or management assistance. They can even help you identify grants, loans, or ven-

ture capital for your business, then help you complete the necessary forms for getting the money. Call your state capitol operator listed on page 370 to get the telephone number of the nearest office.

U.S. Small Business Administration

This is the most frequently used government office for starting a business, but because of the heavy demand for their services you might experience some difficulty getting through to the exact office that you need. They offer a variety of programs, including loans, technical assistance, mentoring programs for women, special loans for people with disabilities, business counseling and help competing for government contracts. To find out more, call 800-8-ASK-SBA.

Your State Department of Commerce

Every state government has special offices that encourage new business and help existing businesses grow. This is how new jobs are created, so these offices are very important to any state. Most states have special loans and even grants to encourage new business activity. Many also have special one-stop business centers or separate offices that will help you find a good location for your business or find and train your employees. Other offices will help you get government contracts or sell your goods and services overseas. Call your state capitol operator listed on page 370 to get the number of your State Department of Commerce or Office of Economic Development.

Catalog of Federal Domestic Assistance

This book is published every six months by the U.S. Government Printing Office and lists every money program available from the federal government. It lists over 1000 loans, grants and other programs especially for businesses, including special help if you want to start a business in a small town or if you want to sell your products overseas. Most any public library should have a copy, or you can purchase a copy from U.S. Government Printing Office, Superintendent of Documents, Washington, D.C. 20402, 202-512-1800.

2. Where Do I Find Money to Go to School?

Whether you are 18 or 80, there is plenty of money out there to help you go to school on either a full-time or part-time basis. Today there are more people on college campuses over the age of 35 than there are 18 and 19-year-olds. The federal government alone gives out more than $32 billion in financial aid every year for tuition, and despite all the talk of government cutbacks, this is enough money to give every college student an average of $3,000. The basic sources are:

U.S. Department of Education

They can tell you about the basic money programs available from the Department of Education. These are by no means all of the programs available, but it is a good starting place. Call 800-4-FED-AID.

Your State Department of Education

Every state has a number of programs that offer grants and loans to student residents. Many of the programs are to encourage people to enter certain professions that are needed in the state, like nursing, teaching, or even accounting. Call your state capitol operator listed on page 370 to get the number of your State Department of Education.

Private Scholarships and Grants

Although government money represents about 80 percent of the total money available to students, that still leaves a sizeable portion available from the private sector. Most of the private money is from foundations and other organizations. Many of them can be found in books at any public library. Ask a good reference librarian and they'll show you everything you need to know.

Catalog of Federal Domestic Assistance

This book is published every six months by the U.S. Government Printing Office and lists every money program available from the federal government. More than 60 programs are only for students, including special money if you are a woman who wants to become an engineer or if you want to become counselor for victims of domestic violence. Most public libraries have a copy of this book, or you can purchase one from the U.S. Government Printing Office, Superintendent of Documents, Washington, D.C. 20402, 202-512-1800.

Financial Aid Departments

Contact the financial aid department of the school you want to attend because they often know of other special programs to help you with tuition. Departments in which you plan to major can also help identify federal programs that offer scholarships for that particular subject area.

3. Where Do I Find Money to Buy or Fix Up a House?

Before you send money to some late night infomercial that promises to make you a million dollars in real estate, or to anyone else who offers you access to money to buy or fix up a house, trailer or condominium, check out the following sources:

HUD USER

This is an information clearinghouse that will provide you with information on all programs available through the U.S. Department of Housing and Urban Development. They have a number of programs that offer everything from financial assistance for real estate developers, to money to buy a condominium. Call 800-245-2691.

Catalog of Federal Domestic Assistance

This book is published every six months by the U.S. Government Printing Office and lists every housing program from the Department of Housing and Urban Development, the Department of Agriculture, the Depart-

ment of Veterans Affairs and the Department of Energy. Most public libraries have a copy, or you can purchase one from the U.S. Government Printing Office, Superintendent of Documents, Washington, D.C. 20402, 202-512-1800.

State Department of Housing

Every state has a number of money programs for people who want to buy or fix up single-family or multi-family dwellings and for first-time home buyers. Many even have programs for nonprofit groups that want to provide housing for special groups. To find out what your state offers, call your state capitol operator listed on page 370 to get the number of your State Department of Housing.

4. Where Can I Learn More About Government Auctions?

One thing to remember about government auctions - you're not going to get a drug dealer's confiscated limousine for only $1.00. But you can get bargains on a ton of other things, usually at discounts of 50 percent to 80 percent. There are a half dozen different agencies that have auctions, including the General Services Administration, the Department of Defense, the Small Business Administration, the Customs Service, the Postal Service, the Internal Revenue Service, and the Department of Housing and Urban Development. The kinds of items you can expect to bid on include everything from

cars, computers, office equipment, cameras, clothing and almost anything you can think of. A few years ago the Internal Revenue Service even auctioned off the Mustang Ranch, a famous brothel in a state where prostitution is legal. To locate the government auctions in your area, contact your local Federal Information Center at 800-688-9889.

Each state government also has auctions and sales of surplus property. You can find out how your state disposes of their goodies by contacting your state government operator listed on page 370.

5. What Are the Best Jobs to Get Into?

Why wait for *U.S. News and World Report* to identify the best jobs for the year 2001?

It's probably written by some journalist who spent only a few days or weeks researching the information and presenting a national overview. Instead, can you can contact the government experts who collect and interpret this information in the first place. They spend millions of dollars to generate data and reports on future job prospects, and definitely know more than the journalists who wrote the article.

Or you can contact non-profit organizations who have experts studying the supply and demand of workers in their area of interest. These sources can give you information, not on a national level but by zip code, and can break down occupations not only by broad categories but also by salary level.

U.S. Department of Labor

200 Constitution Ave NW
Washington, D.C. 20210
202-219-5000

U.S. Department of Commerce

14th & Constitution Ave NW
Washington, D.C. 20230
202-482-2000

Your State Department of Labor Information

Contact your state capitol operator listed on page 370.

Gales *Encyclopedia of Associations*

This book lists thousands of trade and professional organizations like the Society for Chemical Engineers or
the Landscapers Association. Such groups can provide
you with information about current job prospects and
anticipated demand in the future for their profession.
The book is available in most public libraries.

6. How Do I Get Help With My Aging Parents?

More than 35 percent of our national budget goes to
seniors, and we've published books that identify more
than 2,000 special programs for seniors. In addition to
Medicare and Medicaid, seniors are eligible for free
transportation, free legal help, free help in writing a liv-

ing will, money to fix up their home, and, in certain cases, even free long-term care. Seniors can also get fun things - college tuition, travel money, free concert and theater tickets and more.

The best place to start finding out about all these programs is by contacting your state office on aging (call your state capitol operator, listed on page 370) or by contacting the ElderCare Locator, National Association of Area Agencies on Aging, 1112 16th St., NW, Washington, D.C. 20024, 800-677-1116.

7. How Can I Travel Overseas for Free?

There are dozens of programs that allow citizens to travel overseas at the government's expense. You can get $17,000 to study a foreign language, or $20,000 to travel abroad studying international farming. High school and college students can receive $2,500 to study and travel in the summer. Here are the major starting places:

Catalog of Federal Domestic Assistance

This book identifies more than 40 programs that provide money opportunities for travel overseas. It is available in most public libraries or you can purchase a copy from the U.S. Government Printing Office, Superintendent of Documents, Washington, D.C. 20402, 202-512-1800.

Money to Travel Abroad and Share Your Expertise

In response to requests from posts overseas, the United States Information Agency sends approximately 600 Americans abroad annually for short-term speaking engagements.

The U.S. Speakers Program is one of the principal vehicles for fostering discussion on major issues with overseas audiences. Experts who qualify are usually in the fields of economics, international affairs, U.S. political and social processes, sports or science and technology. A U.S. Speaker's tour generally includes informal lectures or discussions, followed by questions and answers with a smaller group of experts from the country where the presentation is made.

For information contact: U.S. Speakers Program, U.S. Information Agency, 301 4th St., SW, Washington, D.C. 20547, 202-619-4764.

The Peace Corps

Jimmy Carter's mother became a volunteer when she was already a grandmother. Volunteers serve for a period of two years, living and working overseas with people who need help with everything from nutrition to building dams. Volunteers are expected to become a part of the local community and to demonstrate, through their voluntary service, that people can be an important impetus for change.

Volunteers receive a stipend and health insurance. Contact: Peace Corps, 1990 K St., NW, Washington, D.C. 20526, 800-424-8580.

Money for Musicians, Dancers and Actors to Perform Overseas

Each year, the government sends abroad a small number of fully-funded performing arts presentations in music, dance, and theater. In addition to performances, overseas tours usually involve workshops or master classes, interviews with foreign media, and representational events such as dinners or receptions.

Contact: Arts America, Bureau of Educational and Cultural Affairs, U.S. Information Agency (USIA), 301 4th St., SW, Room 567, Washington, D.C. 20547, 202-619-4779.

Work for the Government Overseas

The federal government hires people to work overseas doing everything from typing to spying, and there are posts all around the world. Those interested in jobs abroad can contact the Office of Personnel Management to learn current job openings and the skills required.

Other government agencies also hire people to work overseas, and you should contact them directly for information on their latest employment opportunities. Contact: Federal Job Information Center, Office of Personnel Management, 1900 E St., NW, Washington, D.C. 20415, 202-606-2700.

8. How Do I Start a Non-Profit Organization?

Contrary to popular belief, you don't have to hire a lawyer and have thousands of dollars in the bank to start your own non-profit group. With as little as $35 - and 30 minutes of paperwork that you can complete sitting at your kitchen table - you can get started raising funds for causes you care about. Here are the best sources for more information.

Filing with the Internal Revenue Service

To become an official non-profit organization, you must complete certain IRS forms. Lawyers charge hundreds or even thousands of dollars to fill out these forms, but you can do it yourself. Don't worry, if you screw them up the IRS will help you get it right. Call the Internal Revenue Service Forms Line at 800-829-3676 and ask for copies of Publication 557, *Tax-Exempt Status for Your Organization* Form 1023, *Application for Recognition of Exemption Under Section 501(c)(3) of the Internal Revenue Code*, and Form 1024, *Application for Recognition of Exemption Under Section 501(a) or for Determination Under Section 120.*

Read them over and fill them out the best you can. If you have questions, contact the Internal Revenue Service Info-Line 800-829-1040. For difficult questions, contact: Exempt Organizations Technical Division, Internal Revenue Service, U.S. Department of the Treasury 1111 Constitution Ave., NW, Room 6411, Washington, D.C. 20224, 202-622-8100.

Filing with the State Government

You also have to file with your state government to become a nonprofit. Call your state information operator on page 370 to see who to talk to about requirements in your state.

Grants and Foundation Support Resource List

Your local Congressional Representative or Senator's Office can send you a free report that's produced by the Congressional Research Service called *Grants and Foundation Support* (IP50G). It describes sources of funding (both government and private), as well as information regarding grant proposal development. Contact their local office or U.S. Capitol, Washington, D.C. 20515, 202-224-3121, 800-972-3524.

The Center for Foundation Support

The Foundation Center is a non-profit organization which gathers and disseminates facts about foundations. The Center's libraries contain copies of foundations' tax returns, collections of books, documents, and reports about the foundation field, and related material. They also publish funding directories specific to certain fields, and offer programs to assist individuals in information searches. You may also request a list of libraries in each state where Center publications containing foundation information are available. The Center has the following regional offices:

- The Foundation Center
  79 Fifth Ave/16th St.

New York, NY 10003-3076
800-424-9836

- The Foundation Center
1001 Connecticut Ave., NW,
Suite 938
Washington, D.C. 20036
202-331-1400

- The Foundation Center
312 Setter St.
San Francisco, CA 94108
415-397-0902

- The Foundation Center
1356 Hanna Bldg.
1422 Euclid Ave.
Cleveland, OH 44115
216-861-1934

9. Where Can I Find the Best Treatment Information for an Ailment or Disease?

As I said in the first part of this book, most doctors suffer from chronic info-fobia. You've seen the headlines. Every day there are new discoveries, treatments and cures for so many illnesses. It's almost impossible for doctors to keep up. They spend their entire day treating patients, not talking to other scientists or reading research reports. You can get more up-to-date information than what your doctor knows by going straight to the source. Start with the following:

National Institutes of Health

9000 Rockville Pike
Bethesda, MD 20894
301-496-4000

The government spends over $12 billion a year re-searching the latest causes and cures of diseases, and a few phone calls can put you in touch with a facility or agency that is studying your problem. This office will often send you information, point you to special-ists in your area or tell you how you can learn about physicians who are getting grants to treat your condi-tion for free.

National Health Information Center

P.O. Box 1133
Washington, D.C. 20013
800-336-4797

This a national information clearinghouse that can di-rect you to either private or public specialists that are studying your condition or disease. They are also help-ful in answering other health-related questions, like where to find medical insurance or even finance a health care career.

10. How Can I Get Free Prescription Drugs?

No one in this country needs to choose between being able to buy food or their medications. Most drug com-

panies, and even some states, offer free medication to those who cannot afford them. Unfortunately, many doctors don't even know these programs exist.

Each drug company has separate requirements for their free prescription programs, usually income-based, however some don't. What I have found is that is that first you have to admit you are having trouble paying for medication, and then your doctor has to sign a form. It's that easy! If your doctor is unwilling to sign, it's time to get a new doctor. To find out more about the programs contact:

Pharmaceutical Research and Manufacturers of America Association

1100 15th St. NW
Washington, D.C. 20005
1-800-PMA-INFO

They will send you a listing of each drug company's program.

Special Committee on Aging

U.S. Senate, SD-G 31
Washington, D.C. 20510
202-224-5364

They will send you a more detailed description of each drug company's program.

State programs

There are about 10 states that offer free or discount prescription drug programs. Contact your state information operator listed on page 370, and ask for your state Department of Health, or your State Office on Aging. Either will be able to explain the programs available in your state.

11. How Can I Deal with Creditors, Or Fix Bad Credit?

There are several issues involved here. First is how to handle people who are harassing you for not paying bills. Bill collectors have to follow certain regulations, and you have rights. They are not allowed to unnecessarily harass you, or call you during certain hours. The Federal Trade Commission can tell you your rights in dealing with bill collectors. They can send you literature or they can even investigate anyone harassing you. Look in your local telephone book for a local regional office or contact their main office at: Federal Trade Commission, Public Reference, Room 130, Washington, D.C. 20580, 202-326-2222.

Another issue is how to get out of debt. There are two major organizations that can help:

Consumer Credit Counseling Services

This is a national organization that helps consumers develop a plan to deal with debt. Although they do good

work in helping people, they also receive a lot of their financing from credit card companies, so the bankruptcy option may not be the first item they place on the table. Read between the lines. You can find a local office by contacting 800-388-2227.

County Cooperative Extension Service

These government-supported offices are located in every county in the United States and offer free credit counseling services. For the office nearest you, contact your state county cooperative extension office on page 374.

Counseling for Homeowners

To help reduce mortgage delinquencies, defaults and foreclosures, the government provides free counseling to homeowners and tenants through local non-profit organizations. Some will even pay your mortgage for a certain period of time, while you get back on your feet. To find the counseling agency nearest you, contact: Single Family Servicing Division, Secretary-Held and Counseling Services, Office of Insured Single Family Housing, U.S. Department of Housing and Urban Development, Washington, D.C. 20410, 800-569-4287.

It seems that every time you turn on the radio, someone is offering to help you change your credit report. You have a right to see the information, as well as a right to have the information corrected, and you don't

need a third party poking their nose in your affairs when you can do it yourself. It's easy if you contact The Federal Trade Commission, Public Reference, Room 130, Washington, D.C. 20580, 202-326-2222.

12. How Can I Deal with Bad Contractors, Auto Dealers or Drycleaners?

Most local service companies and contractors are regulated at the state level, and there are offices in your state government that will investigate any of your complaints. Often you don't even have to call these offices, you just have to mention that you are going to call them if the situation is not fixed to your liking. If a contractor or company doesn't deliver on their promise, up the ante. Tell them you will report them, and name the agency. Watch them turn pale and offer to correct the problem for free. They know that if they lose an argument with the state, it can put them out of business. Call your state capitol operator on page 370 and ask for the state office of consumer affairs, or the office of the Attorney General.

13. How Do I Deal with a Crummy Lawyer?

Almost every professional group - lawyers, doctors, accountants, even real estate folks - has a state organization that regulates their activities. Any wrongdoing,

or potential wrongdoing, can be reported to these offices, and they will investigate. As with contractors and drycleaners, just the threat of contacting these offices can be enough to get your problem solved. To find the office in your state, contact the state capitol operator, listed on page 370.

14. How Do I Sue My Insurance Company or Bank?

Like the doctors and dry cleaners, insurers and banks are regulated by the state, and there are offices that will investigate any complaint you have against them. Call your state capitol operator, listed on page 370, and ask for the office of the banking or insurance commissioner. In the case of a bank, you can also contact the Federal Deposit Insurance Corporation, Office of Consumer Affairs, 550 17th St., NW, Room F-130, Washington, D.C. 20429, 202-898-3535, 800-934-3342.

15. How Can I Find Out About My Neighbor, My Boss, or My Lost Lover?

There is a lot of public information on individuals that most people would be scared to know is available. Use the following:

Where Do They Live?

The Postal Service will provide you with forwarding addresses and the Social Security Administration will lo-

cate lost loved ones for you. The Division of Motor Vehicles in most states will provide you with an address, and all the military services have locator services for past and present members. Look in the government section of your telephone book for current numbers to these offices.

Who Do They Owe?

Anytime you borrow money and put up an asset as collateral, that information is open to the public. The information is filed at the state capitol under the Uniform Commercial Code, usually in the office of the Secretary of State. Contact your state capitol operator on page 370.

Do They Own Cars and Houses?

Most states will tell you the owner of a vehicle, or which vehicles any individual owns. Contact your state capitol operator on page 370 and ask for the Division of Motor Vehicles. All cities also have offices where you can find out who owns a home and how much they paid for it. Contact your city government for this information.

Home Addresses of Businesses and Post Office Boxes

You can also get the names, and in many cases even the home addresses, of the owners of any business. Contact the state Office of Corporations. Call your

state capitol operator on page 370. You can also find out the owner of a box number by contacting the post office.

16. Where Do I Get Help with My Invention?

Unless you have a ton of money, the last thing you want to do if you have great invention is call one of those companies that advertise on TV. They charge big bucks and guarantee nothing. You can get the same help for free.

Protect Your Idea for Only $10

Instead of getting a full patent, you can file a Disclosure Statement with the Patent and Trademark Office and they will keep it in confidence as evidence of the date of conception of your invention or idea.

Contact: Disclosure Statement, Commissioner of Patents and Trademarks, Patent and Trademark Office, Washington, D.C. 20231, Recorded Message 703-557-3158, Disclosure Office and Legal Counsel 703-308-HELP.

Free Consulting for Inventors

Most cities around the country have offices called Small Business Development Centers. These are state and federally supported centers that will work with you in obtaining a patent, developing a prototype, locating a

manufacturer, and even finding money. Most of their services are free or cost very little.

For an office near you contact your state capitol operator listed on page 370, and ask for the state Department of Economic Development. They will be able to direct you to your local Small Business Development Center.

Evaluations of Your Idea

There are non-profit and government supported organizations that will evaluate your idea at fees ranging from $0 to $295. Contact any or all of the following:

- Innovation Assessment Center
  2001 6th Ave. Suite 2608
  Seattle, WA 98121
  206-464-5450
  - a $295 fee

- Wisconsin Innovation Service Center
  402 McCutchan Hall
  University of Wisconsin-Whitewater
  Whitewater, WI 53190
  414-472-1365
  - a $165 fee

- Inventure Program
  Benjamin C. Swartz
  Inventure Program
  Drake Business Center
  2507 University
  Des Moines, IA 50311

515-271-2655
- no charge

- The Wal-Mart Innovation Network (WIN)
  Center for Business Research and Development
  College of Business Administration
  Southwest Missouri State University
  901 S. National Avenue
  Springfield, MO 65804
  417-836-5667/5680
  - a $150 fee

- U.S. Department of Energy
  CE-521, Mail Stop SE-052
  1000 Independence Ave., SW
  Washington, D.C. 20585
  202-586-1605
  - no charge for energy related inventions

17. How Do I Get a Patent, Trademark or Copyright?

Copyrights are simple to get. Trademarks are a little more difficult, but you can probably do it all yourself. And patents take a bunch of work, but a lot of it can be done by yourself at local libraries. The Patent Office will help you along the way, but at some point you may want to consider getting help. Here are the sources to start:

- Patents and Trademarks
  U.S. Department of Commerce
  U.S. Patent and Trademark Office

P.O. Box 9
Washington, D.C. 20231
703-308-HELP

- Copyrights
Library of Congress
Copyright Office
Washington, D.C. 20559
202-479-0700 or 202-707-3000

18. Tired of Bureaucratic Runaround?

This is not an uncommon problem, and if the government is doing it to you, there are some simple actions to take. If it's a federal office messing you over, simply call the office of your Representative or Senator. They will be happy to investigate. After all, they want your vote. Congress has power over the other branches of government, because that's who approves their budget. Most government agencies even have special offices that only deal with requests, like yours, from Congress. Their messages go on different color paper. Their letters go into different color envelopes. They can get action like you and I can't. And don't forget, you have three places to turn, two Senators and one Representative. If one fails, try the others. If a state office is at fault, use the same procedure at the state level. You have local Representatives or Senators that represent you in your state capitol. If you don't know who they are, memorize their names and numbers.

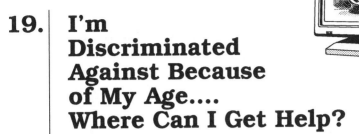

19. I'm Discriminated Against Because of My Age.... Where Can I Get Help?

According to the law, anyone over age 40 is protected by the Age Discrimination in Employment Act. The law prohibits age discrimination in hiring, pay, promotions and too many other factors to list. You can contact the government to see if you have a valid complaint. If so, they will investigate your case and even bring a lawsuit against the employer. Contact: Equal Employment Opportunity Commission, 1801 L Street, NW, Washington, D.C. 20507, 800-669-4000.

20. How Can I Fight the IRS?

If you ever feel mistreated by the Internal Revenue Service, you don't have to hire an expensive attorney. Congress has set up special offices that will fight the IRS for you. These offices are called Problem Resolution Centers, and you can find your local office by looking in the blue pages of your local telephone directory under U.S. Department of Treasury, or by contacting Problem Resolution Staff, Taxpayer Ombudsman, Internal Revenue Service, U.S. Department of Treasury, 1111 Constitution Ave, NW, Room 1027, Washington, D.C. 20224, 202-622-4300.

375 Organizations That Will Do Research for You for Free

Animals and Agriculture

Agriculture Exports Clearinghouse

Foreign Agricultural Service
U.S. Department of Agriculture
Room 5074
Washington, DC 20050
202-720-7115
Fax: 202-720-1727

www: http://www.usda.gov/fas
E-mail: fasinfo@ag.gov

The Foreign Agricultural Service compiles and disseminates agricultural trade and commodity production information to agribusinesses and the general public. They offer private companies and cooperatives assistance in marketing their products overseas by collecting and publicizing information on foreign buyers and advertising U.S. export availability. They have a monthly magazine, commodity and trade reports, publications, and fact sheets (many of which are free). They can answer such questions as:

1) What are the market prospects for U.S. food and farm products in Japan?

2) What are some overseas markets and buying trends for a particular product?

3) What are some overseas promotional activities?

4) How do I begin an export business?

5) How do I advertise my product directly to buyers overseas?

Economic Research Service (Agriculture)

U.S. Department of Agriculture
1301 New York Ave., NW, Room 110
Washington, DC 20005-4788
202-219-0515
Fax: 202-219-0112
Fax on Demand: 202-219-1107

 www: http://www.econ.ag.gov
E-mail: service@econ.ag.gov

The Economic Research Service conducts research on the economic and socio-demographic issues of rural America; the marketing, trade, and consumption of farm commodities; U.S. and foreign economic policies and their effects on trade; and more. They produce monographs and journal articles ranging from very technical research reports to easy-to-read leaflets. They offer situation and outlook reports providing a mixture of outlook and in-depth analysis of current commodity, trade, resource, and policy issues. Most of the information is available free of charge. They can answer such questions as:

1) What are the links between development and world trade?

2) What information exists on the U.S. and world markets for agricultural products?

3) How can farmers better conserve water resources?

4) What are the benefits of organic farming?

5) How can farmers adjust their techniques to keep pace with global market trends?

National Agricultural Statistics Service

USDA South Building
U.S. Department of Agriculture (USDA)
Washington, DC 20250
202-720-3896
Fax: 202-690-1311

www: http://www.usda.gov/nass/
E-mail: nass@nass.usda.gov

The National Agricultural Statistics Service collects data on crops, livestock, poultry, dairy, chemical use, prices, and labor, and publishes the official USDA State and national estimates through its Agricultural Statistics Board. There are nearly 400 reports annually covering domestic agriculture, such as estimates of production, stocks, inventories, prices, disposition, utilization, farm numbers and land, and other factors. They provide national profiles from regular surveys of thousands of farmers, ranchers, and agribusinesses that voluntarily provide data on a confidential basis. Publications are available and range from free to $12. They can answer such questions as:

1) How has the use of a specific chemical for crop growth changed over the past five years?

2) Has the size of farms increased or decreased over the past ten years?

3) What statistics exist on wildlife damage to crops?

4) How has the weekly crop weather effected crop growth?

5) What data is there on livestock slaughter?

Alternative Farming Systems Information Center

U.S. Department of Agriculture
National Agricultural Library
10301 Baltimore Blvd., Room 304
Beltsville, MD 20705-2351
301-504-6559
Fax: 301-504-6409

www: http://www.nal.usda.gov
E-mail: nalafsic@nal.usda.gov

The Alternative Farming Systems Information Center encourages research, education, and information delivery about farming systems that preserve the natural resource base while maintaining economic viability. The Center is the focal point for information on all types of alternative farming practices. They can refer you to organizations or experts, identify current research, furnish you with bibliographies, and more. Brief data base searches are free, while exhaustive searches are conducted on a cost recovery basis. They can answer such questions as:

1) How do you establish and maintain an organic garden?

2) What is involved in building a compost pile?

3) What are the effects of herbicide and fertilizer run off?

4) How can I avoid ground water contamination?

5) What are some solar energy alternatives for agriculture?

Animal Welfare Information Center

National Agricultural Library
U.S. Department of Agriculture
10301 Baltimore Blvd.
Beltsville, MD 20705
301-504-6212
Fax: 301-504-7125

 www: http://www.nal.usda.gov/answers/answers.html
E-mail: awic@nal.usda.gov

The Animal Welfare Information Center is the focal point for all aspects of animal welfare. They have information on the care, handling, and management of animals used in research; training guides and manuals for animal care personnel; ethical issues; animal behavior; and pain control. They have a publications list of free fact sheets, bibliographies, and other resources. They can answer such questions as:

1) What information is there on the ethical and moral issues relating to animals and the philosophy of animal rights?

2) What alternatives are there to the use of live animals in research?

3) What videos exist on the care of animals?

4) What are some of the legislation regarding animal welfare?

5) What are some of the resources available regarding the raising of poultry?

Aquaculture Information Center

National Agricultural Library
U.S. Department of Agriculture
10301 Baltimore Blvd.
Beltsville, MD 20705
301-504-5558
Fax: 301-504-6409

www: http://www.nal.usda.gov/answers/answers.html
E-mail: aic@nal.usda.gov

The Aquaculture Information Center collects information on
the culture of aquatic plants and animals in freshwater, brack-
ish, and marine environments. Examples include: catfish farming, oyster culture, salmon ranching, and trout farming. They
have a publications list of free fact sheets, bibliographies, and
other resources. They can answer such questions as:

1) How do you start a catfish farm?

2) What are the effects of sodium, cadmium, and lead on
aquatic plants?

3) What types of algae are edible?

4) What is involved in raising snails?

5) What can be done to stop the pollution of freshwater environments?

Food and Nutrition Information Center

National Agricultural Library
U.S. Department of Agriculture
10301 Baltimore Blvd., Room 304
Beltsville, MD 20705
301-504-5719
Fax: 301-504-6409

www: http://www.nal.usda.gov/answers/answers.html
E-mail: fnic@nal.usda.gov

The Food and Nutrition Information Center serves many types of users including educators, students, researchers, and consumers. Reference services are provided. Subjects covered include human nutrition research and education, diet and diet-related diseases, food habits, food composition, nutrition education, and more. The Center offers a variety of services which include answers to specific questions, lending books and audiovisuals, and providing computerized literature searches. A publications list is available, many of which are free. They can answer such questions as:

1) What studies exist on the effects of the school breakfast program?

2) What information can you provide to parents concerned about their overweight children?

3) Do you have information on anorexia nervosa?

4) Is it dangerous to consume caffeine while pregnant?

5) Are canned peaches as nutritious as fresh?

Horticulture Clearinghouse

U.S. Department of Agriculture
10301 Baltimore Blvd.
Beltsville, MD 20705
301-504-5204
Fax: 301-504-6927

www: http://www.nal.usda.gov

The Horticulture Clearinghouse covers technical horticultural or botanical questions, economic botany, wild plants of possible use, herbs, bonsai, and floriculture. They can answer such questions as:

1) How can you grow lavender commercially as a source of essential oils?

2) How do you grow and dry herbs?

3) How much would landscaping improve the worth of a home?

4) Which plants can be used for medicinal purposes?

5) How can I control garden insects without using chemical sprays?

Meat and Poultry Hotline

Food Safety and Inspection Service
U.S. Department of Agriculture
Washington, DC 20250
800-535-4555
Fax: 202-690-2859

www: http://www.usda.gov

The Meat and Poultry Hotline takes calls from consumers regarding cases of meat or poultry food poisoning or complaints about meat or poultry spoilage, due to improper packaging or processing. They can also provide you with health-oriented information on safe handling and storage of meats and poultry. They can answer such questions as:

1) What should be done during a power outage?

2) What is salmonella and how can people be protected?

3) What are the different type of foodborne illnesses?

4) How long should you cook poultry?

5) What information should be included on meat and poultry labels and what does it mean?

Organic Gardening

Public Information Center, 3404
U.S. Environmental Protection Agency
401 M St., SW

Washington, DC 20460
202-260-7751
Fax: 202-260-6257

www: http://www.epa.gov
E-mail: public-access@epamail.epa.gov

The Public Information Center has free information sheets on organic gardening, composting, and recycling. They can answer such questions as:

1) What plants should be planted near each other to deter pests?

2) What are the dangers of pesticides?

3) Who can I talk to regarding composting and recycling?

4) What are the advantages of organic fertilizers?

5) What is required to maintain a lawn?

Plant Information Service

U.S. Botanic Garden
245 1st St., SW
Washington, DC 20024
202-226-4082
Fax: 202-225-1561

The U.S. Botanic Garden serves as a center for plant information offering a telephone information service as well as responding to written inquiries, Monday through Friday from 9:00 to 11:30 a.m. They can answer such questions as:

1) What are the benefits of organic gardening?

2) How can I use insects to control garden pests?

3) Which house plants are poisonous?

4) What are the dangers of chemical fertilizers?

5) Which herbs grow best indoors?

Rural Information Center

National Agricultural Library
U.S. Department of Agriculture (USDA)
10301 Baltimore Blvd.
Beltsville, MD 20705
301-504-5372
800-633-7701
Fax: 301-504-5181

www: http://www.nal.usda.gov/answers/answers.html
E-mail: ric@nal.usda.gov

The Rural Information Center is designed to provide information and referral services to local government officials, businesses, community organizations, and rural citizens working to maintain the vitality of America's rural areas. The Center provides: customized information products to specific inquiries; refers users to organizations or experts in the field; performs database searches; furnishes bibliographies; identifies current USDA research and Cooperative Extension System programs; and assists users in accessing the National Agricultural Libraries' extensive collection. There is a cost recovery fee for photocopying articles and searches. They can answer such questions as:

1) Which organizations focus on rural health issues?

2) What resources for the historic preservation of farmland are available in rural areas?

3) How can tourism be promoted in small towns?

4) What are examples of the more innovative economic development projects in rural communities?

5) What rural organizations focus specifically on research and development?

Seafood Hotline

Office of Seafood
Food and Drug Administration
200 C St., SW
Washington, DC 20201
800-332-4010
Fax: 202-401-3532

www: http://www.fda.gov_.
E-mail: oco@fdacf.sw.dhhs.gov

The Seafood Hotline can provide consumers with information on how to buy and use seafood products, including storing and handling of seafood, and questions on seafood labeling and nutrition. The Hotline has many free publications on a variety of seafood issues. They can answer such questions as:

1) Can fish be kept frozen for a year?

2) What kind of fish is escolar?

3) What are the dangers of eating raw shellfish?

4) What information is available on canned tuna?

5) What are some seafood safety concerns for people with particular medical conditions?

Business and Industry

Advertising Practices

Federal Trade Commission (FTC)
6th and Pennsylvania Ave., NW
Washington, DC 20580
202-326-3131
Fax: 202-326-3259

www: http://www.ftc.gov
E-mail: consumerline@ftc.gov

This division of the Federal Trade Commission (FTC) promotes the distribution of truthful information to the public through law enforcement and oversight activities in the following areas: general advertising for deceptive claims; advertising claims for food and over-the-counter drugs, particularly claims relating to safety or effectiveness; tobacco advertising; and performance and energy-savings claims for solar products, furnaces, window coverings, wood burning products, and more. They can answer such questions as:

1) How do you file a complaint with the FTC?

2) When and where is the advertising of tobacco products legal, and what are the reasons behind this?

3) How long are over-the-counter drugs tested before they are released on the market?

4) What penalties are levied against a company that has been charged with deceptive advertising?

5) How effective are over-the-counter diet pills?

Federal Aviation Administration

Office of Public Affairs
800 Independence Ave., SW
Washington, DC 20591
202-366-4000

www: http://www.dot.gov
E-mail: gramick@postmaster2.dot.gov

The Federal Aviation Administration (FAA) is the starting place for any information on airlines, airports, and aircraft. The FAA regulates air commerce, develops civil aeronautics, installs and operates airports, conducts aeronautic research and provides guidance and policy on accident prevention in general aviation. They keep statistics on air travel, accidents, and more. There are free publications on airline careers, aviation, and airplanes, as well as videos and curriculum guides. They can answer such questions as:

1) Which airlines had the worst on time rate for a given month?

2) What videos are available on aviation?

3) What historical information is available on women in aviation?

4) What are the current statistics on air traffic accidents?

5) What methods are used to reduce the noise level of new aircraft?

Board of Governors
of the Federal Reserve System (Banking)

Publications Services
20th and C Sts., NW
Washington, DC 20551
202-452-3244
Fax: 202-728-5886

www: http://www.bog.frb.fed.us

The Federal Reserve System, the central bank of the United States, is charged with administering and making policy for the Nation's credit and monetary affairs. The Federal Reserve helps to maintain the banking industry in sound condition, capable of responding to the Nation's domestic and international financial needs and objectives. It has publications and audiovisual materials prepared which are designed to increase public understanding of the functions and operations of the Federal Reserve System, monetary policy, financial markets and institutions, consumer finance, and the economy. They can answer such questions as:

1) How did the Federal Reserve begin and how does it function today?

2) What is the history of the U.S. monetary policy and how is it formulated?

3) Is there a brief overview available on banking regulation?

4) What is the evolution of money?

5) How are checks used, processed, and collected?

Business Assistance Service

Office of Business Liaison
Room 5062
U.S. Department of Commerce
Washington, DC 20230
202-482-1360
Fax: 202-482-4054

The Office of Business Liaison provides information and guidance on programs throughout the federal government. Although it cannot provide legal advice or intervene on an inquirer's behalf with a federal agency, it can alleviate the necessity of making numerous attempts to locate or obtain federal information, programs, and services. Most requests are for information having to do with government procurement, exporting, marketing, statistical sources, and regulatory matters. They can answer such questions as:

1) Where can someone get information on what the government is buying and what steps are required to sell to the government?

2) Who can advise a business on unfair trade practices?

3) Where are the statistics on a specific type of business?

4) Where is there information on federal databases?

5) Is there U.S. tariff information available?

Central and Eastern Europe Business Information Center

U.S. Department of Commerce
International Trade Administration
14th and Constitution Ave., NW, Room 7414
Washington, DC 20230
202-482-2645
Fax: 202-482-4473

www: http://www.iep.doc.gov

The Central and Eastern Europe Business Information Center serves as a clearinghouse for information on business conditions in Eastern European countries, and on emerging trade and investment opportunities in those countries. It also serves as a source of information on U.S. government programs supporting private enterprise, trade, and investment in Eastern Europe. The Center also serves as a referral point for voluntary assistance programs. A variety of printed materials are available directly from the Center, as are bibliographies on data available from other sources. Most of the services are free of charge. They can answer such questions as:

1) What are the export procedures for a particular product to Poland?

2) What are the population, economic, commercial, and trade statistics on Romania?

3) Is there a list of contacts for export information in Bulgaria?

4) What political and economic issues should be considered when investing in businesses in Eastern Europe?

5) How can I advertise directly in Eastern European countries?

Commodity Futures Trading Commission

Office of Communication and Education Services
Commodity Futures Trading Commission
3 Lafayette Center, NW
1155 21st St.
Washington, DC 20581
202-418-5080
Fax: 202-418-5525

www: http://www.cftc.gov/cftc/

The Commodity Futures Trading Commission (CFTC) promotes economic growth, protects the rights of customers, and ensures fairness of the marketplace through regulation of futures trading. CFTC regulates the activities of numerous commodity exchange members, public brokerage houses, commodity trading advisers, and others, as well as approves the rules under which an exchange operates. They have free publications and can refer you to other offices within CFTC for specific information. They can answer such questions as:

1) What is the purpose of futures trading?

2) How do you read a commodity futures price table?

3) Do brokers have to be registered, and if so, how does one check on a broker?

4) What are some of the important issues that people should be aware of before entering the futures market?

5) What do I do if I suspect my broker of dishonest or unethical behavior?

Federal Communications Commission

1919 M St., NW
Washington, DC 20554
202-418-0200
Fax: 202-418-2830

www: http://www.fcc.gov
E-mail: fccinfo@fcc.gov

The Federal Communications Commission regulates interstate and foreign communications by radio, television, wire, satellite, and cable. It is responsible for the development and operation of broadcast services and the provision of rapid, efficient nation-wide and worldwide telephone and telegraph services at reasonable rates. They take complaints and have free information on all areas falling within their responsibility. They can answer questions such as:

1) What can be done if someone is having trouble with their cable company or does not understand their cable bill?

2) Where do you complain if you find the local D.J.'s show to be offensive?

3) What are the rules regarding pay per call services?

4) Where can you learn more about cellular radio regulations?

5) What happens when radio signals are picked up by consumer electronic products?

Export Country Experts

U.S. Foreign and Commercial Services
Export Promotion Services
U.S. Department of Commerce
Room 2810
Washington, DC 20230
202-482-3809
Fax: 202-482-5819

www: http://www.doc.gov

The Country Desk Officers at the U.S. Department of Commerce can provide businesses with information on a market, company, or most any other aspect of commercial life in a particular country. These specialists can look at the needs of an individual U.S. firm wishing to sell in a particular country in the full context of that country's overall economy, trade policies, and political situation, and also in light of U.S. policies toward that country. Desk officers keep up to date on the economic and commercial conditions in their assigned countries. Each desk officer collects information on the country's regulations, tariffs, business practices, economic and political developments, trade data and trends, market size, and growth. They have free reports and other information available or they can refer callers to other country specialists. They can answer such questions as:

1) How can I expand my business through a foreign franchise?

2) How can I reduce my company's distribution and transportation costs overseas?

3) What type of export opportunities exist for computer manufacturing companies who want to expand to Germany?

4) What are some recent foreign labor trends in Japan?

5) Which markets are growing the fastest overseas?

Economic Research Service

U.S. Department of Agriculture
1301 New York Ave., NW
Room 110
Washington, DC 20005-4788
202-219-0515
Fax: 202-219-0112
Fax on Demand: 202-219-1107

www: http://www.econ.ag.gov
E-mail: service@econ.ag.gov

The Economic Research Service conducts research on the economic and socio-demographic issues of rural America; the marketing, trade, and consumption of farm commodities; U.S. and foreign economic policies and their effects on trade; and more. They produce monographs and journal articles ranging from very technical research reports to easy-to-read leaflets. Situation and outlook reports providing a mixture of outlook and in-depth analysis of current commodity, trade, resource, and policy issues are also available. Most of the information is free of charge. They can answer such questions as:

1) What are the links between development and world trade?

2) What information exists on the U.S. and world markets for agricultural products?

3) How can farmers better conserve water resources?

4) What are the benefits of organic farming?

5) How can farmers adjust their techniques to keep pace with global market trends?

Economics: National, Regional, and International

Bureau of Economic Analysis
U.S. Department of Commerce
1441 L St., NW
Washington, DC 20230
202-606-9900
Fax: 202-606-5310

 www: http://www.bea.doc.gov

The Bureau of Economic Analysis (BEA) provides information on national and regional economics. BEA collects basic information on such key issues as economic growth, inflation, regional development, and the Nation's role in the world economy. It distributes a number of publications that measure, analyze and forecast economic trends, and are available on recorded messages, online through the Economic Bulletin Board, and in BEA reports. They can answer such questions as:

1) What is the average per capita income in the United States?

2) Will the rate of inflation increase or decrease over the next five years, and by what percent?

3) What percentage of the Gross National Product (GNP) does the government spend on health care?

4) How does the United States' national unemployment rate compare to other industrialized countries?

5) What was the unemployment rate in Pennsylvania from 1989-1993?

Exporter's Hotline

Trade Information Center
U.S. Department of Commerce
Washington, DC 20230
800-USA-TRADE
Fax: 202-482-4473

www: http://www.ita.doc.gov/ita_

The Trade Information Center is a comprehensive one-stop shop for information on U.S. Government programs and activities that support exporting efforts. This hotline is staffed by trade specialists who can provide information on seminars and conferences, overseas buyers and representatives, overseas events, export financing, technical assistance, and export counseling. They also have access to the National Trade Data Bank, which provides basic export information, country-specific information, and industry-specific information. They can provide a great deal of free assistance, but there is a fee charged for data bank searches and other technical assistance. They can answer such questions as:

1) What countries are increasing or decreasing imports of a particular product, and at what rates?

2) What 10 countries are the top importers of a specific product?

3) How can a businessman meet prescreened prospects who are interested in a product or service?

4) How can a business assess their export potential?

5) How can a businessman obtain background data on potential foreign partners?

Fishery Statistics Division

Office of Research and Environmental Information
National Marine Fisheries Service
National Oceanic and Atmospheric Administration
U.S. Department of Commerce
1335 East-West Highway, Room 12362
Silver Spring, MD 20910
301-713-2328
Fax: 301-713-4137

 www: http://remora.ssp.nips.gov/mrfss

The Fisheries Statistics Division publishes statistical bulletins on marine recreational fishing and commercial fishing, and on the manufacture and commerce of fishery products. This Division has several annual and biannual reports available. They can answer such questions as:

1) How many fish were imported in a year, and what kind?

2) What is the most popular fish to export?

3) What kinds of fish are frozen?

4) What statistics exist on processed fish?

5) How many fish were caught by weekend fishermen?

Office of Industries

United States International Trade Commission
500 E St., SW
Washington, DC 20436
202-205-3296
Fax: 202-205-3161

www: http://www.usitc.gov
E-mail: cunningham@usitc.gov

The Office of Industries at the U.S. International Trade Commission has experts assigned to every commodiity imported into the U.S. These experts are responsible for investigation of the customs laws of the United States and foreign countries; the volume of imports in comparison with domestic production; the effects relating to competition of foreign industries; and all other factors affecting competition between articles of the U.S. and imported articles. They are knowledgeable about the domestic and foreign industry, and have statistical and factual information. They also have information regarding the tariff schedules. There is no charge for this information. They can answer such questions as:

1) What is the rate of duty for a product from a particular country?

2) What is the rate of import-export, the size of the market and the major producers of women's sweaters?

3) How much of a product is exported and what is the size of the potential market?

4) What happens if someone suspects an imported article is being subsidized or sold at less then fair value?

5) What can a company do if they feel they are being unfairly effected by import trade?

Technical Data Center (Job Safety)

Technical Data Center
Occupational Safety and Health Administration
U.S. Department of Labor
200 Constitution Ave., NW, Room N2625
Washington, DC 20210
202-219-7500
Fax: 202-219-5046

The Technical Data Center compiles technical information on all industries covered by the Occupational Safety and Health

Administration (OSHA). The Center maintains a library of 8,000 volumes and 250 journals, as well as an extensive microfilm collection of industry standards and OSHA rule-making records. The Center is also the docket office and holds the hearing records on standards, the comments, and final rules. Literature searches are conducted free of charge. They can answer such questions as:

1) What are some hazard training programs that can be implemented in the workplace to teach employees to work safely in a variety of situations?

2) When was a particular company inspected and what violations were found?

3) What are the health hazards of a particular chemical?

4) What are some dangers of working around chemicals while pregnant?

5) Have there been similar reports of spinal cord injuries in a particular job?

Labor-Management Relations Clearinghouse

Federal Mediation and Conciliation Service (FMCS)
2100 K St., NW
Washington, DC 20427
202-606-8100
Fax: 202-606-4251

The Federal Mediation and Conciliation Service represents the public interest by promoting the development of sound and stable labor-management relationships; preventing or minimizing work stoppages by assisting labor and management in settling their disputes through mediation; advocating collective bargaining, and much more. They can answer such questions as:

1) What is "alternative dispute resolution", and how can it be used?

2) How can companies work to develop effective labor-management committees?

3) What statistics exist on dispute mediation, preventive medication, work stoppages, and contract mediation?

4) What are some steps that companies can take to improve communication between labor and management?

5) What happens when a Federal agency and employee representative reach a negotiation impasse?

Federal Labor Relations Authority

Federal Labor Relations Authority
607 14th St., NW
Washington, DC 20424-0001
202-482-6550
Fax: 202-482-6636
Bulletin Board: 202-512-1387

Telenet or FTP: fedbbs.access.gpo.gov

The Federal Labor Relations Authority oversees the Federal service labor-management relations program. It administers the law that protects the right of employees of the Federal Government to organize, bargain collectively, and participate through labor organizations of their own choosing. They can answer such questions as:

1) What laws protect Federal employees?

2) What steps can be taken when labor and management have reached an impasse?

3) How does an employee file a union grievance procedure?

4) How do I get a copy of my local union's collective bargaining agreement?

Labor Statistics Clearinghouse

Office of Publications
Bureau of Labor Statistics
U.S. Department of Labor
2 Massachusetts Ave., NE, Room 2860
Washington, DC 20212

202-606-7828
Fax: 202-606-7890

 www: http://stats.bls.gov
E-mail: labstat.helpdesk@bls.gov

The Bureau of Labor Statistics (BLS) is the principal data-gathering agency of the Federal Government in the field of labor economics. The Bureau collects, processes, analyzes, and disseminates data relating to employment, unemployment, and other characteristics of the labor force; prices and consumer expenditures; wages, other worker compensation, and industrial relations; productivity; economic growth and employment projections; and occupational safety and health. This office can also provide you with a release schedule for BLS major economic indicators and the recorded message number. BLS can refer you to experts within the Bureau who can answer your specific question, provide you with historical information, and refer you to tables and charts for data. The BLS has publications, periodicals, magnetic tapes, diskettes, and more for sale. They can answer questions such as:

1) What are the employment statistics and the outlook for a particular occupation?

2) What is the unemployment rate for a particular state?

3) What is the current wage for a word processor in Seattle, and what are the usual benefits associated with that position?

4) What is the employment projection for a specific job?

5) What is the consumer/producer price index and how has it changed over time?

Mine Safety Clearinghouse

Office of Information and Public Affairs
Mine Safety and Health Administration
U.S. Department of Labor
4015 Wilson Blvd.
Arlington, VA 22203

703-235-1452
Fax: 703-235-4323

 www: http://199.115.12.200

The Mine Safety and Health Administration develops mandatory safety and health standards, ensures compliance with such standards, assesses civil penalties for violations, and investigates accidents. It cooperates with and provides assistance to states in the development of effective state mine safety and health programs and improves and expands training programs. The Clearinghouse can provide general information regarding the Mine Safety and Health Administration, as well as free brochures, manuals, and other publications regarding mine safety and health. They can answer such questions as:

1) How can mine operators train miners effectively to prevent accidents and to avoid unsafe conditions?

2) What are the inspection procedures for a mine?

3) What is the latest information on the treatment and prevention of black lung and other respiratory diseases that are common to miners?

4) What is the latest research on robotics and automation in the mining industry?

5) What mines have been ordered to close because of safety concerns?

Mineral Commodity Information

Minerals Information Office
U.S. Department of the Interior
Reston, VA 22092
703-648-4460
Fax: 703-648-4888

The U.S. Geological Survey (USGS) National Center Minerals Information Office is staffed by mineral experts who distribute a wide variety of mineral-related information and publications to meet and support the needs of the public, as well as government agencies and the scientific and industrial sectors. The staff provides information on the most current as well as past published reports pertaining to minerals, mining, processing, and research. They have statistics on import sources, uses, government stockpile, reserves, world resources, and substitutes. Dozens of commodity specialists are also available to assist you. They can answer such questions as:

1) What will the price of silver be over the next five years?

2) What is the role of gold in the international monetary system?

3) How can industries improve the quality of domestic steel?

4) How many tons of coal did U.S. industries produce last year?

5) What methods are used to recycle scrap metal?

Minority Energy Information Clearinghouse

Office of Minority Economic Impact
U.S. Department of Energy
Forrestal Building, Room 5B-110
1000 Independence Ave., NW
Washington, DC 20585
202-586-5876
Fax: 202-586-3075

www: http://www.doe.gov

The Minority Energy Information Clearinghouse develops and disseminates information related to energy programs that have an impact upon minorities, minority business enterprises, minority educational institutions, and other minority organizations. They can direct callers to government programs that will assist minority businesses in entering the energy field, as well as giving information about educational programs for minority students who are energy majors. They can answer such questions as:

1) What type of fellowships are available to minority college students attending Historically Black Colleges and Universities who want to pursue energy-related careers?

2) What types of energy-related loans are available to minority businesses?

3) Can I receive a listing of minority energy conferences or workshops?

4) How does the Clearinghouse's electronic bulletin board work?

5) How has recent energy legislation had an impact upon minority businesses?

Overseas Private Investment Corporation

Investor Information Service
1100 New York Ave., NW
MS 7412
Washington, DC 20527
202-336-8663
Fax: 202-408-5155

Investor Information Service assists U.S. firms in gathering information on foreign countries and their business environments, as well as facilitating the flow of information about developing countries to potential U.S. investors. OPIC created the Investor Information Service (IIS). Country-specific information is available in kit form on more than 100 countries, as well as on 16 regions. Kits include materials covering the economies, trade laws, business regulations, political conditions and investment incentives of developing countries and regions. Kit costs range from $10-$420. They can answer such questions as:

1) What information exists for someone who wants to set up a fast food business in Greece?

2) What is the latest information on the foreign economic trends and their implications for the U.S. in Hungary?

3) What issues should be considered in purchasing an overseas venture?

4) Is it possible to meet with local business representatives, and experienced U.S. investors, and to attend briefings by the U.S. Ambassador in a foreign country?

5) What is the current investment climate in France? Is it favorable to new U.S. businesses?

Pension Benefit Guaranty Corporation

Public Affairs
1200 K St., NW
Washington, DC 20005
202-326-4040
Fax: 202-326-4042

 www: http://www.pbgc.gov

The Pension Benefit Guaranty Corporation works to ensure the solvency and viability of company-sponsored pension plans. They can provide you with information and publications on pension plans, as well as information pertaining to laws and regulations on pensions. They can answer questions such as:

1) What is the Federal pension law?

2) What are pensions plans and how do they operate?

3) What information on plans is a company required to give to members?

4) What are the rights and options of participants?

5) What is the employer's responsibilities regarding pension plans?

Pension and Welfare Benefits Administration

U.S. Department of Labor
200 Constitution Ave., NW
N5656
Washington, DC 20210
202-219-8921
Fax: 202-219-5362

The Pension and Welfare Benefits Administration (PWBA) helps to protect the economic future and retirement security of working Americans. It requires administrators of private pension and welfare plans to provide plan participants with easily understandable summaries; to file those summaries with the agency; and to report annually on the financial operation of the plans. PWBA has publications and other information available. They can answer questions such as:

1) What is the effect of job mobility on pension plans?

2) What is the Employee Retirement Income Security Act (ERISA)?

3) What studies have been done on the investment performance of ERISA plans?

4) What information are pension plans required to provide to participants?

5) What employee benefit documents are available from the Department of Labor?

Federal Procurement Data Center

General Services Administration
7th and D St., SW
Washington, DC 20407
202-401-1529
Fax: 202-401-1546

www: http://www.gsa.gov

The Federal Procurement Data Center stores information about Federal procurement actions, from 1979 to present, that totaled $25,000 or more. The systems contains information on purchasing or contracting office; date of award; dollars obligated; principal product or service; name and address of contractor; and more. Searches and printouts are available on a cost recovery basis. They can answer such questions as:

1) How many contracts did a particular company receive in a given year?

2) Who in the government is buying winter parkas?

3) What types of contracts are being awarded in Franklin county?

4) What has the National Park Service purchased in the last month?

5) Who do I need to talk to in order to sell my particular product?

Science and Technology Division

Library of Congress
Washington, DC 20540
202-707-5639

 www: http://www.loc.gov

The Science and Technology Division's collection numbers 3.5 million books, nearly 60,000 journals, and 3.7 million technical reports. The collections include such treasures as first editions of Copernicus and Newton and the personal papers of the Wright Brothers and Alexander Graham Bell. The Division has primary responsibility for providing reference and bibliographic services and for recommending acquisitions in the broad areas of science and technology. Reference services are provided to users in person, by telephone, and by correspondence. Indirect reference service is provided through bibliographic guides (Tracer Bullets) and research reports prepared by Division subject specialists and reference librarians. Copies of reference guides are available at no charge. They can answer such questions as:

1) Where can someone begin looking for information on lasers and their applications?

2) What are good sources of information on volcanoes?

3) What resources exist on extraterrestrial life?

4) Where could someone find sources for information on medicinal plants?

5) How would someone go about creating a hologram?

U.S. Securities and Exchange Commission

Office of Public Affairs
450 5th St., NW
Washington, DC 20549
202-942-0020
Fax: 202-942-9654

www: http://www.sec.gov

The Securities and Exchange Commission (SEC) administers federal securities laws that seek to provide protection for investors; to ensure that securities markets are fair and honest; and to provide the means to enforce securities laws through sanctions. They have free publications, a public reference room, disclosure reports, and information on how individuals can protect themselves. They can answer such questions as:

1) What are pyramid schemes and how do they work?

2) Where can someone find out if there have been complaints about a particular broker or adviser?

3) How does someone choose investments safely?

4) Who needs to register with the SEC and what is required?

5) What is the SEC and how does it operate?

U.S. Small Business Administration

Answer Desk
409 3rd St., SW
Washington, DC 20416
800-827-5722
202-205-6400
Fax: 202-205-7064

www: http://www.sbaonline.sba.gov

The Small Business Administration (SBA) aids, counsels, assists, and protects the interests of small business, and ensures that small business concerns receive a fair portion of government purchases, contracts, and subcontracts. SBA also makes loans and licenses, and regulates small business investment companies. The Small Business Answer Desk helps callers with questions on how to start and manage a business, where to get financing, and other information needed to operate and expand a business. They have a publications catalogue, with most items available for under $5.00. They can answer such questions as:

1) What programs or forms of assistance are available to women entrepreneurs?

2) What help exists for a business interested in developing an export market?

3) Is there a way a business can receive free management consulting?

4) Are there programs designed specifically for businesses in small towns?

5) How does a company enter the federal procurement market?

National Center for Standards and Certification

National Institute of Standards and Technology
Building 411, Room A163
Gaithersburg, MD 20899
301-975-4040
Fax: 301-926-1559

The National Center for Standards and Certification Information provides a free service which will identify standards for selling any product to any country in the world. This federal agency will tell you what the standard is for a given product or suggest where you can obtain an official copy of the standard. They can answer such questions as:

1) What U.S. industries standards pertain to certain products?

2) What foreign standards apply to a product?

3) What is the latest GATT information on proposed foreign regulations?

4) Where can I locate the organizations that have standards information?

5) How are military standards different for U.S. standards?

Transportation Research Information Services

2101 Constitution Ave., NW
Washington, DC 20418
202-334-2934
Fax: 202-334-2003

www: http://www.nas.edu

The Transportation Research Information Services (TRIS) is the prime source of transportation research information in the United States. TRIS is an information clearinghouse designed to identify worldwide sources of transportation research information. TRIS contains more than 250,000 abstracts of completed research and summaries of research projects in progress. TRIS is regularly used by transportation administrators, operators, academics, planners, designers, engineers, and managers. TRIS contains information on various modes and aspects of transportation including planning, design, finance, construction, maintenance, traffic operations, management, marketing, and other topics. They can answer such questions as:

1) What is the latest research on airport capacity?

2) What information exists on the privatization of toll roads?

3) What data should be considered when building a bypass?

4) What studies have been conducted on land traffic getting to and from airports?

5) What technology exists to weigh trucks in motion rather than at weigh stations?

Women's Bureau Clearinghouse

U.S. Department of Labor
200 Constitution Ave., NW, Room S3306
Washington, DC 20210
800-827-5335
202-219-4486
Fax: 202-219-5529

www: http://www.dol.gov/dol/wb/dol
E-mail: wb-wwc@dol.gov

The Women's Bureau Clearinghouse was designed and established to assist employers in identifying the most appropriate policies for responding to the dependent care needs of employees seeking to balance their dual responsibilities. They can also provide information on women's issues, as well as work force issues that affect women. They offer information and guidance in areas such as women-owned businesses, women workers, alternative work schedules, dependent care issues, and much more. They also have publications and other information available, much of which is free. They can answer such questions as:

1) What are some elder care program options?

2) What is the earning difference between men and women?

3) How does flex time work in companies similar to mine?

4) What are some examples of alternate work schedules and how do they work?

5) What literature and other resources are available on employer-supported child care?

Office of American Workplace

U.S. Department of Labor
200 Constitution Ave., NW
Washington, DC 20210
202-219-6098
Fax: 202-219-8762

www: http://www.dol.gov/dol/oaw/

Working together, labor and management in every sector of the American economy are creating joint programs devoted to productivity, organizational efficiency, and a better work environment. The Office of American Workplace seeks to gather information about the various programs, as well as labor and management efforts. They have a free newsletter, as well as other information on this topic. They can answer such questions as:

1) Which firms and organizations in the private sector have labor-management programs?

2) How can a program be instituted to improve labor-management relations?

3) What types of cooperative arrangements have been attempted in companies similar to mine?

4) What involvement have labor unions had in starting these programs in the workplace?

Consumer and Housing

Animal Welfare Information Center

National Agricultural Library
U.S. Department of Agriculture
10301 Baltimore Blvd.
Beltsville, MD 20705
301-504-6212
Fax: 301-504-7125

www: http://www.nal.usda.gov/answers/answers.htm
E-mail: awic@nal.usda.gov

The Animal Welfare Information Center is the focal point for all aspects of animal welfare. They have information on the care, handling, and management of animals used in research; training guides and manuals for animal care personnel; ethical issues; animal behavior; and pain control. They have a publications list of free fact sheets, bibliographies, and other resources. They can answer such questions as:

1) What information is there on the ethical and moral issues relating to animals and the philosophy of animal rights?

2) What alternatives are there to the use of live animals in research?

3) What videos exist on the care of animals?

4) What are some of the legislation regarding animal welfare?

5) Are there resources available regarding the raising of poultry?

Auto Safety Hotline

Office of Defects Investigation (NEF-10)
National Highway Traffic Safety Administration
U.S. Department of Transportation
400 7th St., SW
Washington, DC 20590
800-424-9393
Fax: 202-366-7882

www: http://www.nhtsa.dot.gov

The Auto Safety Hotline can provide information on recalls, defects, investigations, child safety seats, tires, drunk driving, crash test results, seat belts, air bags, odometer tampering, and other related topics. They also accept reports of automobile safety problems. The Hotline publishes the New Car Assessment Program, which provides comparable data on the frontal crashworthiness of selected new vehicles. They have free fact sheets and publications on these topics and more. They can answer such questions as:

1) What is the safest new car?

2) Which child car seats have been recalled?

3) What should you do if you suspect an odometer has been tampered with?

4) How many states have seat belt laws, and what are the statistics regarding their use and benefits?

5) What are the statistics for drunk driving, and what information exists for alcohol's involvement in fatalities?

6) What is the fuel efficiency of a particular car?

Federal Communications Commission

1919 M St., NW
Washington, DC 20554
202-418-0200
Fax: 202-418-2809

www: http://www.fcc.gov

The Federal Communications Commission regulates interstate and foreign communications by radio, television, wire, satellite, and cable. It is responsible for the development and operation of broadcast services and the provision of rapid, efficient nationwide and worldwide telephone and telegraph services at reasonable rates. They take complaints and have free information on all areas falling within their responsibility. They can answer questions such as:

1) What can be done if someone is having trouble with their cable company or does not understand their cable bill?

2) Where do you complain if you find the local D.J.'s show to be offensive?

3) What are the rules regarding pay per call services?

4) Where can you learn more about cellular radio regulations?

5) What happens when radio signals are picked up by consumer electronic products?

Consumer Product Safety Commission

Office of Information and Public Affairs
U.S. Consumer Product Safety Commission
Washington, DC 20207
800-638-2772
Fax: 301-504-0862

 E-mail: info@cpsc.gov
Gopher: cpsc.gov

The Consumer Product Safety Commission (CPSC) protects the public against unreasonable risks of injury from consumer products; assists consumers in evaluating the consumer products and minimizes conflicting state and local regulations; and promotes research and investigation into the causes and prevention of product-related deaths, illnesses, and injuries. The CPSC Hotline can provide you with information on product recalls and will take reports of hazardous products or product-related injuries. You can write to the CPSC for a complete list of publications which describe some of the common hazards associated with the use of consumer products, recommending ways to avoid these hazards. They can answer such questions as:

1) What toys are currently being recalled?

2) What types of consumer products are the most dangerous?

3) What safety information exists for the classroom?

4) Are there special precautions you should take for the elderly?

5) What is some current information regarding poisons?

Credit Information

Office of Consumer Affairs
Federal Deposit Insurance Corporation
550 17th St., NW, Room F-130
Washington, DC 20429
202-942-3100
800-934-3342

www: http://www.fdic.gov
E-mail: consumer@fdic.gov

The Federal Deposit Insurance Corporation (FDIC) was established to promote and preserve public confidence in banks, protecting the money supply through provision of insurance coverage for bank deposits and periodic examinations of insured state-chartered banks that are not members of the Federal Reserve System. The FDIC can provide you with information and an overview of the FDIC, and the major consumer and civil rights laws and regulations that protect bank customers. They can answer questions on such topics as:

1) Equal Credit Opportunity and Age

2) Equal Credit Opportunity and Women

3) Fair Credit Billing

4) Fair Credit Reporting Act

5) Truth in Lending

National Credit Union Administration

Public Information
1775 Duke St.
Alexandria, VA 22314-3428
703-518-6330
Fax: 703-518-6429

www: http://www.ncva.gov

The National Credit Union Administration is responsible for chartering, insuring, supervising, and examining federal credit unions and administering the National Credit Union Share Insurance Fund. They have free publications and can refer you to the correct office for more information on credit unions. They can answer such questions as:

1) How are credit unions chartered?

2) What are the rules and regulations regarding the organization of credit unions?

3) Is there a master list of all federally insured credit unions?

4) How are credit unions liquidated?

5) How are credit unions insured?

Fair Housing Information Clearinghouse

P.O. Box 9146
McLean, VA 22102
800-343-3442
Fax: 703-821-2098

www: http://www.hud.gov

The Fair Housing Information Clearinghouse can put you in touch with a reference specialist who can assist you in identifying materials regarding fair housing. They have guidebooks, manuals, reports, and audiovisual materials that may be of interest. In addition, they maintain a database of discrimination cases decided by the U.S. Department of Housing and Urban Development (HUD) and HUD's Administrative Law Judges. For a fee, a reference specialist will search the database to identify cases of interest to you. For more information regarding the Clearinghouse contact the office listed above. A publications list (listing many free publications), is available. They can answer questions such as:

1) What is the Fair Housing Act?

2) What should be done if you suspect discrimination in the housing market?

3) What are some referrals to other sources of information on fair housing?

4) What are the accessibility requirements for certain buildings?

5) How much will it cost to create accessible housing?

Food and Nutrition Information Center

National Agricultural Library
U.S. Department of Agriculture
10301 Baltimore Blvd., Room 304
Beltsville, MD 20705
301-504-5719
Fax: 301-504-6409

www: http://www.nal.usda.gov/answers/answers.html
E-mail: fnic@nal.usda.gov

The Food and Nutrition Information Center serves many types of users including educators, students, researchers, and consumers. Reference services are provided. Subjects covered include human nutrition research and education, diet and diet-related diseases, food habits, food composition, nutrition education, and more. The Center offers a variety of services which includes answers to specific questions, lending books and audiovisuals, and providing computerized literature searches. A publications list is available, many of which are free. They can answer such questions as:

1) What studies exist on the effects of the school breakfast program?

2) What information can you provide to parents concerned about their overweight children?

3) Do you have information on anorexia nervosa?

4) Is it dangerous to consume caffeine while pregnant?

5) Are canned peaches as nutritious as fresh?

Federal Trade Commission (Fraud)

Public Reference Branch
Pennsylvania Ave. at 6th St., NW
Washington, DC 20580
202-326-2222
Fax: 202-326-2050

 www: http://www.ftc.gov

The Federal Trade Commission (FTC) protects consumers against unfair, deceptive, or fraudulent practices. The FTC enforces a variety of consumer protection laws enacted by Congress, as well as trade regulation rules issued by the Commission. Its actions include individual company and industry-wide investigations, administrative and federal court litigation, rulemaking proceedings, and consumer and business education. The FTC has a wealth of information and free publications on a variety of topics. They can answer such questions as:

1) What are the laws regarding shopping by mail or phone?

2) What are some things people should know before looking for a job with a head hunter?

3) What information exists for people checking out mortgages or refinancing?

4) What should someone do if their lifetime membership in a health club expires?

5) What can be done to protect against credit card fraud?

Horticulture Clearinghouse

U.S. Department of Agriculture
10301 Baltimore Blvd.
Beltsville, MD 20705
301-504-5204
Fax: 301-504-6927

www: http://www.nal.usda.gov

The Horticulture Clearinghouse covers technical horticultural or botanical questions, economic botany, wild plants of possible use, herbs, bonsai, and floriculture. They can answer such questions as:

1) How can you grow lavender commercially as a source of essential oils?

2) How do you grow and dry herbs?

3) How much might landscaping improve the worth of a home?

4) Which plants can be used for medicinal purposes?

5) How can I control garden insects without using chemical sprays?

HUD USER (Housing)

P.O. Box 6091
Rockville, MD 20850
800-245-2691
Fax: 301-251-5767

www: http://www.huduser.org

HUD USER, a service of the U.S. Department of Housing and Urban Development, is an information source for housing and community development researchers and policymakers that collects, creates, and distributes a wide variety of materials. You can find information on low-income housing, community development strategies, environmental hazards, land development regulations, population shifts, and housing for elderly and disabled people. A free monthly newsletter and a publications catalogue is available. They can answer such questions as:

1) What information is there on housing for people with special needs?

2) How does one remove lead-based paint from their home?

3) What are "enterprise zones" and what are their goals?

4) What are some federal programs and other sources of assistance for homelessness?

5) What video programs are there on housing issues?

Housing Discrimination

Fair Housing Enforcement Division
Office of Fair Housing and Equal Opportunity
U.S. Department of Housing and Urban Development (HUD)
Washington, DC 20410-2000
800-669-9777

The U.S. Department of Housing and Urban Development administers the law that prohibits discrimination in housing on the basis of race, color, religion, sex, and national origin; investigates complaints of housing discrimination; and attempts to resolve them through conciliation. Two common forms of discrimination are redlining and steering. Redlining is the illegal practice of refusing to originate mortgage loans in certain neighborhoods on the basis of race or ethnic origin. Steering is the illegal act of limiting the housing shown by a real estate agent to a certain ethnic group. HUD refers complaints to state and local fair housing agencies. They can answer such questions as:

1) How do I file a discrimination complaint?

2) What are the regulations regarding housing discrimination?

3) Is sexual harassment a violation of the Fair Housing Act?

4) Can someone be denied housing because of a mental disability?

5) Do landlords have to pay for physical changes to your apartment if you need them, such as grab bars in the bathroom or wider doors?

Public Housing Drug Strategy Clearinghouse

Drug Information and Strategy Clearinghouse
U.S. Department of Housing and Urban Development (HUD)
P.O. Box 6424
Rockville, MD 20850
800-578-3472
Fax: 301-251-5767

Sponsored by the Department of Housing and Urban Development, the Drug Information and Strategy Clearinghouse provides housing officials, residents, and community leaders with information and assistance on drug abuse prevention and drug trafficking control techniques. They have created a database containing information on improving resident screening procedures, strengthening eviction policies, increasing cooperation with local law enforcement, implementing drug tip hotlines, forming resident patrols, starting child care centers, and organizing drug education/prevention activities. The clearinghouse also provides information packages, resource lists, HUD regulations, referrals, and a newsletter. There is no charge for most information. They can answer such questions as:

1) How can housing authorities apply for government grants?

2) What are some anti-drug strategies that have been successfully carried out in public housing units?

3) What are the latest drug abuse prevention theories and have there been demonstration projects based on these models?

4) What resident patrols and related programs have been successful in building drug-free neighborhoods?

5) How can there be an increase in cooperation with local law enforcement and other agencies?

National Injury Information Clearinghouse

U.S. Consumer Product Safety Commission
4330 East-West Highway
Washington, DC 20207
301-504-0424
Fax: 301-504-0025

E-mail: info@cpsc.gov
Gopher: cpsc.gov

The National Injury Information Clearinghouse maintains thousands of detailed investigative reports of injuries associated with consumer products. It has access to automated databases with several million incidents of injuries that have been reported by a nationwide network of hospital emergency departments. You can find the victim's background, including age, race, injury diagnosis, consumer product involved, and more. The Clearinghouse distributes documents and will fulfill search requests, usually at no charge. They can answer such questions as:

1) How many children under the age of five are injured each year while playing with toys?

2) Are all-terrain vehicles considered dangerous?

3) How many injuries/deaths have been reported within the last five years for all-terrain vehicles?

4) How many fires are caused each year by electric range/ovens?

5) Which children's clothing manufacturers produce flame retardant materials and how effective are they?

U.S. Postal Service (Mailing)

Office of Consumer Affairs
475 L'Enfant Plaza, SW, Room 5821
Washington, DC 20260-2200
202-268-2281
Fax: 202-268-2304

www: http://www.usps.gov

The Postal Service provides mail processing and delivery services to individuals and businesses and protects the mail from loss or theft. They can answer all your postal service questions and provide you with publications and referrals to other postal service departments. They can answer such questions as:

1) How can a business protect itself against mail fraud?

2) What services does the Postal Service offer?

3) How does a business set up a mail room?

4) What international mail services are offered?

Meat and Poultry Hotline

Food Safety and Inspection Service
U.S. Department of Agriculture
Washington, DC 20250
800-535-4555
Fax: 202-690-2859

www: http://www.usda.gov

The Meat and Poultry Hotline takes calls from consumers on cases of meat or poultry food poisoning or complaints about meat or poultry spoilage due to improper packaging or processing. They can also provide you with health-oriented information on safe handling and storage of meats and poultry. They can answer such questions as:

1) What should be done during a power outage?

2) What is salmonella and how can people be protected?

3) What are the different type of foodborne illnesses?

4) How long should you cook poultry?

5) What information should be included on meat and poultry labels and what does it mean?

Mortgage Information Center

Program Evaluation Division
Assistant Secretary for Housing
U.S. Department of Housing and Urban Development (HUD)
451 7th St., SW
Attn: B133
Washington, DC 20410
202-755-7470 ext. 145
Fax: 202-755-7455
Bulletin Board: 202-708-3563

Monthly reports are compiled by the Program Evaluation Division of HUD in areas relating to the mortgage market, securities, taxation, market trends, interest rates, among others. You can receive a free survey of mortgage lending activity and a survey of FHA and conventional mortgage rates. They can answer such questions as:

1) What are the average mortgage rates for different parts of the country?

2) What is the difference in mortgage rates over the past 10 years?

3) What is the average interest rate on new home loans versus existing home loans?

4) What is the number of unsold new houses in a given month?

5) What is the current FHA rate?

Organic Gardening

Public Information Center, 3404
U.S. Environmental Protection Agency
401 M St., SW
Washington, DC 20460
202-260-7751
Fax: 202-260-6257

www: http://www.epa.gov
E-mail: access@epamail.epa.gov

The Public Information Center has free information sheets on organic gardening, composting, and recycling. They can answer such questions as:

1) What plants should be planted near each other to deter pests?

2) What are the dangers of pesticides?

3) Who can I talk to regarding composting and recycling?

4) What are the advantages of organic fertilizers?

5) What is required to maintain a lawn?

Pension Benefit Guaranty Corporation

Public Affairs
1200 K St., NW
Washington, DC 20005
202-326-4040
Fax: 202-326-4042

www: http://www.pbgc.gov

The Pension Benefit Guaranty Corporation works to ensure the solvency and viability of company-sponsored pension plans. They can provide you with information and publications on pension plans, as well as laws and regulations on pensions. They can answer questions such as:

1) What is the federal pension law?

2) What are pensions plans and how do they operate?

3) What information on plans is a company required to give to members?

4) What are the rights and options of participants?

5) What is the employer's responsibilities regarding pension plans?

Pension and Welfare Benefits Administration

U.S. Department of Labor
200 Constitution Ave., NW
N5656
Washington, DC 20210
202-219-8921
Fax: 202-219-5362

The Pension and Welfare Benefits Administration (PWBA) helps to protect the economic future and retirement security of working Americans. It requires administrators of private pension and welfare plans to provide plan participants with easily understandable summaries; to file those summaries with the agency; and to report annually on the financial operation of the plans. PWBA has publications and other information available. They can answer questions such as:

1) What is the effect of job mobility on pension plans?

2) What is the Employee Retirement Income Security Act (ERISA)?

3) What studies have been done on the investment performance of ERISA plans?

4) What information are pension plans required to provide to participants?

5) What employee benefit documents are available from the Department of Labor?

Plant Information Service

U.S. Botanic Garden
245 1st St., SW
Washington, DC 20024
202-226-4082
Fax: 202-225-1561

The U.S. Botanic Garden serves as a center for plant information offering a telephone information service, as well as responding to written inquiries from Monday through Friday, from 9:00 to 11:30 a.m. They can answer such questions as:

1) What are the benefits of organic gardening?

2) How can I use insects to control garden pests?

3) Which house plants are poisonous?

4) What are the dangers of chemical fertilizers?

5) Which herbs grow best indoors?

Seafood Hotline

Office of Seafood
Food and Drug Administration
200 C St., SW
Washington, DC 20201
800-332-4010
Fax: 202-401-3532

www: http://www.fda.gov_.
E-mail: oco@fdacf.sw.dhhs.gov

The Seafood Hotline can provide consumers with information on how to buy and use seafood products, including storing and handling of seafood, and questions on seafood labeling and nutrition. The Hotline has many free publications on a variety of seafood issues. They can answer such questions as:

1) Can fish be kept frozen for a year?

2) What kind of fish is escolar?

3) What are the dangers of eating raw shellfish?

4) What information is available on canned tuna?

5) What are some seafood safety concerns for people with particular medical conditions?

Social Security Administration

Social Security Administration
Public Inquiries
6401 Security Blvd.
Baltimore, MD 21235
410-965-7700

www: http://www.ssa.gov

The Social Security Administration administers the Social Security and Medicare programs. They can assist certain beneficiaries in claiming reimbursement and developing and adjudicating claims. They can answer such questions as:

1) If you were to retire today, how much would you receive in benefits?

2) What should be done once you turn 65?

3) What is supplemental security income and how do you apply for it?

4) What disability insurance benefits do you qualify for?

5) What survivor benefits are available to children?

Internal Revenue Service (Taxes)

U.S. Department of Treasury
1111 Constitution Ave., NW
Washington, DC 20224
800-829-1040
Fax on Demand: 703-487-4160

www: http://www.irs.ustreas.gov

The Internal Revenue Service is responsible for administering and enforcing the internal revenue laws and related statutes. It's mission is to collect the proper amount of tax revenue at the least cost to the public. They can answer such questions as:

1) How do you get copies of your back tax forms?

2) What is required when you deduct your home office?

3) What are the rules about writing off a vacation/work trip?

4) What happens if you can't pay your taxes?

5) Can you deduct your mother as a dependent if she lives with you?

Women's Bureau Clearinghouse

U.S. Department of Labor
200 Constitution Ave., NW, Room S3306
Washington, DC 20210
800-827-5335
202-219-4486
Fax: 202-219-5529

www: http://www.dol.gov/dol/wb/dol
E-mail: wb-wwc@dol.gov

The Women's Bureau Clearinghouse was established to assist employers in identifying the most appropriate policies for responding to the dependent care needs of employees seeking to balance their dual responsibilities. They can also provide information on women's issues, as well as work force issues that affect women. They can offer information and guidance in areas such as women-owned businesses, women workers, alternative work schedules, dependent care issues, and much more. They also have many free publications and other information available. They can answer such questions as:

1) What are some elder care program options?

2) What is the earning difference between men and women?

3) How does flex time work in companies similar to mine?

4) What are some examples of alternate work schedules and how do they work?

5) What literature and other resources are available on employer-supported child care?

Criminal Justice

National Institute of Justice AIDS Clearinghouse

National Criminal Justice Reference Service
U.S. Department of Justice
Box 6003
Rockville, MD 20849-6003
800-458-5231
Fax: 301-251-5343

 www: http://cdcnac.aspensys.com:86
E-mail: aidsinfo@cdc.nac. aspensys.com

This National Institute of Justice AIDS Clearinghouse is the only centralized source of information on the impact of AIDS on criminal justice professionals and their work. Staff specialists are available to answer questions, make referrals, and suggest publications relating to AIDS and the criminal justice system. They can answer such questions as:

1) What precautions are necessary when searching or transporting inmates who may be infected with the AIDS virus?

2) Are there AIDS training materials to be used in lock up situations?

3) What are the issues surrounding the testing of inmates for the AIDS virus?

4) What are some different AIDS policies adopted by various police departments around the country?

5) Are there materials or speakers available for an AIDS-focused seminar?

Bureau of Alcohol, Tobacco, and Firearms

Distribution Center
U.S. Department of Treasury
P.O. Box 5950
Springfield, VA 22150-5950
703-455-7801

The Bureau of Alcohol, Tobacco, and Firearms (ATF) is responsible for enforcing and administering firearms and explosives laws, as well as those laws covering the production, use, and distribution of alcohol and tobacco products. ATF can provide you with a wealth of information, statistics, and publications. They can answer such questions as:

1) What explosive incidents and stolen explosives occurred in a year by state and by type of explosives?

2) What are the different types of firearms available?

3) What are the license requirements for a given state to carry a weapon?

4) How do law enforcement officials trace firearms?

The United States Commission on Civil Rights Clearinghouse Division

624 9th St., NW
Washington, DC 20425
202-376-8113
Fax: 202-376-7597

The U.S. Commission on Civil Rights serves as a national clearinghouse for information on discrimination or denial of equal protection of the laws because of race, color, religion, sex, age, handicap, or national origin. The library contains 50,000 reference works and a comprehensive collection of reports, transcripts, and civil rights texts. They have a free quarterly newsletter, and a catalogue of publications, as well as two on-line database systems. They can answer such questions as:

1) What is the overall economic status of Americans of Asian descent?

2) What is the extent of racial imbalance in the schools?

3) What is the current analysis of the earnings gap between black and white men?

4) What can my community do to remedy civil rights violations by police officers?

5) What information exists on the role of women and minorities in network news?

National Criminal Justice Reference Service

National Institute of Justice/NCJRS
Box 6000
Rockville, MD 20850
800-851-3420
Fax: 301-251-5212

www: http://ncjrs.aspensys.com:81/ncjrshome.html
E-mail: askncjrs@aspensys.com

The National Criminal Justice Reference Service brings the latest criminal justice research findings to criminal justice policymakers, practitioners, and researchers from around the world. Their database features summaries of books, reports, articles, and audiovisual materials. They have a free bi monthly catalogue which lists new publications (many of which are free), upcoming conferences, and more. They can answer such questions as:

1) What videotapes are there on criminal justice topics?

2) What information exists on community safety issues?

3) How effective is parole and probation?

4) What drug abuse programs are in place for offenders?

5) What is date rape?

Drug and Crime Data Center and Clearinghouse

1600 Research Boulevard
Rockville, MD 20850
800-666-3332

www: http://ncjrs.aspensys.com:81/ncjrshome.html
E-mail: askncjrs@aspensys.com

The Data Center and Clearinghouse serves the drugs-and-crime information needs of federal, state, and local policy makers, criminal justice and public health practitioners, researchers and universities, private corporations, the media, and the general public. The most current data is available on illegal drugs, drug law violations, drug-related crime, drug-using offenders in the criminal justice system, and the impact of drugs on criminal justice administration. The Clearinghouse maintains a database of some 1,500 annotated bibliographies of statistical and research reports, books, and journal articles on drugs and crime. All documents are free. They can answer such questions as:

1) What are the economic costs of drug-related crime?

2) What data exists on the quantity and flow of illicit drugs from cultivation to consequences?

3) What percentage of high school seniors used cocaine last year?

4) What tactics have been used to build integrity and reduce drug corruption in police departments?

5) What percentage of rapists report that their victims were well known to them?

National Clearinghouse on Election Administration

Federal Election Commission
999 E St., NW
Washington, DC 20463
202-219-3670
800-424-9530
Fax: 202-219-8500

www: http://www.fec.gov

The National Clearinghouse on Election Administration is an agency of the Federal Election Commission. Its overall objective is to enhance the honesty, integrity, and efficiency of the federal election process by providing information and assistance to state and local election officials, to state legislatures and legislative reference bureaus, and to other interested organizations regarding the conduct of Federal elections. They can answer such questions as:

1) What research reports are available on state campaign finance laws?

2) Where can I obtain advice and assistance in making polling places more accessible to the elderly and handicapped?

3) What statistics exist that could summarize state and national voting age populations, the number of registered voters, turnout, and results in presidential elections for 1960 through 1988?

4) What landmark judicial decisions have been made involving elections over the past twenty years?

5) What are the registration techniques and procedures in a particular state?

Equal Employment Opportunity Commission (EEOC)

Publications and Information Center
P.O. Box 12549
Cincinnati, OH 45212-0549
800-669-EEOC
Fax: 513-489-8695

The purpose of the Equal Employment Opportunity Commission is to eliminate discrimination based on race, color, religion, sex, national origin, or age in hiring, promoting, firing, setting wages, testing, training, and all other terms and conditions of employment. The Commission conducts investigations of alleged discrimination, and provides voluntary assistance programs for employers, unions, and others. They have free publications and information available. They can answer such questions as:

1) What questions cannot be asked in an employment interview?

2) What constitutes sexual harassment?

3) What federal law prohibits employers from discriminating between men and women in the payment of wages, and to whom does the law apply?

4) What can be done if you feel you have been unfairly discriminated against?

5) What information exists to train personnel officers on the prevailing laws and regulations?

Bureau of Justice Assistance Clearinghouse

P.O. Box 6000
U.S. Department of Justice
Rockville, MD 20850
800-688-4252
Fax: 301-251-5212

www: http://ncjrs.aspensys.com:81/ncjrshome.html
E-mail: askncjrs@aspensys.com

The Bureau of Justice Assistance Clearinghouse (BJA) informs state and local criminal justice practitioners about BJA products and programs. They provide federal funding and technical assistance to state and local units of government to improve the criminal justice system. They can answer such questions as:

1) What information is available regarding a variety of anti-drug programs?

2) What programs are in place to improve the efficiency of the criminal justice system?

3) What are the estimated costs of drug testing for a pretrial service program?

4) What training programs exist for narcotics enforcement?

5) What are the treatment alternatives to street crimes?

Justice Statistics Clearinghouse

Bureau of Justice Statistics
U.S. Department of Justice
Box 6000
Rockville, MD 20850
800-732-3277

www: http://ncjrs.aspensys.com:81/ncjrshome.html
E-mail: askncjrs@aspensys.com

The Bureau of Justice Statistics (BJS) supports this clearinghouse for those seeking crime and criminal justice data. In addition to distributing BJS publications, the Clearinghouse responds to statistics requests by offering document database searches, statistics information packages, referrals, and other related products and services. They can answer such questions as:

1) What is the annual national estimate of the amount of crime against persons and households?

2) What are some of the characteristics of victims?

3) How differently are juveniles handled from adults?

4) How prevalent is organized crime?

5) What is the recidivism rate, and when criminals are rearrested, with what crimes are they normally charged?

Juvenile Justice Clearinghouse

National Criminal Justice Reference Service
U.S. Department of Justice
Box 6000
Rockville, MD 20850
800-638-8736

www: http://ncjrs.aspensys.com:81/ncjrshome.html
E-mail: askncjrs@aspensys.com

The Juvenile Justice Clearinghouse disseminates publications, re-search findings, and program evaluations supported by the Office of Juvenile Justice and Delinquency Prevention. In addition, the staff can prepare customized responses to information requests. They can answer such questions as:

1) How do juvenile courts vary in handling drug and alcohol cases?

2) What can a community do in response to youth gangs?

3) What methods have been successful in dealing with juvenile reinstitution?

4) How many juveniles were arrested last year for possession of illegal drugs?

5) What methods are effective in reducing violence in the schools?

National Clearinghouse For Legal Services, Inc.

205 W. Monroe, 2nd Floor
Chicago, IL 60605
312-263-3830
Fax: 312-263-3846

The National Clearinghouse for Legal Services is the most comprehensive source for information concerning civil poverty law. Also, the Clearinghouse has many publications dealing with issues of vital interest to the non poverty lawyer. Problems with health care, housing, and social security strike people in all economic situations. These are just some of the 20 major areas of law that Clearinghouse publications cover, providing practical information useful to people in all economic and social strata. The Clearinghouse, as a resource center and a legal research system, offers the most complete source of civil poverty law publications that can be found. They have a free publications list. They can answer such questions as:

1) What information exists on the eligibility requirements for Medicare home health care?

2) What models exist on establishing pro bono programs?

3) What are the various issues concerning the tax burden on the poor?

4) What are the litigation issues concerning homeless persons and emergency shelter?

5) Where can information be obtained on child custody cases?

National Center for Missing and Exploited Children

2101 Wilson Blvd., Suite 550
Arlington, VA 22201
800-843-5678
Fax: 703-235-4067

www: http://www.missingkids.org

The National Center for Missing and Exploited Children serves as a clearinghouse of information on missing and exploited children; provides technical assistance to citizens and law-enforcement agencies; offers training programs to law-enforcement and social service professionals; distributes photos and descriptions of missing children nationwide; coordinates child protection efforts with the private sector; networks with nonprofit service providers and state clearinghouses on missing persons; and provides information on effective state legislation to ensure the protection of children. They can answer such questions as:

1) How can a parent work through the civil and criminal justice systems in order to regain custody of the child her ex-husband stole from her?

2) How can a parent protect children against day care abuse?

3) What are some of the warning signs of child sexual exploitation?

4) What is the profile of a runaway and the patterns of runaway behavior?

5) What information is available to help a child testify in court?

Office for Victims of Crime Resource Center

U.S. Department of Justice
Box 6000
Rockville, MD 20850
800-627-6872
Fax: 301-251-5212

www: http://ncjrs.aspensys.com:81/ncjrshome.html
E-mail: askncjrs@aspensys.com

The Office for Victims of Crime Resource Center is sponsored by the Office of Victims of Crime. It can provide access to resources, such as more than 7,000 victim-related books and articles, national victimization statistics, federally sponsored victim-related research studies, and information on state victim compensation programs. From the Clearinghouse, you can get free publications, borrow hard-to-find publications, and buy selected videotapes. Information specialists can also conduct database searches. They can answer such questions as:

1) What is the relationship between child abuse and delinquency?

2) What information is there for police when confronting a domestic violence incident?

3) What are some of the programs which compensate victims of crime?

4) What is the criminal justice response to victim harm?

5) How can one improve the use and effectiveness of the Neighborhood Watch program?

Education And The Arts

ERIC Clearinghouse on
Adult, Career, and Vocational Learning

Ohio State University Center on Education and
  Training for Employment
1900 Kenny Rd.
Columbus, OH 43210
800-848-4815
Fax: 614-292-1260

E-mail: ericacve@magnus.acs.ohio_state.edu

The Clearinghouse on Adult, Career, and Vocational Learning
provides materials covering all levels of adult and continuing
education from: basic literacy training through professional skill
upgrading; vocational and technical education covering all service areas for secondary, postsecondary, and adult populations;
and career education and career development programs for all
ages and populations. A publications list and price sheet are
available. They can answer questions such as:

1) What research exists on the effectiveness of flex time and
   job share programs?

2) What is the job placement rate of graduates from vocational schools?

3) What are the statistics on job satisfaction and wage earnings?

4) What are the benefits of vocational education?

5) What information exists on how people can find a job and
   make effective career choices?

ERIC Clearinghouse on Educational Assessment and Evaluation

Catholic University of America
Room 210 O'Boyle Hall
Washington, DC 20064
202-319-5120
Fax: 202-319-6692

E-mail: eric_ae@cua.edu

The Clearinghouse on Assessment and Evaluation provides information on the assessment and evaluation of education projects or programs, tests and other measurement devices, methodology of measurement and evaluation, and more. A publications list and price sheet are available. They can answer such questions as:

1) Do statistics show that tests discriminate against certain minority groups?

2) What tests are given to handicapped children and what is the research behind these tests?

3) Is the Scholastic Aptitude Test (SAT) an effective tool of measurement?

4) What is computer-assisted testing?

5) How often are SAT tests updated and who designs the questions?

Bilingual Education Clearinghouse

National Clearinghouse for Bilingual Education
1118 22nd St., NW
Washington, DC 20037
202-467-0867
Fax: 800-531-9347

E-mail: askncbe@ncbe.gwu.edu

The Bilingual Education Clearinghouse provides information to practitioners in the field on curriculum materials, program models, methodologies, and research findings on the education of limited English proficient (LEP) individuals. They also offer an electronic information system, free to users, where access is available to a database of curriculum materials and literature related to the education of LEP persons. An electronic bulletin board is also available which contains news from federal, state, and local education agencies, conference announcements, and other current information. Their newsletter and other publications are available, many of which are free of charge. They can answer such questions as:

1) How do you mainstream language minority students?

2) What computer programs exist to assist in teaching limited English proficient students?

3) What are some of the issues and practices involved in meeting the needs of gifted and talented minority language students?

4) How can parents become involved in the education of limited English students?

5) How can teachers integrate multi-cultural materials in instructional programs?

ERIC Clearinghouse on Counseling and Personnel Services

School of Education
101 Park Building
University of North Carolina at Greensboro
Greensboro, NC 27412-5001
800-414-9769
Fax: 910-334-4116

 www: http://www.uncg.edu/~ericcas2

The Clearinghouse on Counseling and Personnel Services provides documents relating to all levels of counseling and personnel services including preparation, practice, and supervision of counselors at all education levels and in all settings; personnel procedures such as testing and interviewing; group work and case work; career planning; and more. They have free publications, and will conduct searches for a fee. They can answer such questions as:

1) How can counselors enhance a student's self-esteem through counseling?

2) What are the emerging priorities for the counseling field in the 1990's?

3) What dropout prevention programs have been effective?

4) What is the current high school dropout rate?

5) What tests are available to students who are undecided on a choice of career?

ERIC Clearinghouse on Disabilities and Gifted Education

The Council for Exceptional Children
1920 Association Dr.
Reston, VA 22091
800-328-0272

E-mail: eric@inet.ed.gov

The Clearinghouse on Disabilities and Gifted Education provides information on all aspects of education and development of handicapped persons, including prevention of handicaps, identification and assessment of handicaps, and intervention and enrichment programs. All aspects of the education and development of gifted persons are covered as well. A publications list and price sheet are available. They can answer such questions as:

1) What are the issues concerning the mainstreaming of a handicapped student?

2) How do you "home school" a gifted child?

3) What is the research concerning the post-school status of learning disabled students?

4) What preschool services are available for children with handicaps?

5) Under what criteria is a child considered gifted?

ERIC Clearinghouse on Educational Management

College of Education
5207 University of Oregon
Eugene, OR 97403-5207
503-346-5043
800-438-8841
Fax: 541-346-2334

 www: http://ericir.sir.edu/eric/eric.html

The Clearinghouse on Educational Management distributes information on the following subjects: the leadership, management, and structure of public and private educational organizations; practice and theory of administration; preservice and inservice preparation of administrators; and tasks and processes of administration. The Clearinghouse also provides information on sites, buildings, and equipment for education, and planning, financing, construction, renovating, and evaluating educational facilities. They can answer such questions as:

1) What are "mentor teachers" and how do you prepare them to assist new teachers?

2) How do you best confront racism in schools?

3) How do you recruit, select, and retain good teachers?

4) What research has been done on the various methods of school discipline?

5) What elements must be considered in the design of a new school?

Educational Research

Office of Educational Research and Improvement's
Information Service
U.S. Department of Education
Education Information Branch
Capitol Plaza Building, Suite 300
555 New Jersey Ave., NW
Washington, DC 20208-5641
800-424-1616

Gopher: ed.gov

The Education Information Branch staff specialists can provide information on topics such as early childhood education, elementary and secondary education, higher education, adult and vocational education, education finance, longitudinal statistical studies, and special education. They have publications and reports, many of which are free. They can answer such questions as:

1) What statistics are there on the number of students who receive loans, grants, and work-study assistance from state sources?

2) What are the statistics on private postsecondary education, such as enrollment, earned degrees conferred, full and part-time faculty members and their salaries, and more?

3) What information is available on how to choose a school for a child and what makes a school good?

4) How can parents help their children become better readers?

5) What are the enrollment outcomes for recent master's and bachelor's degree recipients?

Educational Resources Information Center

ACCESS ERIC
Aspen Systems Corporation
1600 Research Blvd.
Rockville, MD 20850

800-538-3742
Fax: 301-309-2084

www: http://www.aspensys.com/eric

Educational Resources Information Center (ERIC) is a nationwide information service set up to collect materials about current developments in education and make them available to the public. The system includes 16 clearinghouses, each of which is responsible for acquiring, processing, and disseminating information about a particular aspect of education. The ERIC database contains bibliographic information, including key descriptors and abstracts, on over 850,000 research documents, journal articles, curricular materials, and resource guides. The Clearinghouses offer a wide variety of services and products, and can answer questions about: subject fields, run computer searches, develop short bibliographies, newsletters, and other free or inexpensive materials; publish monographs; publish handbooks; and develop materials to help you use ERIC.

ACCESS ERIC is the main center for the ERIC clearinghouses. It answers all questions on how to use ERIC and helps anyone stay up-to-date on the latest developments in the education field. They can answer such questions as:

1)   How can I use ERIC to answer my education question?

2)   What is required to have a database search run on a topic?

3)   How can I have something that I have written entered into the ERIC system?

4)   Where can I find the latest statistics on an education topic?

5)   How can school administrators develop new management tools and practices?

ERIC Clearinghouse on Elementary and Early Childhood Education

University of Illinois
805 West Pennsylvania Ave.
Urbana, IL 61801

217-333-1386
Fax: 217-333-3767

www: http://ericps.ed.vivc.edu/nccic/nccichome.html
E-mail: askeric@ericir.syr.edu

The Clearinghouse on Elementary and Early Childhood Education provides information covering all aspects of the cognitive, emotional, social and physical development, and education of children from birth through early adolescence, excluding specific elementary school curriculum areas. Among the topics covered are: prenatal and infant development and care; child care programs and community services for children at local, state, and federal levels; parent, child, and family relationships; home and school relationships; foster care and adoption; and more. A publications list and price sheet are available. They can answer such questions as:

1) How do you start a day care center?

2) How do you choose a day care center and how do you assess a preschooler's development?

3) How can parents become involved in the education of their children?

4) How do you meet the needs of homeless children?

5) How do you help children with their social development?

ERIC Clearinghouse on Higher Education

George Washington University
One Dupont Circle
Washington, DC 20036-1183
202-296-2597
Fax: 202-296-8379

E-mail: eric@inet.ed.gov

The Clearinghouse on Higher Education provides information covering education beyond the secondary level that leads to a four-year, masters, doctoral or professional degree and that includes courses and programs designed to enhance or update skills obtained in these degree programs. Areas include: academic advising, faculty, continuing education, legal issues, curriculum development, and more. They can answer such questions as:

1) What research and assessments are available on the trends and issues in higher education today?

2) What percentage of staff of higher education facilities are minorities and women?

3) What information is available on the issue of student stress?

4) How do we raise academic standards as a country?

5) What techniques are useful in improving a student's organizational skills?

ERIC Clearinghouse on Information and Technology

Syracuse University School of Education
4-194 Center for Science and Technology
Syracuse, NY 13244-4100
315-443-3640
Fax: 315-443-5448

 www: http://ericib.syr.edu

The Clearinghouse on Information and Technology provides information covering educational technology and library and information science at all levels. Instructional design, development, and evaluation with emphasis on educational technology; computers, audio and video recordings, and more. They can answer such questions as:

1) What is the latest research on the value of using computers and applying video technology to enhance learning?

2) What are the various studies comparing the different types of computer based media?

3) Is there an overview of instructional television and its effectiveness for teaching children?

4) At what grade level are computers introduced in the classroom, on average?

5) Are audio recordings an effective tool for teaching foreign languages?

ERIC Clearinghouse on Junior Colleges

University of California at Los Angeles
3051 Moore Hall
Los Angeles, CA 90024
310-825-3931
Fax: 310-206-8095

www: http://www.gseis.ucla.edu/eric/eric.html

The Clearinghouse on Junior Colleges provides information covering the development, administration, and evaluation of two-year public and private community and junior colleges, technical institutes, and two-year branch university campuses. They have free publications and will conduct database searches for a fee. They can answer such questions as:

1) What are the main problems involved with transfer students?

2) How many students working on A.A. degrees in nursing are mothers and other women returning to further their education?

3) How do you implement a cultural exchange or study abroad program?

4) How do you recruit and retain minorities and women at junior colleges?

5) What percentage of students attending two-year programs receive financial assistance?

ERIC Clearinghouse on Languages and Linguistics

Center for Applied Linguistics
1118 22nd St., NW
Washington, DC 20037
202-429-9292
Fax: 202-659-5641

 www: http://www.cal.org

The Clearinghouse on Languages and Linguistics provides information on languages and language sciences; all areas of foreign language, second language, and linguistics instruction; cultural and intercultural context of languages; international exchanges; teacher training; and more. Mini-bibliographies and fact sheets are available free of charge. Ready-made search printouts are available for a fee, and prices vary for specific searches. They can answer such questions as:

1) How do you institute teaching English as a second language in the workplace?

2) How do you develop a curriculum and training program for volunteer tutors for limited-English proficient adults?

3) What are the pros and cons of language immersion programs in schools?

4) What are the issues regarding the foreign language requirement?

5) What are some available opportunities abroad for teaching English as a foreign language?

National Clearinghouse on Literacy Education

Center for Applied Linguistics
1118 22nd St., NW
Washington, DC 20037
202-429-9292
Fax: 202-659-5641

www: http://www.cal.org

The National Clearinghouse on Literacy Education produces and disseminates materials summarizing current research and information available on selected topics; develops a directory of effective adult literacy programs and projects; and supports a user services program to respond to information requests. They have a publications list available, and many of the items are free. They can answer such questions as:

1) What organizations offer programs for senior citizens interested in learning to read and write?

2) How can workplaces promote English as a second language?

3) What free resources are available to adult literacy instructors?

4) What percentage of U.S. immigrants are illiterate? What programs exist to help them?

5) What type of educational materials and programs are available to teach English to out-of-school youth?

Museum Reference Center

Smithsonian Institution
Office of Museum Programs
900 Jefferson Dr., SW
Washington, DC 20560
202-786-2271
Fax: 202-357-2311

www: http://www.sii.si.edu

The Museum Reference Center serves as a clearinghouse for museum programs providing professional development training, advisory assistance, and research services to the national and international museum community and the Smithsonian staff. The Center participates through the sponsorship of workshops, internships, and professional visitor programs, an audiovisual production loan program, publications, and more. They can answer such questions as:

1) Where can information be obtained regarding internship programs for museum careers?

2) What is the latest research on climate control and security for museums?

3) What information exists on how to train docents and volunteers?

4) Where can examples of exhibit designs be found?

5) Where can information be found on collection sharing?

Performing Arts Library

John F. Kennedy Center for the Performing Arts
2700 F St., NW
Washington, DC 20566
202-416-8780

The Performing Arts Library is a joint project of the Library of Congress and the Kennedy Center, and offers information and reference assistance on dance, theater, opera, music, film, and broadcasting. The Performing Arts Library serves the research and information needs of the public, artists, and staff of the Center. The Library also identifies and locates the creative and resource materials necessary to develop new works and productions in the performing arts. Reference service is available by phone, in person, or by mail. They can answer such questions as:

1) How can an orchestral program of Irish composers be tailored for a young audience?

2) What information exists on different dance companies based in New York?

3) Is there information on what is required to start a record company?

4) Are their recordings of interviews or videotapes of famous actresses discussing their works?

5) Where can recordings be located on poetry readings?

ERIC Clearinghouse on Reading and Communication Skills

Indiana University
Smith Research Center
Suite 150
2805 East Tenth St.
Bloomington, IN 47408-2698
812-855-5847
Fax: 812-855-4220

www: http://www.indiana.edu/~eric_rec

The Clearinghouse on Reading and Communication Skills provides information on reading, English, communication skills, identification, diagnosis and remediation of reading problems, and more. A catalogue of publications including prices is available. The Clearinghouse will also conduct custom database searches for a fee. They can answer such questions as:

1) How do you teach elementary students listening skills?

2) How can parents help their child to read?

3) How do you help a quiet student communicate in the classroom?

4) Where can teachers obtain written activities for junior high social studies classes?

5) Is there information on sex stereotypes in children's literature?

ERIC Clearinghouse for Science, Mathematics, and Environmental Education

1929 Kenny Rd.
Columbus, OH 43210
614-292-6717
Fax: 614-292-0263

E-mail: ericse@osu.edu

The Clearinghouse for Science, Mathematics, and Environmental Education acquires educational literature on the following topics: development of curriculum and instructional materials; teachers and teacher education; learning theory; educational programs; and computer applications. They can answer such questions as:

1) Is there information on how to teach a lesson on environmental education?

2) What can be done to boost students' enthusiasm for math?

3) What are some of the common safety hazards in science classrooms?

4) Where can teachers obtain free science instructional materials?

5) Are there financial aid programs available to teachers interested in continuing education?

ERIC Clearinghouse for Social Studies/Social Science Education

Social Studies Development Center
Indiana University
Smith Research Center
2805 East Tenth St., Suite 120
Bloomington, IN 47405
812-855-3838
Fax: 812-855-0455

 E-mail: ericso@indiana.edu

The Clearinghouse for Social Studies/Social Science Education acquires journal articles and documents at all levels of social studies and social science education, including anthropology, economics, geography, sociology, social psychology, civics, and political science, as well as on history and social topics. A publications catalogue is available, including prices. They can answer such questions as:

1) What are some interesting learning activities designed to teach social studies?

2) What resources exist to supplement teachers' lessons on Africa and African Culture?

3) How do you teach geography at home?

4) How can you teach the law incorporating Supreme Court cases?

5) How can teachers stimulate children's interest in anthropology?

ERIC Clearinghouse on Teacher Education

American Association of Colleges for Teacher Education
One Dupont Circle, NW
Suite 610
Washington, DC 20036
202-293-2450
Fax: 202-457-8095

 www: http://www.aacte.org

The ERIC Clearinghouse on Teacher Education acquires, publishes, and disseminates documents conveying research, theory, and practice in teacher education and in all aspects of health education, physical education, recreation education, nutrition education, and more. They can answer such questions as:

1) What are the teacher certification requirements?

2) How effective are student teachers in the classroom?

3) What computer games are there to help kids learn math?

4) What techniques can a teacher use to improve classroom productivity?

5) What are "at risk" students and how can they best be served?

ERIC Clearinghouse on Urban Education

Teachers College
Columbia University Institute for Urban and Minority Education
Main Hall, Room 303, Box 40
525 West 120th St.
New York, NY 10027
212-678-3433
Fax: 212-678-4012

 www: http://eric_web:tc.colombia.edu
E-mail: ericcue@colombia_edu

The Clearinghouse on Urban Education provides information on the programs and practices in schools in urban areas. In addition, the education of racial/ethnic minority children and youth in various settings is studied: on the local, national, and international level; theory and practice of education equity; and urban and minority experiences. A publications list and price sheet are available. They can answer such questions as:

1) What is the current research on effective programs for reducing the dropout rates among inner city high school students?

2) What research is available on the number of pregnant, minority teenagers who obtain their high school diplomas in inner city schools?

3) What information is there on mentoring programs?

4) What issues are involved in linking schools with human service agencies?

5) Are urban schools financed equitably?

Energy and Environment

EPA Control Technology Center Hotline (Air Pollution)

U.S. Environmental Protection Agency (EPA)
AEERL
Research Triangle Park, NC 27711
919-541-0800

ttnbbs.rtpnc.epa.gov

The EPA Control Technology Center Hotline provides technical support to state and local agencies and to EPA regional offices in implementing air pollution control programs. They can answer such questions as:

1) What type of computer software can my company use to assess pollution control problems and evaluate potential solutions?

2) What impacts have control technologies had on air pollution?

3) What type of air pollution permits does my company need to operate in my state?

4) How can my company reduce its air pollution control costs?

5) What are the best cost-effective methods to maintain my company's air pollution control equipment?

BACT/LAER Clearinghouse (Air Pollution)

U.S. Environmental Protection Agency (EPA)
Control Technology Center
Research Triangle Park, NC 27711
919-541-5432
Fax: 919-541-5742

ttnbbs.rtpnc.epa.gov

The BACT/LAER Clearinghouse assists state and local air pollu-tion control agencies in selecting the best available control tech-nology (BACT) and the lowest achievable emission rate (LAER). It controls new or modified sources in a nationally consistent manner. They can answer such questions as:

1) How can my agency get assistance in compiling inventories of air toxic emissions?

2) How does the EPA estimate air toxic emissions?

3) Where can I get a listing of national emissions estimates and factors for air that is made toxic from motor vehicles?

4) Where can I find out about the toxic emissions for a particu-lar consumer product?

5) How can my company achieve the lowest achievable emis-sion rate for our product?

Asbestos Ombudsman Clearinghouse

U.S. Environmental Protection Agency (EPA)
401 M St., SW
Washington, DC 20460
800-368-5888
Fax: 703-305-6462

 www: http://www.epa.gov

The assigned mission of the Asbestos Ombudsman Clearing-house is to provide to the public sector, including individual citi-zens and community services, information on the handling and abatement of asbestos in schools, the workplace, and the home. In addition, interpretation of the asbestos-in-school re-quirements and publications are provided to explain recent legis-lation. The EPA Asbestos Ombudsman receives complaints and requests for information and provides assistance with regard to them. They can answer such questions as:

1) What is asbestos, and in what era was it used?

2) How do I know if I have asbestos in my home or at work and how do I find help to contain or eliminate it?

3) What do I do if I have been exposed to asbestos?

4) How can I safe-proof my house from asbestos?

5) Are the schools in my particular neighborhood safe from asbestos?

Boating Safety Hotline

Consumer and Regulatory Affairs Branch
Auxiliary, Boating, and Consumer Affairs Division
Office of Navigation Safety and Waterways Services
U.S. Coast Guard
U.S. Department of Transportation
2100 2nd St., SW
Washington, DC 20593
800-368-5647
Fax: 202-267-4285

www: http://www.navcen.uscg.mil

The Boating Safety Hotline can provide you with information on such topics of interest to boaters as safety recalls, publications, Coast Guard department contacts and addresses, public education courses, and free Coast Guard Services. They have a wealth of free information and publications to share. They can answer such questions as:

1) What statistics exist on boating accidents?

2) How can parents teach children about water safety?

3) What things do people need to consider in evaluating floatation devices?

4) What licenses or regulations should boaters be aware of before they hit the water?

5) Where can people receive information on water charts and other navigational aids?

National Climatic Data Center

National Oceanic and Atmospheric Administration
U.S. Department of Commerce
Federal Building
151 Patton Ave., Room 120
Asheville, NC 28801
704-271-4800
Fax: 704-271-4876

 E-mail: orders@ncdc.noaa.gov

The National Climatic Data Center (NCDC) provides an important historical perspective on climate. Through the use of over a hundred years of weather observations, reference databases are generated. NCDC's data and information are available to everyone including the general public, the legal profession, engineering, industry, agriculture, and government policy makers. They can answer such questions as:

1) What were the weather conditions like in a particular part of a state on a specific day, and can this information be used for a court case?

2) In what parts of the country is the climate moderate allowing energy bills to be held to a minimum?

3) What information is available on severe storms, such as the occurrences of storms, data on the paths of individual storms, deaths, injuries, and estimated property damage?

4) Are droughts becoming more widespread?

5) Is the greenhouse theory becoming a reality?

Energy Efficiency and Renewable Energy Clearinghouse

P.O. Box 3048
Merrifield, VA 22116
800-363-3732

Fax: 703-893-0400
Bulletin Board: 800-273-2955

www: http://www.eren.doe.gov

The Energy Efficiency and Renewable Energy Inquiry and Referral Clearinghouse can provide information on how to save energy, as well as information on solar, wind, or any other aspect of renewable energy. They have the latest research on renewable energy technologies and energy conservation, and can refer you to other valuable resources. A list of free publications is available. They can answer questions such as:

1) How can you convert a home to solar heat?

2) How do heat pumps work and are they efficient?

3) What should you look for in a wood-burning appliance?

4) What can be done to improve the energy efficiency of a home?

5) Is the wind a practical source of energy?

Safe Drinking Water Hotline

U.S. Environmental Protection Agency (EPA)
401 M St., SW
Washington, DC 20460
800-426-4791
Fax: 202-260-8072

www: http://www.epa.gov/epaoswer/hotline.htm
E-mail: hotline_sdwa@ epamail.epa.gov

The Safe Drinking Water Hotline responds to questions concerning the Safe Drinking Water Act, water standards, regulations, and the Underground Injection Program. It will also provide selected free publications. They can answer such questions as:

1) How do I find out if there is lead in my drinking water?

2) What is the Underground Injection Program?

3) What are some of the newer techniques for removing and disposing of water pollutants?

4) What research is being done to develop safer drinking water?

5) What can I do if there is too much fluoride in my drinking water?

EROS Data Center (Earth Resources)

U.S. Geological Survey
Mundt Federal Bldg.
Sioux Falls, SD 57198
605-594-6511
Fax: 605-594-6589

 www: http://edu.www.cr.usgs.gov/eros_hom.html

The Earth Resources Observation Systems (EROS) Data Center is a national archive, production, and research facility for remotely sensed data and other forms of geographic information. It receives, processes, and distributes data from the U.S.' Landsat satellite sensors and from airborne mapping cameras. The Center houses over 2,000,000 worldwide scenes of Earth acquired by Landsat satellites and nearly 6,000,000 aerial photographs of U.S. sites. Maps and photographs range from $6 to $65 and can be obtained from the Center's customer service department. The staff can answer such questions as:

1) How can I receive a listing of aerial photographs of a particular hurricane that I am studying?

2) How do the Landsat satellite sensors work?

3) How can EROS help my company's geologic exploration projects?

4) How can EROS help my company form a geochemical assessment of a potential land site that we are interested in developing?

5) Can the Center furnish me with a printout of land owner-
ship lists in my particular county?

Earth Science Information Centers

U.S. Geological Survey
507 National Center
Reston, VA 22092
703-648-6892
800-USA-MAPS
Fax: 703-648-5548

www: http://www.usgs.gov/
E-mail: esicmail@usgs.gov

Earth Science Information Centers (ESIC) offer nationwide information and sales service for U.S. Geological Survey map products and earth science publications. This network of ESICs provides information about: geologic, hydrologic, and land use
maps, books, and reports; aerial, satellite, and radar images
and related products; earth science and map data in digital for-
mat and related applications software; and geodetic data.
ESICs can fill orders for custom products and provide information about earth science materials from many public and private producers. They can answer such questions as:

1) Where can maps of Indian lands be located?

2) What earth-science teaching aids are available?

3) Where can accurate topographic maps be found which
show the location and measurable elevation of natural and
man made features?

4) Where can out-of-print maps be located?

5) Where can wetlands be found in the state of Ohio?

National Earthquake Information Center

U.S. Geological Survey
Mail Stop 967
Box 25046, Federal Center

Denver, CO 80225
303-273-8500
Fax: 303-273-8450

E-mail: sedas@neis.cr.usgs.gov

National Earthquake Information Center compiles, computes, and distributes digital and analog data on earthquakes that have occurred around the world. They have information on seismograms, earthquake magnitudes, intensities, and epicenter locations. They can answer such questions as:

1) What information exists on the most recent earthquake in California?

2) How many fault lines are known in California and where are they located?

3) What should people do in the event of an earthquake?

4) Where has there been seismic activity around the world in a given month?

5) What is the largest earthquake on record?

Emergency Planning and Community-Right-To-Know Information Hotline

Booz, Allen & Hamilton, Inc.
1725 Jefferson Davis Highway
Arlington, VA 22202
800-535-0202
Fax: 703-412-3333

www: http://www.epa.gov/epaoswer/hotline.htm

The Emergency Planning and Community-Right-To-Know Information Hotline (EPCRA) provides information on what types of waste may be hazardous to the public's health. All information is open to local agencies, citizens, attorneys, consultants, and communities. EPCRA helps answer questions on the best ways to remove and store hazardous and solid waste. They can answer such questions as:

1) What constitutes a hazardous chemical release?

2) Which releases are especially dangerous?

3) What type of emergency planning is available for those working around or in contact with hazardous waste?

4) How are companies and communities regulated?

5) What documents are available to the average citizen concerned about waste?

Emissions Clearinghouse

Emission Factor Clearinghouse, MD-14
U.S. Environmental Protection Agency (EPA)
Research Triangle Park, NC 27711
919-541-5477

The Emissions Clearinghouse is a means of exchanging information on air pollution control matters. It addresses the criteria pollutants and toxic substances from stationary and area sources, as well as mobile sources. The *Emission Factor Clearinghouse Newsletter* is issued quarterly, and contains information on recent publications, inquiries about EPA emission inventory policy, newly developed emission factors, and requests for assistance in dealing with general or specific air pollution emissions. The Clearinghouse does have a database for which there is a user fee. They can answer such questions as:

1) How can I get a FAX Chief system?

2) What information exists on the underground storage of fuel tanks?

3) How can I find an engineer to assist me with my emissions questions?

4) What are atmospheric tanks and how are they used?

National Energy Information Center

U.S. Department of Energy
1F048 Forrestal Building
1000 Independence Ave., SW

Washington, DC 20585
202-586-8800
Fax: 202-586-0727

www: http://www.eia.doe.gov

The National Energy Information Center provides general reference services on U.S. Department of Energy data. It can provide statistical and analytical data, information, and referral assistance on a wide variety of energy-related issues. A publications directory, including many free publications, is available. They can answer such questions as:

1) What energy-related educational materials exist for elementary and secondary students?

2) What are some of the issues surrounding the Clean Air Act Amendments?

3) What is the short-term energy outlook?

4) What companies have purchased uranium and how much?

5) What is the petroleum supply statistics for a particular month?

National Environmental Data Referral Service

NEDRES Office
National Oceanic and Atmospheric Administration
U.S. Department of Commerce
Environmental Information Services
1305 East-West Highway
Silver Spring, MD 20910
301-713-0572
Fax: 301-713-1249

www: http://www.esdim.noaa.gov/
E-mail: barton@esdim.noaa.gov

The National Environmental Data Referral Service (NEDRES) is designed to provide convenient, economical, and efficient access to widely scattered environmental data. NEDRES is a publicly

available service which identifies the existence, location, characteristics, and availability conditions of environmental data sets.
NEDRES database contains only descriptions, and not the actual data. Major subject categories include climatology and
meteorology, oceanography, geophysics and geology, geography, hydrology and limnology, terrestrial resources, toxic and
regulated substances, and satellite remotely sensed data. For
more information on the NEDRES database, contact the office
listed above. They can provide the information and pointers to
data on such questions as:

1) What data exists on the air quality in the U.S.?

2) Where can information be found on the Chesapeake Bay?

3) Where can data be located on the estuarine water of California?

4) How has acid rain affected the environment?

5) How has pollution affected the ocean environment?

Environmental Financing Information Network

Labat-Anderson, Inc.
401 M St., SW, 3304
Washington, DC 20460
202-260-0420

The Environmental Financing Information Network is an online
database service. They help state and local officials find different ways to finance and improve the environment in which we
live. They assist towns in locating funds to update wastewater
treatment plants and other environmental projects all the way
down to the sewage system. Information on State Revolving
Funds and Public-Private Partnerships is included. They can answer such questions as:

1) How can we get financial funding for a non-profit organization?

2) What are the pros and cons of forming a public or private
partnership?

3) What other cities have revamped their waste management system?

4) How can towns or cities find technical assistance to help with new waste technology?

5) What ways can a state economically enhance their waste treatment systems?

U.S. Environmental Protection Agency (EPA)

Public Information Center
401 M St., SW
Washington, DC 20460
202-260-2080
Fax: 202-260-6257

www: hhtp://www.epa.gov
E-mail: public_access@epamail.epa.gov

The Public Information Center of the Environmental Protection Agency should be the first point of contact for all environmental issues. They have free publications on a variety of environmental topics, and can refer you to other experts within the EPA for more specific responses to your inquiries. They can answer such questions as:

1) What cars have the best gas mileage?

2) What are the current pesticide regulations?

3) What environmental education materials exist for teachers?

4) What can be done to reduce pollution?

5) What is radon, and how can it be removed from a home?

Center for Environmental Research Information

Research and Technology Transfer
U.S. Environmental Protection Agency (EPA)
26 W. Martin Luther King Dr.
Cincinnati, OH 45268

513-569-7369
513-569-7562 (to order publications)
Fax: 513-569-7566

 www: http://www.epa.gov/docs/ord/

The Office of Research and Development (ORD) has centralized most of its information distribution and technology transfer activities in the Center for Environmental Research Information (CERI). CERI also serves as a central point of distribution for ORD research results and reports. They have statistics, regulations, and publications available at no charge. They can answer such questions as:

1) How can I protect my home from pesticides and pollution?

2) What types of pollution can cause harm to my family?

3) What safety guidelines must a company or lab follow?

4) How can a business get grant money to do research?

5) What certifications must companies meet in regulating their pollution?

National Marine Fisheries Service

Public Affairs
National Oceanic and Atmospheric Administration
U.S. Department of Commerce
1335 East-West Highway, Room 9272
Silver Spring, MD 20910
301-713-2370
Fax: 202-501-2953 (constituent services)

www: http://www.noaa.gov

The National Marine Fisheries Service (NMFS) manages the country's stocks of saltwater fish and shellfish for both commercial and recreational interests. NMFS enforces the Magnuson Fishery Conservation and Management Act to assure that fishing stays within sound biological limits. Scientists conduct research relating to these management responsibilities in science and research centers and have special knowledge of the fish in their geographical area. They can answer such questions as:

1) What is currently being done to protect whales and what statistics exist regarding these mammals?

2) What are some issues currently under discussion regarding fishing on an international level?

3) What is the Habitat Conservation Program and where can someone find out more information about it?

4) What information exists on seafood inspection?

5) What is currently being done to restore the marine habitat in the Chesapeake Bay?

Forest Service

U.S. Department of Agriculture
Public Affairs
201 14th and Independence Ave., SW
Washington, DC 20250
202-205-1760
Fax: 202-205-0885

 www: http://www.fs.fed.us

This country's national forests offer more than 114,300 miles of trails, a Scenic Byway System consisting of nearly 5,000 miles of highways in 32 states, 70 wild and scenic rivers covering nearly 3,500 miles and much more. *A Guide to Your National Forest* lists regional offices, several private and one Forest Service Interpretative Association, and a list of State Boards of Tourism where camping information may be obtained. They can answer such questions as:

1) What state forests in Maryland offer good sailing opportunities?

2) How far in advance must I reserve a campsite?

3) What is the best time of year to plan a camping trip in Tennessee?

4) Which rivers in North Carolina are recommended for canoeing or rafting?

5) How do I receive a listing of national scenic and historic trails?

Geologic Inquiries Group

U.S. Geological Survey (USGS)
907 National Center
Reston, VA 22092
703-648-4383
Fax: 703-648-4888

 www: http://www.usgs.gov

The Geologic Inquiries Group is the primary information group of the Geologic Division of the USGS. The Group can provide information and answers to questions concerning all aspects of geology, such as the geology of specific areas, energy and mineral resources, earthquakes, volcanoes, geochemistry, geophysics, and other geoscience disciplines, and geologic map coverage. They have publications available, some of which are free. They can answer such questions as:

1) Where can information be obtained on a particular volcano?

2) Where can geologic maps for a specific area of a state be located?

3) What educational materials exist for teachers who want to teach their students about geology?

4) What geologic information is available on earthquakes?

5) What help is available for someone doing a science project on volcanoes?

National Geophysical Data Center

National Oceanic and Atmospheric Administration
Mail Code E/GC
325 Broadway, Dept. NGB

Boulder, CO 80303
303-497-6419

www: http://meridian.ngdc.noaa.gov/ngdc.html

The National Geophysical Data Center (NGDC) combines in a single center all data activities in the fields of solid earth geophysics, marine geology and geophysics, and solar-terrestrial physics. NGDC fills thousands of requests each year for data services and publications. Typical specialized data services may include digitization of analog charts, derivation of geomagnetic indexes, and customized computer graphics. They can answer such questions as:

1) Where can historical earthquake data be obtained?

2) Where can data on solar flare activity be located?

3) What causes avalanches, and what methods are used to ensure the safety of skiers in areas where avalanches typically occur?

4) Where are thermal springs and thermal wells located in Nevada?

5) Where can information on earthquake damage to transportation systems be obtained so that new systems can better withstand the effects of an earthquake?

National Response Center (Hazardous Chemicals)

U.S. Coast Guard Headquarters
2100 2nd St., SW, Room 2611
Washington, DC 20593
800-424-8802

The National Response Center receives notification and calls reporting oil spills, hazardous chemical releases, biological and radiological releases that have spilled into the environment. They pass the accidents on to a Federal On-Scene Coordinator, who coordinates and begins the clean-up efforts. The Hotline is open to the general public and to companies to call with sightings. Most of the information available from the Center is free. They can answer such questions as:

1) Has there ever been a report of hazardous waste spilled in a specific neighborhood or location?

2) How can I get a report released about a company regarding hazardous waste?

3) What is hazardous waste?

4) How does the Environmental Protection Agency enforce hazardous waste storage?

RCRA Hotline (Hazardous Waste)

U.S. Environmental Protection Agency (EPA)
401 M St., SW
Washington, DC 20460
800-424-9346
703-412-9810
Fax on Demand: 202-651-2060

www: http://www.epa.gov

RCRA stands for the Resource Conservation and Recovery Act which has the goals of: protecting human health and the environment from the potential hazards of waste disposal; conserving energy and natural resources; reducing the amount of waste generated, including hazardous waste; and ensuring that wastes are managed in an environmentally sound manner. They can answer questions regarding recycling, hazardous waste, solid waste issues, and much more. They have a catalogue of publications, as well as a publication, *Solving the Hazardous Waste Problem: EPA's RCRA Program*, which provides an overview of RCRA. They can answer such questions as:

1) What are the hazardous waste disposal regulations in my state?

2) Which plant pesticides are considered safe?

3) What are the laws and regulations concerning hazardous waste transportation?

4) How can I begin a recycling program in my community?

5) What are some of the most recent technologies and management strategies for hazardous waste control?

National Water Information Center

U.S. Geological Survey
12201 Sunrise Valley Dr.
Reston, VA 22092
800-426-9000

www: http://www.usgs.gov
E-mail: h20@info.gov

The National Water Information Center answers general questions on hydrology, water as a resource, and hydrologic mapping, as well as providing information on the products, projects, and services of the Water Services Division. The Center also provides information and materials for specific needs and is a reference office for Water-Resources Investigation reports released before 1982. The Information Center has maps showing a wide range of water-resources information. The staff can answer such questions as:

1) How can my company improve its waste disposal practices?

2) Where can I receive information on water resource conditions in my state?

3) What can people do to help reduce the problem of acid rain?

4) How can my company prevent ground water contamination?

5) Where can I receive introductory information on ground water hydraulics?

Indoor Air Quality Information Clearinghouse

P.O. Box 37133
Washington, DC 20013
800-438-4318
Fax: 202-484-1510

E-mail: iaquinfo@aol.com

The Indoor Air Quality Information Clearinghouse of the Environmental Protection Agency can provide information and assistance on indoor air quality problems. It brings together information on more than 17 issues (from asbestos to wood preservatives), for the range of agencies involved in addressing those issues, from health agencies to energy departments. This office also has information on home humidifiers, residential air cleaners, Sick Building Syndrome, indoor air quality, new carpet, and more. They can answer such questions as:

1) What is Sick Building Syndrome, and what agency do I contact if I suspect my building is unsafe?

2) How do I identify and eliminate radon gas from my home?

3) How do I determine if the paint in my home is lead based?

4) What is the most recent legislation concerning asbestos-in-school requirements?

5) What is the Toxic Substance Control Act?

Bureau of Land Management

Office of Public Affairs
U.S. Department of the Interior
1849 C St., NW, Room 5600
Washington, DC 20240
202-208-3801
Fax: 202-208-5242

There are close to 270 million acres of public lands located primarily, but not exclusively, in the West and in Alaska comprising one-eighth of our nation's land area. It is the charge of the Bureau of Land Management (BLM) to administer and care for these lands. To accomplish this task, the BLM has a variety of programs and activities, from the very new Heritage Education program aimed at involving and educating young people about America's cultural heritage to finding out about the availability of public lands for sale. They have free publications and can direct you to other resources within the BLM. They can answer such questions as:

1) Where are campgrounds located on BLM lands and what facilities or recreational areas do they have?

2) What videos are available concerning rivers?

3) How can I find out which public lands are for sale in my state?

4) How do I stake a mining claim on federal lands?

5) How can I receive a listing of wildlife habitats on public lands?

U.S. Nuclear Regulatory Commission

Public Document Room
Washington, DC 20555
202-634-3273
Fax: 202-634-3343

 www: http://www.nrc.gov

The Nuclear Regulatory Commission (NRC) licenses and regulates civilian use of nuclear energy to protect public health and safety and the environment. The NRC licenses persons and companies to build and operate nuclear reactors and other facilities, and to own and use nuclear materials. The Commission makes rules, sets standards, and carefully inspects companies to ensure that they do not violate existing safety rules. They can answer such questions as:

1) What information exists on abnormal occurrences in nuclear facilities?

2) What is the construction permit process for nuclear facilities?

3) What specific operational information must nuclear facilities submit to the NRC?

4) What statistics are available related to nuclear power?

5) How are radioactive materials packaged for transport?

National Oceanic and Atmospheric Administration

14th St. and Constitution Ave.
Washington, DC 20230
202-482-6090
Fax: 202-482-3154

www: http://www.noaa.gov

The National Oceanic and Atmospheric Administration gathers data, conducts research, and makes predictions about the state of the environment in which we live. NOAA charts the seas and skies, and enriches our understanding of the oceans, atmosphere, space, and sun. They can refer you to other offices and experts for specific questions, and they also offer a variety of publications and films. They can answer such questions as:

1) What research is being conducted on tropical weather and how can we better predict hurricanes?

2) How has the greenhouse effect changed the environment?

3) What are the physical and chemical processes that occur within the Earth's atmosphere?

4) What is being done to protect marine mammals?

5) What research exists on the solar activity in the upper atmosphere?

Oceanographic Information

National Oceanographic Data Center (NODC)
National Environmental Satellite, Data, and Information Service
National Oceanic and Atmospheric Administration
U.S. Department of Commerce
1315 East West Highway
Silver Spring, MD 20910
301-713-3277
Fax: 301-713-3300

www: http://www.nodc.noaa.gov

The National Oceanographic Data Center (NODC) provides global coverage of oceanographic data and services. NODC's databases cover physical and chemical properties of the world's oceans, seas, and estuaries, plus information on selected continental shelf and coastal waters. Simple questions usually can be answered without charge by telephone or mail, but more complicated ones requiring research or computer processing normally carry a fee. They can answer such questions as:

1)   How does the Pacific Ocean temperature vary over a year?

2)   How has the Atlantic Ocean been effected by pollution and what data exists on this topic?

3)   What are the responsibilities of the NODC and what directories of information do they maintain?

4)   Is there any bottom current data on the South China Sea?

5)   Is the water warmer in Miami Beach or Myrtle Beach?

National Park Service

Office of Public Inquiries
U.S. Department of the Interior
P.O. Box 37127
Washington, DC 20013-7127
202-208-4747

 www: http://www.nps.gov

Along with other responsibilities, the Park Service administers 350 maintained areas in the National Park System, collects the National Register of Historic Places and a registry of natural sites, and manages the Urban Park and Recreation Recovery Program. It provides technical assistance in planning, acquisition and development of recreation resources, conducts surveys of historic buildings and engineering works, has available programs and resources for teachers, and administers a program in interagency archeological services. Information, including brochures, maps, and a publications catalogue can be ordered from the Government Printing Office. The Office of Public Inquiries can refer you to other Park Service offices and can answer such questions as:

1) What archeological digs are currently in progress and where are they located?

2) What statistics are available on Park Service use, such as total visits, visits by region and state, and overnight stays?

3) Where can I locate videos on historic people or national landmarks?

4) How do I find out whether or not my home is eligible for listing on the National Historic Register?

5) How can I receive a listing of the lesser known National Parks?

National Pesticide Telecommunication Network

Oregon State University
NPTN Ag Chem Extension
333 Weniger
Corvallis, OR 97331-6502
800-858-PEST (7378)
Fax: 541-737-0761

The National Pesticide Telecommunication Network (NPTN) is a toll-free telephone service that provides a wide variety of information on pesticides. Phones are staffed by pesticide specialists with agricultural, environmental, and public health backgrounds. Inquiries are also answered by graduate students in such fields as biology, anatomy, biochemistry, and entomology. They can answer such questions as:

1) Where can I get information on pesticides that might be found in drinking water wells?

2) What are some guidelines for the safe use of pesticides by farmers?

3) What plants have a natural ability to repel insects?

4) How do I make the transition from pesticide lawn control to natural pest control?

5) What is the toxicity and proper use of the pesticide R-11? How can I dispose of it safely?

Pollution Prevention Information Clearinghouse

Labat-Anderson, Inc.
401 M St., SW
Washington, DC 20460
202-260-1023
Fax: 202-260-0178

 E-mail: ppic@epamail.epa.gov

The Pollution Prevention Information Clearinghouse is designed to help national and international industries reduce pollutants that are released into our environment. They specialize in using education and public awareness to prevent excessive pollution. The Clearinghouse has four information exchange directories that can be ordered. There is no charge for any service. They can answer such questions as:

1) How can pollution prevention benefit businesses?

2) How do you implement a pollution prevention program?

3) Are there training opportunities for pollution control/waste management?

4) How do you get technical assistance for pollution control?

5) What are the differences between large and small waste generators?

EPA Radon Office

U.S. Environment Protection Agency (EPA)
401 M St., SW (MS6604J)
Washington, DC 20460
202-233-9370
Fax: 202-333-9597

The EPA Radon Office can answer all your questions concerning radon. The staff can answer such questions as:

1) What is radon? How does it affect people?

2) How do I determine whether or not my home has a radon problem?

3) How can I obtain a radon detector for my home? How does it work?

4) What are some effective radon prevention methods?

5) What are some control methods for eliminating radon in well water?

National Sea Grant Depository

Pell Library Building
The University of Rhode Island
Bay Campus
Narragansett, RI 02882
401-874-6114
Fax: 401-874-6160

www: http://nsgd.gso.uri.edu

The National Sea Grant Depository provides a wide variety of information on America's oceans, Great Lakes, and coastal zones. It maintains the only complete collection of publications generated by the National Sea Grant College Program. Publications include information on: oceanography, marine education, fisheries, coastal zone management, aquaculture, marine recreation and law. The collection includes journal reprints, technical and advisory reports, handbooks, charts, maps, manuals, directories, books, audiovisual materials, computer programs, annual reports, conference proceedings, and newsletters produced by Sea Grant funded researchers. The staff can answer such questions as:

1) What are some of the most common fish found in Alaska?

2) How do I begin a fish culture enterprise?

3) What is the impact of pollution on the marine environment?

4) What can people do to prevent the pollution of coastal waters?

5) What are some of the potential risks to coastal investment?

Small Business Ombudsman Clearinghouse

U.S. Environmental Protection Agency (EPA)
Small Business Ombudsman, 1230C
401 M St., SW
Washington, DC 20460
800-368-5888
Fax: 703-305-6462

 www: http://www.epa.gov

The Small Business Ombudsman Clearinghouse helps your business comply with all environmental regulations. They provide information on current policies, safety precautions, and general information on keeping the air you breathe healthy. They are available to assist private citizens, small communities, enterprises, trade associations, technical consultants, and laboratories. Listings on all aspects of current EPA regulatory developments are available at no charge. Over 200 EPA publications are maintained for distribution. They can answer such questions as:

1)   Am I covered under the new Clear Air Act requirements?

2)   How do I get an I.D. number for hazardous waste disposal?

3)   What are the requirements for any underground storage waste?

4)   How do I know if my community is following proper safety guidelines?

5)   What type of waste material could be hazardous to my community?

National Snow and Ice Data Center

World Data Center-A For Glaciology
CIRES, Box 449
University of Colorado
Boulder, CO 80309
303-492-5171
Fax: 303-492-2468

www: http://www_nsidc.colorado.edu
E-mail: nsidc@kyros.colorado.edu

The National Snow and Ice Data Center provides a national and international focus for snow and ice data information services. The Center provides: broad user access to snow and ice data through specialized data reports and inventories in Glaciological Data; through special data sets maintained in the Center; through tailored bibliographies; and through access to the Snow and Ice Library. There is a small fee for some services. They can answer such questions as:

1) How does exhaust from jet aircraft affect cloud cover?

2) Where can data be accessed on glacier fluctuations?

3) How has snow cover varied over time in North America?

4) What current research is being undertaken regarding avalanches?

5) What is the difference between fresh water ice and sea ice?

Solid Waste Information Clearinghouse

P.O. Box 7219
1100 Wayne Ave., Suite 700
Silver Spring, MD 20907-7219
800-67-SWICH
Fax: 301-589-7068

www: http://www.swana.org
E-mail: swana@millkern.com

The Solid Waste Information Clearinghouse (SWICH) is concerned with how state and local offices and industries get rid of solid waste. The general public is also welcome to request information. SWICH can show how to economically and ecologically get rid of waste by source reduction, recycling, composting, planning, education, public training, public participation, legislation and regulation, waste combustion, and collection. They can answer such questions as:

1) How can I implement a recycling program in my community?

2) What is the most economical way to dispose of a waste product?

3) How have other communities started and benefited from recycling?

4) What types of disposal is available to my community or business?

National Space Science Data Center

National Aeronautics and Space Administration
Goddard Space Flight Center
Greenbelt, MD 20771
301-286-7354
Data Request: 301-286-6695
Fax: 301-286-1771

www: http://nssdc.gsfc.nasa.gov/
E-mail: request@nssdca.gsfca.nasa.gov

The National Space Science Data Center (NSSDC) is an organization that provides a variety of valuable services for scientists throughout the world. The Center furthers the use of data obtained from space and earth science investigations, maintains an active data repository, and supports scientific research. The data are contained on more than 120,000 magnetic tapes, tens of thousands of film products, and optical, video, and magnetic disks. NSSDC works with individual users to address their specific requirements. There is a charge for most data, but it is only on a cost recovery basis. They can answer such questions as:

1) What satellites are currently operating in space and which ones are planned for future launch?

2) What data from space can provide estimates of marine phytoplankton in the ocean?

3) Where can photographs taken from APOLLO be located?

4) What data is available to researchers studying the ozone?

5) What information exists on a particular rocket launch?

Technology Transfer Competitiveness

Administrator
Federal Laboratory Consortium
P.O. Box 545
Sequim, WA 98382
360-683-1005
Fax: 360-683-6654

 www: http://www.zyn.com/slc/

The mission of the Federal Laboratory Consortium is to facilitate technology transfer among government, business, and academic entities in order to promote American economic and technological competitiveness. It sponsors conferences and seminars and publishes a free monthly newsletter. For very specific questions from researchers who find themselves at an impasse, the Consortium will conduct a database search to refer the inquirer to an appropriate lab. Write or call for a free general information packet explaining the organization, how to access its services, facilities available for testing, and examples of technology transfers. They can answer such questions as:

1) How can the heat pipes used to cool satellites be converted for use in a business?

2) How can toothpaste used by astronauts benefit those that are used on Earth?

3) What research is being conducted on electric cars?

4) Where can a business locate information on humidity control for a warehouse?

Technology Transfer Program

NASA Scientific and Technical Information Facility
Technology Transfer Office
NASA-CASI
800 Elkridge Landing Rd.
Linthicum Heights, MD 21090-2934

410-859-5300, ext. 242
Fax: 301-621-0134

 www: http://www.nasa.gov

Technology Transfer is an ideal way to apply the National Aeronautics and Space Administration's (NASA) experience and discoveries to your research or business. The transfer of aerospace technology which embraces virtually every scientific and technical discipline is paying off in a broad spectrum of practical applications in industry. The Technology Transfer System is a network of specialized organizations dedicated to helping industry access, apply, and utilize NASA's pool of innovations and technical resources. This allows you to access a wide range of information, products, services and technical expertise. A staff of experts assists you in pinpointing problems, identifying needs, and exchanging ideas. They can answer such questions as:

1) How can ultra-sensitive measuring devices used to measure space dust be put to use measuring environmental pollutants?

2) How can standard doorknobs be replaced with electronic openers?

3) Is it possible to convert spacesuits for use by firefighters or workers in industrial situations?

4) What lunar tool technology can be used in designing cordless power tools?

Toxic Substance Control Act

U.S. Environmental Protection Agency (EPA)
Environmental Assistance Division
401 M St., SW
Washington, DC 20460
202-554-1404
Fax: 202-554-5603

 E-mail: tsca_hotline@epamail.epa.gov

The Toxic Substance Control Act (TSCA) regulates the storage and removal of toxic substances and spills. They are concerned with safely containing toxic substances that may be harmful to our environment. TSCA is open to the general public as well as to industries and environmental groups. They can answer such questions as:

1) What chemicals can a manufacturer produce, and are they on the toxic inventory list?

2) What can I do if a toxic substance was spilled or contained on my property?

3) What are the latest regulations regarding production and handling of toxic substances?

4) How can I get a listing of places where toxic waste is stored?

Undersea Research

National Undersea Research Program
National Oceanic and Atmospheric Administration (NOAA)
U.S. Department of Commerce
R/OR2, Room 11853
Building SSMC-3
1315 East-West Highway
Silver Spring, MD 20910
301-713-2427
Fax: 301-713-0799

The National Undersea Research Program (NURP) develops programs and provides support to scientists and engineers to accomplish research underwater for the study of biological, chemical, geological, and physical processes in the world's oceans and lakes. NURP provides investigators with modern undersea facilities including submersibles, habitats, air and mixed gas SCUBA, and remotely operated vehicles. They can answer such questions as:

1) How do I get a grant from NURP?

2) What is the appropriate undersea center for me to contact in my region?

3) How deep in the sea does NURP support scientists work?

4) What kind of research expenses will be covered under a NURP grant?

5) Does NURP support coral reef research?

EPA National Small Flows Clearinghouse (Wastewater)

West Virginia University
P.O. Box 6064
Morgantown, WV 26506
800-624-8301
Fax: 304-293-3161

The National Small Flows Clearinghouse is the center for small systems wastewater technology transfer. The Clearinghouse provides training resources and expertise in management and maintenance of small wastewater systems. It assists small communities in meeting environmental goals and water quality requirements. The Clearinghouse offers products and services to aid consultants, local officials, and developers in designing, constructing, operating, and managing small wastewater systems. Its products and services include databases, publications, video programs, workshops, and seminars. The staff can answer such questions as:

1) How can I find out more about the use of constructed wetlands that are used to treat domestic wastewater?

2) How can I find out more about sequencing batch reactors? How do they compare with conventional continuous waste treatment systems?

3) What should I look for when hiring qualified wastewater personnel?

4) How can our community get the most out of our existing wastewater resources and facilities?

5) What are some current technologies for cleansing polluted water?

Watershed Resource Information System

U.S. Environmental Protection Agency (EPA)
1717 K St., NW
Suite 801
Washington, DC 20006
800-726-LAKE (5253)

www: http://www.epa.gov

The Watershed Resource Information System is an information resource on lake restoration, protection, and management. Its Watershed Information Resource Database contains abstracts and citations of technical materials and information and bibliographies. A specialist will conduct a database search for you for a fee of $25, plus $.10 per page per reference. You may purchase the system for $250 or a demo disk for $20. The staff can answer such questions as:

1) What information exists on different methods for restoring polluted lakes?

2) How can I find out about a particular lake's water quality?

3) What are some effective watershed management techniques?

4) What techniques can be used to reduce the incidence of acidification in lakes?

5) What are some effective methods of reducing toxic substances in lakes?

National Weather Service

National Oceanic and Atmospheric Administration
1325 East-West Highway
Silver Spring, MD 20910
301-713-0622

www: http://www.nws.noaa.gov

The National Weather Service, through a network of field offices, predicts the nation's weather and issues storm and flood warnings. They also publish a weekly series of daily weather maps which include the highest and lowest temperatures chart and the precipitation areas. They can send anyone interested a sample copy or subscription information on this material. They also have publications on a variety of weather conditions, as well as films, videos, and slides. They can answer such questions as:

1) What should be done in the event of a hurricane?

2) What is a tornado?

3) How are severe storms forecast and where can more information be obtained about them?

4) Is there information available on monthly and seasonal predictions of temperature and precipitation?

5) What is a flash flood?

Wetlands Protection Hotline

Labat-Anderson, Inc.
401 M St.
MC4502F
Washington, DC 20460
800-832-7828
Fax: 703-525-0201

 www: http://www.epa.gov

The Wetlands Protection Hotline is a toll-free telephone service that responds to questions about the value and function of wetlands in our world. The staff is interested in protecting our wetlands and showing how wetlands play an important role in our changing environment. They have free publications and fact sheets available. They can answer such questions as:

1) Where can I get the *1987 Corps of Engineers Wetlands Delineation Manual*?

2) Is there any information available on constructed wetlands?

3) Is it legal to dig out a wetlands area?

4) What is the White House's policy on the protection of wet-lands?

5) What regulations must farmers comply with when they have wetlands on their property?

Health

National Institute on Aging

P.O. Box 8057
Gaithersburg, MD 20898-8057
800-222-2225
Fax: 301-496-1072

The National Institute on Aging conducts research related to the aging process and looks at diseases and other special problems related to the needs of the aged. They have a publications list of free items dealing with a variety of consumer issues. They can answer such questions as:

1) What is a good exercise program for an elderly person?

2) What information exists on menopause and how can symptoms be treated?

3) How can the elderly improve their diet?

4) What is osteoporosis and what can be done to minimize its effects?

5) What factors should people be aware of when taking certain medications?

National AIDS Information Clearinghouse

P.O. Box 6003
Rockville, MD 20849
800-458-5231
Fax: 301-251-5343

www: http://cdcnac.aspensys.com:86
E-mail: aidsinfo@cdc.nac.aspensys.com

The National AIDS Hotline offers 24-hour service seven days a week to respond to any question about HIV infection and AIDS.

Information specialists can refer you to groups in your area, and can direct you to local counseling and testing centers. The Clearinghouse can also connect people with the Clinical Trials Information Center, where they can learn what trials are currently taking place and what the requirements are for participants. They have free resources and publications on AIDS and HIV infection. They can answer such questions as:

1) What videos are available on AIDS that are appropriate for kids?

2) What are the signs and symptoms of infection?

3) How can parents most effectively discuss AIDS with their children?

4) What information exists on AIDS clinical trials?

5) Where can someone get information on caring for an AIDS patient at home?

National Clearinghouse for Alcohol and Drug Information

P.O. Box 2345
11426 Rockville Pike
Rockville, MD 20852
800-729-6686

www: http://www.health.org

The National Clearinghouse for Alcohol and Drug Information (NCADI) gathers and disseminates current information on alcohol and drug-related subjects, and can make referrals to other alcohol, tobacco, and drug resource experts. The Clearinghouse is the national resource center for information on the latest research results, popular press and scholarly journal articles, videos, prevention curricula, print materials, and program descriptions. Services include subject searches on an in-house database and response to inquiries for statistics and other information. NCADI can make referrals to self-help organizations, and can provide information on drug and alcohol abuse treatment. They have a publications catalogue listing, booklets, videos, and posters which range in price from free to $25. They can answer such questions as:

1) How do you implement a drug-free workplace program, and what are the laws regarding drug testing at the workplace?

2) How do you teach kids about the dangers of drugs and alcohol, and what are the warning signs parents should know?

3) What are the effects of Fetal Alcohol Syndrome and where can people turn for more information about it?

4) What are some statistics on drug abuse among college students and what prevention programs exist?

5) What research is being done on children of alcoholics and are there support groups in place for them?

National Institute
of Allergy and Infectious Diseases

Building 31, Room 7A50
9000 Rockville Pike
Bethesda, MD 20892
301-496-5717
Fax: 301-402-0120

 www: http://www.niaid.nih.gov/

The National Institute of Allergy and Infectious Diseases (NIAID) conducts and supports research to study the causes of allergic, immunologic, and infectious diseases, and to develop better means of preventing, diagnosing, and treating these illnesses. Some studies look at the role of the immune system in chronic diseases, such as arthritis, and at disorders of the immune system, as in asthma. NIAID has become the lead component at the National Institutes of Health for coordinating and conducting AIDS research. They have publications, journal articles, and more. They can answer such questions as:

1) What research is currently being done on allergies to pollen?

2) What is the current research being undertaken on AIDS?

3) How can I help my child handle asthma?

4) What is Chronic Fatigue Syndrome and what are the options for treating it?

5) What research exists on problems associated with the immune system?

Alzheimer's Disease Education And Referral Center

P.O. Box 8250
Silver Spring, MD 20907
800-438-4380
Fax: 301-495-3334

www: http://www.alzheimers.org/adear
E-mail: adear@alzheimers.org

The Alzheimer's Disease Education and Referral Center distributes information about Alzheimer's disease to health professionals, patients and their families, and the general public. The Center provides information about the diagnosis and treatment of Alzheimer's disease, research, and services available to patients and family members. The bibliographic references of the Center are included in a computerized index that includes references to patient and professional education materials, including information about health promotion programs. A list is available of free publications, in addition to a free newsletter. They can answer such questions as:

1) What are the symptoms of Alzheimer's disease and what are the causes?

2) What research has been done to evaluate special long-term care units for Alzheimer patients?

3) Where are research centers located which deal with Alzheimer's?

4) What are some statistics on Alzheimer's?

5) What help is available for families caring for an Alzheimer's patient at home?

National Arthritis and Musculoskeletal and Skin Diseases Information Clearinghouse

1 AMS Circle
Bethesda, MD 20892-3675
301-495-4484
Fax: 301-587-4352

The National Institute of Arthritis and Musculoskeletal and Skin Diseases handles inquiries on arthritis, bone diseases, and skin diseases. They conduct and support basic and clinical research concerning the causes, prevention, diagnosis, and treatment of these diseases. They serve as an information exchange for individuals and organizations involved in public, professional, and patient education. The Clearinghouse has free publications on a variety of topics and can search their database for other information that might be needed. They can answer questions such as:

1) What can be done to prevent osteoporosis and who is most at risk for acquiring this disease?

2) Does chocolate cause acne and how can acne be treated?

3) What information exists on joint replacement for people who suffer from severe arthritis?

4) What are some different types of birth marks, and how can they be removed?

5) What educational materials are there for a continuing education forum on arthritis?

Asthma Clearinghouse

National Asthma Education Program
P.O. Box 30105
Bethesda, MD 20824-0105

301-251-1222
Fax: 301-251-1223

www: http://www.nhlbi.nih.gov/nhlbi/nhlbi.html

The Asthma Clearinghouse is a new clearinghouse providing publications, reports, resources, and referrals to experts in the field of asthma. One report, *The Executive Summary: Guidelines for the Diagnosis and Management of Asthma*, explains the diagnosis, therapy, and other important considerations for those that suffer from asthma. They can answer such questions as:

1) What materials are available for kids that explain the causes and treatment of asthma?

2) What conditions trigger an asthma attack?

3) Are there different types of asthma?

4) What are some forms of treatment for asthma sufferers?

5) What are the guidelines for treatment of asthma?

Blood Resources

National Blood Resource Education Program
P.O. Box 30105
Bethesda, MD 20824-0105
301-251-1222
Fax: 301-251-1223

www: http://www.nhlbi.nih.gov/nhlbi/nhlbi.html

The National Blood Resource Education Program was established to ensure an adequate supply of safe blood and blood components to meet our country's needs, ensuring that blood and blood components are transfused only when therapeutically appropriate. The Program helps health professionals understand the risks and benefits of blood transfusions, and ensures that patients receive appropriate information regarding transfusions. They also work to increase public awareness that donating blood is a safe process. They can answer such questions as:

1) What should people should be aware of when donating blood?

2) Is it still possible to get AIDS from blood transfusions?

3) Can you donate your own blood before you undergo surgery in the event you might require a transfusion?

4) How long can blood be kept before it is no longer usable?

5) What are some of the problems that people encounter when they have unusual blood types?

The Cancer Information Service

National Cancer Institute
Building 31, Room 10A24
9000 Rockville Pike
Bethesda, MD 20892
800-4-CANCER
800-422-6237
Fax: 301-402-0555

 www: http://www.nci.nih.gov/

The toll-free Cancer Information Service can provide accurate, up-to-date information about cancer and cancer-related resources in local areas. A wide variety of free publications on specific types of cancer, treatment methods, coping methods, and other cancer-related subjects are distributed. A database is available, that can access information on clinical trials and treatment options. The Cancer Information Service can help you locate materials and research on a specific type of cancer. They can answer such questions as:

1) Is the new prostate cancer test accurate, and to what degree?

2) How often should you get a mammogram and at what age should you begin?

3) What are the side effects of a particular anti-cancer drug?

4) What are the different stages of breast cancer?

5) What are clinical trials and where can I participate in them?

Clearinghouse
on Child Abuse and Neglect Information

P.O. Box 1182
Washington, DC 20013
800-FYI-3366
Fax: 703-385-3206

E-mail: nccanch@calib.com

The Clearinghouse on Child Abuse and Neglect Information was established to help professionals and concerned citizens locate information on child abuse and neglect. They collect and disseminate a wide variety of information including publications, audiovisuals, public awareness materials, and more, and can refer you to other resources. Stock publications and many other services are provided at no cost to the user. User fees are required however, for services such as custom database searches and bibliographies. They can answer such questions as:

1) What statistics exist on the incidence of child abuse and neglect?

2) What laws exist that protect children against child abuse?

3) What is the role of the courts in child protection?

4) What funding sources are there for child abuse and neglect programs?

5) What role do teachers play in the prevention and treatment of child abuse?

National Institute
of Child Health and Human Development

P.O. Box 2911
Washington, DC 20040
301-496-5133
Fax: 301-496-7101

The National Institute of Child Health and Human Development conducts and supports research in maternal and child health and the population sciences. They will respond to individual inquiries on related topics such as studies on reproductive biology and contraception, fertility, mental retardation, and developmental issues. They have free publications and can refer you elsewhere for additional information. They can answer such questions as:

1) What is anorexia nervosa?

2) What are the possible causes of Down Syndrome?

3) What are some important issues to think about when considering a vasectomy?

4) Where is there research being conducted on mental retardation?

5) What are the newest forms of birth control being used?

National Information Center
for Children and Youth with Disabilities

P.O. Box 1492
Washington, DC 20013
202-884-8200
Fax: 202-884-8441

www: http://www.aed.org/nichcy
E-mail: nichcy@aed.org

The National Information Center for Children and Youth with Disabilities operates a national clearinghouse providing free information to assist parents, educators, caregivers, advocates, and others in helping children and youth with disabilities to become active members of the community. The staff provides personal responses to specific questions, as well as information on local, state, or national disability groups for parents, prepared information packets, publications on current issues, and technical assistance to parent and professional groups. They can answer such questions as:

1) How can I help my hyperactive child?

2) At what age do public schools begin mainstreaming students?

3) Can the Center provide a listing of national Down Syndrome support groups?

4) Where can I obtain captioned films for the deaf?

5) How do I make my home more wheelchair accessible? Are there any financial assistance programs available to help me accomplish this?

Cholesterol Information

National Cholesterol Education Program Information Center
National Heart, Lung, and Blood Institute
P.O. Box 30105
Bethesda, MD 20824-0105
301-251-1222
Fax: 301-251-1223

www: http://www.nhlbi.nih.gov/nhlbi/nhlbi.html

Do you know your cholesterol number or has your doctor advised you to change your diet? The National Cholesterol Education Program (NCEP) is for you. NCEP aims to raise awareness and understanding about high blood cholesterol as a risk factor for coronary heart disease and the benefits of lowering cholesterol levels as a means of preventing coronary heart disease. They have specialists on staff to answer questions and they provide printed information on cholesterol, diet, and high blood pressure to the public and health professionals. They can answer such questions as:

1) Is it possible to eat bacon on a low cholesterol diet?

2) Are medications required when trying to lower cholesterol levels?

3) How does exercise affect cholesterol levels?

4) What are the different types of home cholesterol test kits available?

5) What do the cholesterol numbers mean and what is meant by good and bad cholesterol?

National Institute on Deafness and Other Communication Disorders Clearinghouse

1 Communication Ave.
Bethesda, MD 20892-3456
800-241-1044
800-241-1055 TDD
Fax: 301-907-8830

E-mail: nidcd@aeric.com

The National Institute on Deafness and Other Communication Disorders disseminates information on normal and disordered processes of human communication. They have information about hearing, balance, smell, taste, voice, speech, and language for health professionals, patients, and the general public. They have fact sheets, bibliographies, information packets, and directories. They can answer such questions as:

1) What are the treatment options for someone who has aphasia?

2) What can be done for children with frequent ear infections?

3) Are all hearing aids created equal?

4) What can be done to help someone who stutters?

5) What are the current statistics on deafness and hearing disorders?

National Institute of Dental Research

Information Office
Building 31, Room 2C35
31 Center Dr.
MSC-2290

Bethesda, MD 20892
301-496-4261
Fax: 301-496-9988

www: http://www.nidr.nih.gov/
E-mail: nidrinso@od31.nidr.nih.gov

The National Institute of Dental Research conducts research on the causes, prevention, diagnosis, and treatment of diseases and conditions of the mouth and teeth. They have free publications and posters on a variety of topics, and can refer people to experts for further information. They can answer such questions as:

1) What are the oral problems related to AIDS?

2) What information exists on fever blisters and canker sores?

3) What are the causes of periodontal disease and what are some effective treatment options?

4) Are fluoride treatments safe and when should they be started?

5) What are dental sealants and how effective are they in preventing cavities?

National Diabetes Information Clearinghouse

1 Information Way
Box NDIC
Bethesda, MD 20892
301-654-3327
Fax: 301-907-8906

www: http://www.niddk.nih.gov/

The National Diabetes Information Clearinghouse was established to increase the knowledge and understanding of diabetes among patients, health professionals, and the general public. The Clearinghouse has a publications list available, with items ranging in price from free to $25, and a free quarterly newsletter featuring news about diabetes. They can also search their database for information on a specific topic. They can answer such questions as:

1) What is the latest research on the ways to manage diabetes, along with nutrition and diet information?

2) What are the issues and reports regarding diabetes and athletics?

3) What is gestational diabetes and the special risks and dangers it presents?

4) What are the types of insulins currently available, along with the time action of the insulin preparations?

5) What are some common foot care problems frequently experienced by diabetics?

National Digestive Diseases Information Clearinghouse

Box NDDIC
Bethesda, MD 20892
301-496-3583
Fax: 301-496-7422

 www: http://www.niddk.nih.gov/

The Digestive Diseases Information Clearinghouse provides information about digestive diseases to educate the public, patients and their families, as well as physicians and other health care providers. The Clearinghouse provides information products and services such as factsheets, as well as an inquiry and referral service, information about research developments, and organizational and governmental activities related to digestive diseases. The Clearinghouse also maintains a database containing references to literature, products, programs, and services. A list of free publications is available. They can answer such questions as:

1) What are the surgical procedures involved in having a gall bladder removed and are there options to surgery?

2) What are the symptoms, causes, and treatments of ulcers?

3) How do you prevent heartburn?

4) What is a hiatal hernia and does it always require surgery?

5) What is pancreatitis?

Disabilities Information Clearinghouse

Clearinghouse on Disability Information Programs
U.S. Department of Education
Mary Switzer Building, Room 3132
Washington, DC 20202
202-205-8241
Fax: 202-401-2608

The Clearinghouse on Disability Information responds to inquiries on a wide range of topics. Information is especially strong in the areas of Federal funding for programs serving individuals with disabilities, Federal legislation affecting the disability community, and Federal programs benefiting people with disabilities. A publications list is available, many of which are free. The Clearinghouse also maintains a database of sources for equipment to assist disabled people. They can answer such questions as:

1) What information exists about housing disabled people?

2) What handicapped assistance loans are available?

3) What is the law regarding Equal Employment Opportunities for handicapped persons?

4) What are the requirements for public education of students with handicaps?

5) How can businesses best accommodate workers with disabilities?

Disease Information

Centers for Disease Control
Information Resources Management Office
Mail Stop C-15
1600 Clifton Rd., NE

Atlanta, GA 30333
404-332-4555
Fax on Demand: 404-332-4565

The Centers for Disease Control (CDC) has developed a Voice Information System that allows anyone using a touch tone telephone to obtain prerecorded information on particular health issues. The materials include information about certain diseases or health areas, symptoms and prevention methods, immunization requirements, current statistics, recent disease outbreaks, and other available printed materials. Currently information is available on AIDS, Chronic Fatigue Syndrome, encephalitis, hepatitis, Lyme disease, malaria, and more. They can answer such questions as:

1) What are the current statistics on AIDS?

2) Have there been recent disease outbreaks and where have they occurred?

3) Are vaccines required for travel to Africa?

4) When should children be immunized?

5) What is Chronic Fatigue Syndrome and where can I learn more about this condition?

Drug Evaluation Clearinghouse

Center for Drug Evaluation and Research
Food and Drug Administration (FDA)
5600 Fishers Lane
Rockville, MD 20857
301-594-1012

www: http://www.fda.gov

The Center for Drug Evaluation and Research responds to inquiries covering a wide spectrum of drug issues. They develop policy with regard to the safety, effectiveness, and labeling of all drug products, as well as evaluate new drug applications. The Center conducts research and develops scientific standards on the composition, quality, safety, and effectiveness of drugs. A list of guidelines is available to help manufacturers comply with the requirements of the regulations. The staff will respond to requests for information regarding the laws, regulations, policies, and functions of the FDA as it pertains to drugs. Materials are available on pharmaceuticals, drug labeling, and consumer education. They can answer such questions as:

1) What are the pros and cons of estrogen?

2) What information exists on the different forms of The Pill?

3) Do over-the-counter hair growth products really work?

4) What research has been done on Norplant?

5) What information is required on drug package labels?

National Eye Institute

Office of Health, Education and Communication
Building 31, Room 6A32
31 Center Dr.
Bethesda, MD 20892-2510
301-496-5248
Fax: 301-402-1065

www: http://www.nei.nih.gov/
E-mail: 2020@b31.nei.nih.gov

The National Eye Institute (NEI) conducts and supports research related to the cause, natural history, prevention, diagnosis, and treatment of disorders of the eye and visual system. NEI distributes information on eye disorders, and can refer people to other organizations. They have free publications on a variety of topics. They can answer such questions as:

1) What is the latest information about cataracts and how can they safely be removed?

2) Are disposable contact lenses safe?

3) What are the causes of blindness?

4) How can glaucoma be detected early and are there treatment options to be considered?

5) What is Senile Macular Degeneration?

Food and Drug Information

Office of Consumer Affairs
Food and Drug Administration
5600 Fishers Lane, HFE 88
Rockville, MD 20857
301-443-3170
Fax: 301-443-9767

 www: http://www.fda.gov

The Food and Drug Administration (FDA) is charged with ensuring that food is safe and wholesome; that drugs, biological products, medical devices are safe and effective; that cosmetics are safe; that the use of radiological products does not result in unnecessary exposure to radiation; and that all of these products are honestly and informatively labeled. The Office of Consumer Affairs of the FDA handles consumer inquiries on issues under the FDA's responsibility, and serves as a clearinghouse for FDA publications (most of which are free). They can also refer callers to the appropriate office for more information. Topics covered include foods, nutrition, federal regulations, cosmetics, drug labeling, medical devices, pharmaceuticals, and more. They can answer such questions as:

1) What nutritional information is available for pregnant women?

2) Are extended wear lenses safe?

3) What information is required on food labels, and what does it mean?

4) What are the different forms of birth control and how effective are they?

5) What is the status of breast implants and where can someone turn for more information on the subject?

National Health Information Center

Office of Disease Prevention and Health Promotion
P.O. Box 1133
Washington, DC 20013
301-565-4167
800-336-4797
Fax: 301-984-4256

www: http://nhic_nt.health.org
E-mail: nhicinfo@health.org

The National Health Information Center is a health information
referral organization that puts people with health questions in
touch with those organizations that are best able to answer
them. The Center's main objectives are to identify health information resources, channel requests for information to these resources, and develop publications on health-related topics of interest to health professionals, the health media, and the
general public. The Center meets these objectives by using a variety of information resource materials, a database of health-related organizations, and an information referral system. There
is a publications catalogue available, with prices ranging from
free to $5, and the Center covers topics such as community
health, school health, worksite health, nutrition, and more.
They can answer such questions as:

1) What health education program materials exist for employers and how can they be implemented at the worksite?

2) What organizations and support groups exist for people suffering from cerebral palsy?

3) What toll-free numbers are available for various health information?

4) What is the latest information about a specific rare disease
and where can people turn for support?

5) How physically fit are America's six-year-olds and what statistics exist on this topic?

Health Care Delivery

Bureau of Primary Health Care
Health Resources and Services Administration
5600 Fishers Lane, Room 7-05
Rockville, MD 29857
301-594-4110

The Bureau of Primary Health Care helps assure that health care services are provided to medically underserved populations and to persons with special health care needs. The Bureau serves as a national focus for the development of primary health care delivery capacity, and for placement of health care professionals in Health Professional Shortage Areas to promote sustained sources of health services. Support for primary health care is provided primarily through Community Health Centers, Migrant Health Centers, Services for Special Populations, Services for Residents of Public Housing, and the National Health Service Corps. They can answer such questions as:

1) How can nurses or doctors get their college loans repaid through service?

2) What programs exist for migrant health care?

3) What programs deal with the special health care needs of the homeless?

4) What research is being undertaken on meeting the health care needs of the elderly in this country?

5) What areas of the country are currently designated as health professional shortage areas?

Health Care Policy Clearinghouse

Agency for Health Care Policy and Research
P.O. Box 8547

Silver Spring, MD 20907
800-358-9295
Fax on Demand: 301-594-2800

www: http://www.ahcpr.gov

The Agency for Health Care Policy and Research (AHCPR) is the primary source of Federal support for research on problems related to the quality and delivery of health services. AHCPR programs evaluate health services, assess technologies, and improve access to new scientific and technical information for research users. Research findings are disseminated through publications, conferences, and workshops. Materials are available on medical treatment effectiveness, health care costs and utilizations, health care expenditures, health information systems, health technology assessment, and funding opportunities for grants and contracts. They can answer such questions as:

1) What are clinical practice guidelines for the treatment of cataracts?

2) What statistics exist on medical expenditures?

3) How effective is a specific treatment strategy for ulcers?

4) What type of person uses a nursing home and what is their average medical condition upon entering such a facility?

5) What are some treatment options for depression and how effective are they?

Clearinghouse on Health Indexes

National Center for Health Statistics
U.S. Department of Health and Human Services
Public Health Service
6525 Belcrest Rd.
Hyattsville, MD 20782
301-436-8500

www: http://www.cdc.gov/nchswww/nchshome.htm

The National Center for Health Statistics provides information assistance in the development of health measures to health researchers, administrators, and planners. The Clearinghouse's definition of a health index is a measure that summarizes data from two or more components and purports to reflect the health status of an individual or defined group. Services provided to users include annotated bibliographies and a reference and referral service. A publications catalogue is available, with items ranging in price from free to $20. They can answer such questions as:

1) What are the typical characteristics of persons with and without health care coverage?

2) What type of health care is provided to adolescents?

3) What method of contraception is used most frequently in the U.S.?

4) What data exists on the current living arrangements of women of childbearing ages in the U.S.?

5) What survey data exists on the firearm mortality among children?

National Heart, Lung, and Blood Institute Information Center

P.O. Box 30105
Bethesda, MD 20824-0105
301-251-1222
Fax: 301-251-1223

 www: http://www.nhlbi.nih.gov/nhlbi/nhlbi.html

The National Heart, Lung, and Blood Institute is responsible for the scientific investigation of heart, blood vessel, lung, and blood diseases. The Information Center can provide the most current information on cholesterol, high blood pressure, asthma, blood products, and more. Subject specialists can provide information in response to inquiries, which may include publications, bibliographies, program descriptions, referrals to other agencies or organizations, and specific answers free of charge. They can answer such questions as:

1) What are the treatment options for someone suffering from emphysema?

2) What should the level of cholesterol be in blood, and how can it be lowered?

3) What information exists on high blood pressure and is medication the only real option to lowering blood pressure?

4) What is the current research on angioplasty?

5) What help is there for children who have asthma?

High Blood Pressure Information

High Blood Pressure Information Center
P.O. Box 30105
Bethesda, MD 20824-0105
301-251-1222
Fax: 301-251-1223

www: http://www.nhlbi.nih.gov/nhlbi/nhlbi.html

The High Blood Pressure Information Center is a source of information on educational materials for consumers, providers, and planners of high blood pressure control services. The goal of the Center is to reduce death and disability related to high blood pressure through programs of professional, patient, and public education. Print and audiovisual materials, as well as research reports are available. A free newsletter, *InfoMemo*, covers topics of interest concerning blood pressure. They can answer such questions as:

1) Is there a way to lower your high blood pressure through diet and exercise?

2) What is the effect of alcohol on blood pressure?

3) What research exists on alternative therapies such as biofeedback in reducing blood pressure?

4) How can a blood pressure education program be instituted in the workplace?

5) What resources exist for health educators who work with patients with high blood pressure?

Homelessness

National Resource Center on Homelessness and Mental Illness
Policy Research Associates, Inc.
262 Delaware Ave.
Delmar, NY 12054
800-444-7415
Fax: 518-439-7612

Under contract with the National Institute of Mental Illness, Policy Research Associates develops and disseminates new knowledge about the coordination of housing and services for homeless mentally ill persons. The Center publishes a newsletter, and has free information packets and can conduct database searches. They can refer you to organizations concerned with homelessness and mental illness, as well as Federal programs in the field. They can answer such questions as:

1) What are some of the health issues particularly related to homeless people?

2) What are grant programs currently available to homeless organizations to improve services?

3) What self-help programs exist for homeless people?

4) What are some of the issues organizations need to consider when dealing with homeless children?

5) What housing demonstration programs have succeeded with the homeless population?

Public Housing
Drug Strategy Clearinghouse

Drug Information and Strategy Clearinghouse
U.S. Department of Housing and Urban Development (HUD)

P.O. Box 6424
Rockville, MD 20850
800-578-3472
Fax: 301-251-5767

Sponsored by the Department of Housing and Urban Development, the Drug Information and Strategy Clearinghouse provides housing officials, residents, and community leaders with
information and assistance on drug abuse prevention and drug
trafficking control techniques. They have created a database
containing information on improving resident screening procedures, strengthening eviction policies, increasing cooperation
with local law enforcement, implementing drug tip hotlines,
forming resident patrols, starting child care centers, and organizing drug education/prevention activities. The Clearinghouse
also provides information packages, resource lists, HUD regulations, referrals, and a newsletter. There is no charge for most
of this information. They can answer such questions as:

1) How can housing authorities apply for government grants?

2) What are some anti-drug strategies that have been successfully carried out in public housing units?

3) What are the latest drug abuse prevention theories and
   have there been demonstration projects conducted that are
   based on these models?

4) What resident patrols and related programs have been particularly successful in building drug-free neighborhoods?

5) How can there be an increase in cooperation with local law
   enforcement and other agencies in preventing drug abuse?

Indian Health Clearinghouse

Indian Health Service
5600 Fishers Lane, Room 635
Rockville, MD 20857

301-443-3593
Fax: 301-443-0507

www: http://www.tucson.ihs.gov

The Indian Health Services provides comprehensive health services through IHS facilities, tribally contracted hospitals, health centers, school health centers, and health stations. Reports, directories, brochures, and pamphlets are available. They can answer such questions as:

1) How can doctors get their student loans repaid by working for the Indian Health Service?

2) Where are there health professional shortages within the Indian Health Service?

3) Where are health service facilities currently located?

4) What are some of the health care needs specific to Native Americans?

5) What research is being conducted on substance abuse programs for Native Americans?

National Kidney and Urologic Diseases Information Clearinghouse

3 Information Way
Bethesda, MD 20892
301-654-4415
Fax: 301-907-8906

www: http://www.niddk.nih.gov/
E-mail: nkudic@aerie.com

The National Kidney and Urologic Disease Information Clearinghouse (NKUDIC) is an information resource and referral organization seeking to increase the knowledge and understanding of kidney and urologic diseases. They can provide education and information on kidney and urologic diseases to patients, professionals, and the public, as well as make referrals to other appropriate organizations. The Clearinghouse provides products and services such as publications, a computerized database of educational materials, and annotated bibliographies and topical literature searches on selected topics. A publications sheet is available, with most items being free. They can answer such questions as:

1) What are the symptoms, diagnosis, and treatment of kidney stones?

2) What are the different types of urinary incontinence that some elderly people experience?

3) What information exists about the success rate of kidney transplant operations?

4) What professionals deal with kidney and urologic diseases in my area and what services do they provide?

5) What help is there for men who suffer from impotence?

National Maternal and Child Health Clearinghouse

8201 Greensboro Dr.
Suite 600
McLean, VA 22102
703-821-8955

The National Maternal and Child Health Clearinghouse provides education and information services in maternal and child health. The Clearinghouse provides current information through the collection and dissemination of publications on maternal and child health topics, and provides technical assistance in educational resource development, program planning, and topical research. They can also refer individuals to other organizations for further information. A publications catalogue is available, with most items free. They can answer such questions as:

1) What are the dangers of lead poisoning, and how can I protect my children?

2) What are the special nutrition needs of pregnant adolescents?

3) What are some of the concerns and issues pregnant women need to know about to ensure a healthy pregnancy?

4) How can parents be sure they are feeding their children nutritious foods?

5) Where can one go for more information on breastfeeding?

Medical Devices Clearinghouse

Center for Devices and Radiological Health
Food and Drug Administration
Division of Consumer Affairs (HFZ-210)
Rockville, MD 20857
301-443-4190

 www: http://www.fda.gov

The Center for Devices and Radiological Health is responsible for analyzing factors affecting the safe and effective use of medical devices and radiation-emitting products by lay users and on patients. They answer consumer inquiries by telephone or mail on general issues relating to medical devices or radiation-emitting products. Inquiries can be answered on such products as thermometers, hearing aids, contact lenses, condoms, magnetic resonance imaging devices, hemodialysis equipment, tampons, medical x-rays, pacemakers, and artificial hearts. Publications cover topics such as pregnancy test kits, IUDs, eyeglass lenses, ultraviolet radiation, including general information on medical devices and radiological health products. They can answer such questions as:

1) How effective are condoms and what standards are they required to meet?

2) Are breast implants still considered unsafe?

3) Is it safe to make your own sterile fluids to wash your contacts?

4) What should people be aware of before they undergo an x-ray?

5) Are ultrasounds safe?

National Library of Medicine

8600 Rockville Pike
Bethesda, MD 20894
301-496-6095
800-338-7657 (regional library)
Fax: 301-496-2809

 www: http://www.nlm.nih.gov/

The National Library of Medicine (NLM) is the world's largest research library in a single scientific and professional field. The collection today stands at four million books, journals, technical reports, manuscripts, microfilms, and pictorial materials. The Library's computer-based Medical Literature Analysis and Retrieval System (MEDLARS) has bibliographic access to NLM's vast store of biomedical information. All of the MEDLARS databases are available through NLM's online network of more than 20,000 institutions and individuals. NLM charges a user fee for access to the system. They can answer such questions as:

1) What videos are available on a specific health topic?

2) How can a researcher access NLM's database from home?

3) How can a search be conducted for a specific health topic?

4) What reference guides exist to help researchers locate materials?

Mental Health Clearinghouse

National Institute of Mental Health
5600 Fishers Ln., Room 7C02

Rockville, MD 20857
301-443-4515
Fax: 301-443-0008
Fax on Demand: 301-443-5158

 www: http://www.nimh.nih.gov/
E-mail: nimhinfo@nih.gov

The National Institute of Mental Health conducts and supports research to learn more about the causes, prevention, and treatment of mental and emotional illnesses. The Institute collects and distributes scientific and technical information related to mental illness, as well as educational materials for the general public. A publications list is available, with items ranging from free to $25. They can answer such questions as:

1) What are the latest statistics and information on bipolar disorder?

2) What are the various treatment options for someone suffering from depression?

3) What current research is available on the causes and treatment of schizophrenia?

4) What information should you be aware of when looking for a mental health professional?

5) What help exists for people who experience panic attacks?

Minority Health Clearinghouse

Office of Minority Health Resource Center
P.O. Box 37337
Washington, DC 20013
800-444-6472
Fax: 301-589-0884

The Office of Minority Health Resource Center's mission is to improve the health status of Asians, Pacific Islanders, Blacks, Hispanics, and Native Americans. Major activities include: the dissemination of accurate and timely information regarding health care issues and status through conferences and workshops; the awarding of grants for innovative community health strategies developed by minority coalitions; and research on risk factors affecting minority health. The Resource Center has information on minority health-related data and information resources available at the federal, state, and local levels and provides assistance and information to people interested in minority health and minority health programs. They have a database of minority health-related publications, as well as organizations and programs that concentrate on minority health. They can answer such questions as:

1) How can minority health goals be achieved?

2) What research is being conducted regarding African Americans and their particular risk for high blood pressure?

3) What are health issues particular to Alaskan Natives?

4) What programs are effective in encouraging pregnant Mexican Americans to seek prenatal care?

5) Are there programs specific to Native Americans with substance abuse problems?

National Institute of Neurological Disorders and Stroke

Building 31, Room 8A06
9000 Rockville Pike
Bethesda, MD 20892
800-352-9424
Fax: 301-402-2186

 www: http://www.nih.gov/ninds/

The National Institute of Neurological Disorders and Stroke conducts and supports research on the causes, prevention, diagnosis, and treatment of neurological disorders and stroke. They have free publications on a wide variety of consumer materials and can refer people to other organizations for further information. They can answer such questions as:

1) What is Bell's Palsy and what are the ways in which it is treated?

2) What are the different forms of multiple sclerosis?

3) What current research is being conducted on strokes?

4) What can be done to minimize or reverse the effects of Parkinson's?

5) Is there relief available for chronic pain sufferers?

Center for Nutrition Policy and Promotion

Center for Nutrition Policy and Promotion
U.S. Department of Agriculture
1120 20th St., NW
Suite 200 North
Washington, DC 20036
Fax: 202-208-2321

 www: http://www.usda.gov

The Center for Nutrition Policy and Promotion conducts applied research in food consumption, nutrition knowledge and attitudes, dietary survey methodology, food composition, and dietary guidance and nutrition education techniques. The Center uses the research data to monitor the food and nutrient content of diets of the American population, assess dietary status and trends in food consumption, further understand the factors that influence consumer food choices, maintain the National Nutrient Data Bank of the nutrient content of foods, provide dietary guidance in food selection and preparation and in food money management. The Center reports results of research in both technical and popular publications, and a publications list is available. They can answer such questions as:

1) What are the dietary guidelines for Americans?

2) What is the composition of specific foods?

3) What data exists on what people eat?

4) What factors influence consumer food choices?

5) How aware are people of the relationship between diet and health?

National Institute
for Occupational Safety and Health

Division of Standard Development and Technology Transfer
Technology Information Branch
4676 Columbia Parkway
Cincinnati, OH 45226-1998
800-35-NIOSH
Fax: 513-533-8573

E-mail: pubstast@niosdt.em.cdc.gov

The National Institute for Occupational Safety and Health provides technical information on programs and issues dealing with occupational safety and health. The Clearinghouse maintains a database through which they can search for journal articles and other materials on a specific topic. They have publications, reports, and bibliographies, many of which are free. They can answer such questions as:

1) Are video display terminals dangerous to the average individual?

2) What is Carpal Tunnel Syndrome and what can be done to treat it?

3) What are some of the dangers of working in a dry cleaning store?

4) How many deaths occurred on a particular job site?

5) What do I do if I suspect a health problem in my workplace?

National Clearinghouse For Primary Care Information

8201 Greensboro Dr.
Suite 600
McLean, VA 22102
703-821-8955

The National Clearinghouse For Primary Care provides information services to support the planning, development, and delivery of ambulatory health care to urban and rural areas that have shortages of medical personnel and services. They distribute publications focusing on ambulatory care, financial management, primary health care, and health services administration. The Clearinghouse provides information on federal guidances and policies affecting primary care delivery. A list is available of free publications on community health centers, migrant health centers, childhood injury prevention efforts, clinical care, and many other health concerns. They can answer such questions as:

1) What information should be considered when establishing a rural medical practice?

2) What are some of the ways older adults can improve their nutrition and is there information that can be distributed to these clients?

3) What are particular health problems of the migrant population and how can these be addressed?

4) What are some of the characteristics of successful dental programs in community and migrant health centers?

5) What is the status of medical personnel shortages in inner city hospitals and what is being done to alleviate this crisis?

National Rehabilitation Information Center

8455 Colesville Rd., Suite 935
Silver Spring, MD 20910
800-34-NARIC

800-346-2742
Fax: 301-587-1967

www: http://naric.com/naric
E-mail: naric@capaccess.org

The National Rehabilitation Information Center (NARIC) is a library and information center on disability and rehabilitation. The Center is funded by the National Institute for Disability and Rehabilitation Research to collect and disseminate the results of federally-funded research projects. In addition, the Center includes commercially-published books and journal articles in its collection. They also maintain a database of disability and rehabilitation materials which they will search for a small fee. NARIC provides quick reference and referral services, database searches, and photocopies of documents in the collection. They publish a newsletter and other directories and provide information specialists to field the many questions on various topics of concern to people. A list of publications is available, with items ranging in price from free to $25. They can answer such questions as:

1) What resources, support, and information are available for people suffering from traumatic brain injury?

2) Where can you buy a computer keyboard which responds correctly to your patterns of movement if you have cerebral palsy?

3) How effective have supported employment programs been in improving employment opportunities for people with severe disabilities?

4) What are the different education methods available to educate a deaf child, and what are some of the factors to consider when making this choice?

5) What information exists on helping someone who has suffered a spinal cord injury?

Office on Smoking and Health

Centers for Disease Control
4770 Buford Highway, NE
Mail Stop K-50
Atlanta, GA 30341
404-488-5705
800-CDC-1311
Fax: 301-986-5001

 www: http://www.cdc.gov/nccdphp/osh/tobacco.htm

The Smoking Hotline can answer all your questions regarding cigarettes and stop smoking methods. They can provide fact sheets, pamphlets, posters and other publications, as well as information in response to inquiries. The Center can access information on the Combined Health Information Database, and their library and reading room are open to the public. The Info-memo newsletter contains information on disease prevention, education, and control. They can answer such questions as:

1) What are the pros and cons of various stop smoking methods?

2) What is the current status report on smoking?

3) How does smoking affect a person's health?

4) What are the ways in which a person over 50 might stop smoking?

5) What are the rules or regulations regarding smoking in an office or other public place?

National Clearinghouse for Professions In Special Education

The Council for Exceptional Children
1920 Association Dr.
Reston, VA 22091
703-620-3660

The National Clearinghouse for Professions in Special Education provides information that will help people in making a
career choice. They have information about the demand for
special educators in the U.S., about college and university programs that prepare people for these careers, about financial assistance available, and more. They can answer such questions
as:

1) What fellowships are available to work with the deaf?

2) How is music therapy used to work with individuals with disabilities?

3) What different sorts of careers are possible in special education?

4) What type of training is required to work with autistic children?

5) How has mainstreaming affected the special education job
market?

Sudden Infant Death Hotline

National Sudden Infant Death Syndrome Clearinghouse
8201 Greensboro Dr.
Suite 600
McLean, VA 22102
703-821-8955

The Sudden Infant Death Clearinghouse was established to provide information and educational materials on Sudden Infant
Death Syndrome (SIDS), apnea, and other related issues. The
staff responds to information requests from professionals, families with SIDS-related deaths, and the general public by sending written materials and making referrals. The Clearinghouse
maintains a library of reference materials and mailing lists of
state programs, groups, and individuals concerned with SIDS.
Their publications include bibliographies on SIDS and self-help

support groups, a publications catalogue, and a newsletter. They can answer such questions as:

1) What is crib death?

2) What are the current views on home monitoring to prevent SIDS?

3) How can parents help the grieving process in children after the death of a sibling?

4) How many children died of SIDS in a given state last year?

5) How can SIDS be distinguished from child abuse and neglect?

Family Violence and Sexual Assault Institute

1310 Clinic Dr.
Tyler, TX 75701
903-595-6600
Fax: 903-595-6799

The goal of the Family Violence and Sexual Assault Institute is to provide information services to practitioners and researchers who are working to prevent family violence and provide assistance for victims. A publications list and price sheet are available. They can answer such questions as:

1) What journal articles and bibliographies are there on elder abuse, as well as what statistics, copies of legislation, and organizations concerned with elder abuse issues exist?

2) What are some of the signs of sexual abuse?

3) What are some centers and organizations concerned with child maltreatment?

4) What bibliographies are there on the characteristics of abusive and neglecting parents?

5) What agency should a person contact first if abuse is suspected?

National and World Affairs

Agriculture Exports Clearinghouse

Foreign Agricultural Service
U.S. Department of Agriculture
Room 5074
Washington, DC 20050
202-720-7115
Fax: 202-720-1727

www: http://www.usda.gov/fas
E-mail: fasinfo@ag.gov

The Foreign Agricultural Service disseminates agricultural trade and commodity production information to agribusinesses and the general public. They offer private companies and cooperatives assistance in marketing their products overseas by collecting and publicizing information on foreign buyers and advertising U.S. export availability. They have a monthly magazine, commodity and trade reports, publications, and fact sheets (many of which are free). They can answer such questions as:

1) What are the market prospects for U.S. food and farm products in Japan?

2) What are some overseas markets and buying trends for a particular product?

3) What are some overseas promotional activities?

4) How do I begin an export business?

5) How do I advertise my product directly to buyers overseas?

Arms Control and Disarmament Agency

Office of Public Information
2201 C St., NW
Washington, DC 20451
202-647-6575

The Arms Control and Disarmament Agency (ACDA) coordinates the ongoing negotiations between the United States and other nuclear powers to reduce their arsenals. This federal agency also takes the lead in other efforts to reduce the risk of war by, for example, verifying other countries' compliance with the Nuclear Non-Proliferation Treaty and other international agreements. Weapons sales to foreign governments, technology transfer, and treaties are also important elements of arms control. The Agency can answer such questions as:

1) What details exist on certain weapons systems and what analyses have been done on the impact that such systems have on arms control agreements, treaties, and negotiations?

2) What are some of the economic issues related to defense strategies?

3) What is the INF Treaty?

4) What is the current status of arms control and disarmament goals?

5) What is the current arms control policy of the U.S.?

Central Intelligence Agency

Public Affairs
Washington, DC 20505
703-482-0623

 www: http://www.odci.gov/cia

The Central Intelligence Agency (CIA) is strictly a foreign intelligence organization and has no domestic or law enforcement duties. The CIA occasionally issues unclassified publications which provide additional research aids to the academic and business communities. The majority of these reports contain foreign or international economic and political information or are directories of foreign officials. They are available for sale. They can answer such questions as:

1) What is the history of the CIA?

2) What are the steps involved in the intelligence cycle?

3) What agencies or departments are involved with the intelligence community?

4) What involvement does the White House have in intelligence activities?

5) Who oversees the CIA?

Export Country Experts

U.S. Foreign and Commercial Services
Export Promotion Services
U.S. Department of Commerce
Room 2810
Washington, DC 20230
202-482-6220
800-872-8723
Fax: 202-482-4473

 www: http://www.ita.doc.gov

The Country Desk Officers at the U.S. Department of Commerce can provide businesses with information on a market, company, and any other aspect of commercial life in a particular country. These specialists can look at the needs of an individual U.S. firm wishing to sell in a particular country in the full context of that country's overall economy, trade policies, and political situation, bearing in mind current U.S. policies toward that country. Desk officers keep up-to-date on the economic and commercial conditions in their assigned countries. Each officer collects information on the country's regulations, tariffs, business practices, economic and political developments, trade data and trends, market size, and growth. They have free reports and other information at their fingertips or they can refer callers to other country specialists. They can answer such questions as:

1) How can I expand my business through a foreign franchise?

2) How can I reduce my company's distribution and transportation costs overseas?

3) What type of export opportunities exist for computer manufacturing companies who want to expand to Germany?

4) What are some recent foreign labor trends in Japan?

5) Which markets are growing the fastest overseas?

Country Officers

U.S. Department of State
2201 C St., NW
Washington, DC 20520
202-647-4000

www: http://www.state.gov

Hundreds of country experts at the U.S. Department of State are responsible for following all activities in their assigned countries, from a political, economic, and social perspective. These officers are in constant contact with embassies, deliver and receive documents from those embassies, and write reports on the current activities in the country. They have several publications they can send, plus up-to-date information on each country's population, culture, geography, political condition, and more. Call to ask for the number of a specific country officer. They can answer such questions as:

1) What is the current political situation of a particular country?

2) What is the current population, as well as the health situation of a country?

3) Are there any travel advisories for a particular country?

4) Is there a brief overview of a specific country available?

5) What is the status of human rights in a particular country?

U.S. Customs Service

Public Information Office
U.S. Department of the Treasury
P.O. Box 7407
Washington, DC 20044
202-927-6724

The U.S. Customs Service collects the revenue from imports and enforces customs and related laws. It assists in the administration and enforcement of over 400 provisions of law on behalf of more than 40 government agencies. They have many free publications and information on customs rules and travel tips. They can answer such questions as:

1) What are the rules regarding the bringing of pets into the U.S.?

2) Is there a limit to the amount of a particular item one can bring into the country?

3) What are duty-free exemptions, and restricted or prohibited articles?

4) What is required when a traveler declares articles?

5) What is the current duty rate for a particular item?

Defense Technical Information Center

8725 John J. Kingman Rd.
Suite 0944
Ft. Belvoir, VA 22060-6218
703-767-8274

 www: http://www.dtic.mil

The Defense Technical Information Center (DTIC) is the clearinghouse within the Department of Defense (DOD) for acquiring, storing, retrieving, and disseminating scientific and technical information to support the management and conduct of DOD research, development, engineering, and studies programs. DTIC services are available to DOD and its contractors and to other U.S. Government organizations and their contractors. Organizations may also become eligible for service under certain programs. DTIC also responds indirectly to the general public's information requests. Most products and services are free, but, there are some fees for technical reports and on-line access. *A DTIC Handbook for Users* is available. They can answer such questions as:

1) What technical reports exist concerning aeronautics?

2) Is there a listing of defense contractors and/or potential contractors?

3) How does a company obtain defense contract work?

4) What type of security clearance procedures are used for defense contractors?

Defense Clearinghouse

Directorate for Public Communication
U.S. Department of Defense
The Pentagon, Room 2E777
Washington, DC 20301
703-697-5737

www: http://www.dtic.dla.mil/defenselink/

The Department of Defense is responsible for providing the military forces needed to deter war and protect the security of our country. The Directorate for Public Communication is a good starting point for Defense Department information. They have publications available, some of which are free, and they can direct you to other sources within the Department. They can answer such questions as:

1) What is the current Department of Defense budget, and how has it changed since the previous year?

2) What is the status of our troops overseas?

3) What is the federal government's security strategies?

4) What Department of Defense bases have closed within the last year?

5) How can I sell my company's products or services to the Army?

Federal Emergency Management Agency

500 C St., SW
Washington, DC 20472
202-646-4600
Fax: 202-646-4086

 www: http://www.fema.gov

The Federal Emergency Management Agency (FEMA) is the part of our government which deals with planning for and/or coordinating relief in various national emergencies. FEMA plans for nuclear attacks, security emergencies, disaster recovery aid, and helps to coordinate food, shelter, and financial aid in the event of any natural or man made disasters. FEMA has a publications catalogue which lists free publications on subjects such as civil defense, earthquakes, floods, hurricanes, tornadoes, and more. They can answer such questions as:

1) How can people best prepare for an earthquake?

2) What information exists on emergency medical services needed during a time of crisis?

3) How can homeowners repair their home after a flood?

4) Are there plans available on how to build an effective fall-out shelter?

5) What are some safety tips for winter storms?

American Foreign Policy Information Clearinghouse

Bureau of Public Affairs
U.S. Department of State
2201 C St., NW
Washington, DC 20520

202-647-6575
Fax: 202-647-7120

 www: http://www.state.gov

The Department of State receives thousands of reports daily, and produces hundreds of publications, speeches, and conferences on foreign policy issues. The Bureau of Public Affairs informs the American people on foreign policy and advises the Secretary of State on public opinion. If unable to answer an inquiry directly, the staff will direct you to the appropriate source. This bureau issues various publications covering U.S. foreign relations, some of which are free. They can answer such questions as:

1) Where can someone get a copy of the PLO-Israel Peace Treaty and what information does it contain?

2) Are there resource materials available that would allow a business to learn more about the relationship between the U.S. and a foreign country before they invest in that country?

3) What information exists on global terrorism?

4) Where could one find out more information on human rights practices in a particular country?

5) How can one access the U.S.'s or a foreign country's diplomatic records?

Immigration and Naturalization Service

Central Office
425 Eye St., NW
Washington, DC 20536
202-514-4316

The Immigration and Naturalization Service (INS) facilitates the entry of persons legally admissible as visitors or as immigrants to the United States, provides assistance to those seeking permanent resident status, and apprehends those who attempt illegal entry into this country. They have established a telephone service system that provides pre-recorded information on immigration and citizenship-related topics. They can answer such questions as:

1) Where is the local INS office located for a particular community?

2) What are the rules regarding the marriage of a foreign citizen to a U.S. citizen?

3) What are the citizenship requirements for children born outside the U.S.?

4) What constitutes political asylum?

5) What are some visa requirements for travel overseas?

Agency for International Development (AID)

Document Information Services Clearinghouse
1500 Wilson Blvd.
Suite 1010
Arlington, VA 22209
703-351-4006
Fax: 703-351-4039

 Gopher: info.osaid.gov

AID's Center for Development Information and Evaluation (CDIE) produces an evaluation publications series which includes a broad range of subjects of interest to those working in international development. The series comprises project impact evaluations, program evaluations, special studies, program design and evaluation methodology reports, and discussion papers. The CDIE Evaluation Publications List is arranged by general subject category and by type of report within each category. Each document is available for $3. They can answer such questions as:

1) What research has been conducted on family planning issues?

2) How do private volunteer organizations assist in the development of a country?

3) How has the emergency food program operated in a particular country?

4) How have health programs been successfully initiated in developing countries and how can they be sustained?

5) What types of agriculture programs have been attempted and what are the results of those programs?

National Clearinghouse for U.S.-Japan Studies

Indiana University
2805 East Tenth St., Suite 120
Bloomington, IN 47408
812-855-3838
Fax: 812-855-0455

The National Clearinghouse for U.S.- Japan Studies is a database system providing timely and comprehensive information about educational resources available to teach about Japan. The Clearinghouse collects, analyzes, abstracts, and creates a database of materials and resources that can assist school systems and individual teachers in developing and implementing curricula and lessons on broad areas of Japanese culture and society, and on U.S.-Japan relationships. The Clearinghouse also includes items such as videos, films, some simulations, artifact kits, and the like, and teacher-developed materials. They can answer such questions as:

1) What information exists on the Japanese educational system?

2) Where can I obtain copies of Japanese War relocation records?

3) What information is available on the Japanese stock market?

4) What are current U.S. trade policies toward Japan?

5) How can I locate programs that offer study abroad opportunities in Japan?

Indoor Air Quality Information Clearinghouse

P.O. Box 37133
Washington, DC 20013
800-438-4318
Fax: 202-484-1510

E-mail: iaquinfo@aol.com

The Indoor Air Quality Information Clearinghouse of the Environmental Protection Agency can provide information and assistance on indoor air quality problems. It brings together information on more than 17 issues (from asbestos to wood preservatives), for the range of agencies involved in addressing those issues, from health agencies to energy departments. This office also has information on home humidifiers, residential air cleaners, Sick Building Syndrome, indoor air quality, new carpet, and more. They can answer such questions as:

1) What is Sick Building Syndrome, and what agency do I contact if I suspect my building is unsafe?

2) How do I identify and eliminate radon gas from my home?

3) How do I determine if the paint in my home is lead based?

4) What is the most recent legislation concerning asbestos-in-school requirements?

5) What is the Toxic Substance Control Act?

Bureau of Land Management

Office of Public Affairs
U.S. Department of the Interior
1849 C St., NW, Room 5600
Washington, DC 20240
202-208-3801
Fax: 202-208-5242

There are close to 270 million acres of public lands located primarily, but not exclusively, in the West and in Alaska comprising one-eighth of our nation's land area. It is the charge of the Bureau of Land Management (BLM) to administer and care for these lands. To accomplish this task, the BLM has a variety of programs and activities, from the very new Heritage Education program aimed at involving and educating young people about America's cultural heritage to finding out about the availability of public lands for sale. They have free publications and can direct you to other resources within the BLM. They can answer such questions as:

1) Where are campgrounds located on BLM lands and what facilities or recreational areas do they have?

2) What videos are available concerning rivers?

3) How can I find out which public lands are for sale in my state?

4) How do I stake a mining claim on federal lands?

5) How can I receive a listing of wildlife habitats on public lands?

U.S. Nuclear Regulatory Commission

Public Document Room
Washington, DC 20555
202-634-3273
Fax: 202-634-3343

 www: http://www.nrc.gov

The Nuclear Regulatory Commission (NRC) licenses and regulates civilian use of nuclear energy to protect public health and safety and the environment. The NRC licenses persons and companies to build and operate nuclear reactors and other facilities, and to own and use nuclear materials. The Commission makes rules, sets standards, and carefully inspects companies to ensure that they do not violate existing safety rules. They can answer such questions as:

1) What information exists on abnormal occurrences in nuclear facilities?

2) What is the construction permit process for nuclear facilities?

3) What specific operational information must nuclear facilities submit to the NRC?

4) What statistics are available related to nuclear power?

5) How are radioactive materials packaged for transport?

National Oceanic and Atmospheric Administration

14th St. and Constitution Ave.
Washington, DC 20230
202-482-6090
Fax: 202-482-3154

www: http://www.noaa.gov

The National Oceanic and Atmospheric Administration gathers data, conducts research, and makes predictions about the state of the environment in which we live. NOAA charts the seas and skies, and enriches our understanding of the oceans, atmosphere, space, and sun. They can refer you to other offices and experts for specific questions, and they also offer a variety of publications and films. They can answer such questions as:

1) What research is being conducted on tropical weather and how can we better predict hurricanes?

2) How has the greenhouse effect changed the environment?

3) What are the physical and chemical processes that occur within the Earth's atmosphere?

4) What is being done to protect marine mammals?

5) What research exists on the solar activity in the upper atmosphere?

Oceanographic Information

National Oceanographic Data Center (NODC)
National Environmental Satellite, Data, and Information Service
National Oceanic and Atmospheric Administration
U.S. Department of Commerce
1315 East West Highway
Silver Spring, MD 20910
301-713-3277
Fax: 301-713-3300

 www: http://www.nodc.noaa.gov

The National Oceanographic Data Center (NODC) provides global coverage of oceanographic data and services. NODC's databases cover physical and chemical properties of the world's oceans, seas, and estuaries, plus information on selected continental shelf and coastal waters. Simple questions usually can be answered without charge by telephone or mail, but more complicated ones requiring research or computer processing normally carry a fee. They can answer such questions as:

1) How does the Pacific Ocean temperature vary over a year?

2) How has the Atlantic Ocean been effected by pollution and what data exists on this topic?

3) What are the responsibilities of the NODC and what directories of information do they maintain?

4) Is there any bottom current data on the South China Sea?

5) Is the water warmer in Miami Beach or Myrtle Beach?

National Park Service

Office of Public Inquiries
U.S. Department of the Interior
P.O. Box 37127
Washington, DC 20013-7127
202-208-4747

www: http://www.nps.gov

Along with other responsibilities, the Park Service administers 350 maintained areas in the National Park System, collects the National Register of Historic Places and a registry of natural sites, and manages the Urban Park and Recreation Recovery Program. It provides technical assistance in planning, acquisition and development of recreation resources, conducts surveys of historic buildings and engineering works, has available programs and resources for teachers, and administers a program in interagency archeological services. Information, including brochures, maps, and a publications catalogue can be ordered from the Government Printing Office. The Office of Public Inquiries can refer you to other Park Service offices and can answer such questions as:

1) What archeological digs are currently in progress and where are they located?

2) What statistics are available on Park Service use, such as total visits, visits by region and state, and overnight stays?

3) Where can I locate videos on historic people or national landmarks?

4) How do I find out whether or not my home is eligible for listing on the National Historic Register?

5) How can I receive a listing of the lesser known National Parks?

National Pesticide Telecommunication Network

Oregon State University
NPTN Ag Chem Extension
333 Weniger
Corvallis, OR 97331-6502
800-858-PEST (7378)
Fax: 541-737-0761

The National Pesticide Telecommunication Network (NPTN) is a toll-free telephone service that provides a wide variety of information on pesticides. Phones are staffed by pesticide specialists with agricultural, environmental, and public health backgrounds. Inquiries are also answered by graduate students in such fields as biology, anatomy, biochemistry, and entomology. They can answer such questions as:

1) Where can I get information on pesticides that might be found in drinking water wells?

2) What are some guidelines for the safe use of pesticides by farmers?

3) What plants have a natural ability to repel insects?

4) How do I make the transition from pesticide lawn control to natural pest control?

5) What is the toxicity and proper use of the pesticide R-11? How can I dispose of it safely?

Pollution Prevention Information Clearinghouse

Labat-Anderson, Inc.
401 M St., SW
Washington, DC 20460
202-260-1023
Fax: 202-260-0178

E-mail: ppic@epamail.epa.gov

The Pollution Prevention Information Clearinghouse is designed to help national and international industries reduce pollutants that are released into our environment. They specialize in using education and public awareness to prevent excessive pollution. The Clearinghouse has four information exchange directories that can be ordered. There is no charge for any service. They can answer such questions as:

1) How can pollution prevention benefit businesses?

2) How do you implement a pollution prevention program?

3) Are there training opportunities for pollution control/waste management?

4) How do you get technical assistance for pollution control?

5) What are the differences between large and small waste generators?

EPA Radon Office

U.S. Environment Protection Agency (EPA)
401 M St., SW (MS6604J)
Washington, DC 20460
202-233-9370
Fax: 202-333-9597

The EPA Radon Office can answer all your questions concerning radon. The staff can answer such questions as:

1) What is radon? How does it affect people?

2) How do I determine whether or not my home has a radon problem?

3) How can I obtain a radon detector for my home? How does it work?

4) What are some effective radon prevention methods?

5) What are some control methods for eliminating radon in well water?

National Sea Grant Depository

Pell Library Building
The University of Rhode Island
Bay Campus
Narragansett, RI 02882
401-874-6114
Fax: 401-874-6160

 www: http://nsgd.gso.uri.edu

The National Sea Grant Depository provides a wide variety of information on America's oceans, Great Lakes, and coastal zones. It maintains the only complete collection of publications generated by the National Sea Grant College Program. Publications include information on: oceanography, marine education, fisheries, coastal zone management, aquaculture, marine recreation and law. The collection includes journal reprints, technical and advisory reports, handbooks, charts, maps, manuals, directories, books, audiovisual materials, computer programs, annual reports, conference proceedings, and newsletters produced by Sea Grant funded researchers. The staff can answer such questions as:

1) What are some of the most common fish found in Alaska?

2) How do I begin a fish culture enterprise?

3) What is the impact of pollution on the marine environment?

4) What can people do to prevent the pollution of coastal waters?

5) What are some of the potential risks to coastal investment?

Small Business Ombudsman Clearinghouse

U.S. Environmental Protection Agency (EPA)
Small Business Ombudsman, 1230C
401 M St., SW
Washington, DC 20460
800-368-5888
Fax: 703-305-6462

 www: http://www.epa.gov

The Small Business Ombudsman Clearinghouse helps your business comply with all environmental regulations. They provide information on current policies, safety precautions, and general information on keeping the air you breathe healthy. They are available to assist private citizens, small communities, enterprises, trade associations, technical consultants, and laboratories. Listings on all aspects of current EPA regulatory developments are available at no charge. Over 200 EPA publications are maintained for distribution. They can answer such questions as:

1) Am I covered under the new Clear Air Act requirements?

2) How do I get an I.D. number for hazardous waste disposal?

3) What are the requirements for any underground storage waste?

4) How do I know if my community is following proper safety guidelines?

5) What type of waste material could be hazardous to my community?

National Snow and Ice Data Center

World Data Center-A For Glaciology
CIRES, Box 449
University of Colorado
Boulder, CO 80309
303-492-5171
Fax: 303-492-2468

www: http://www_nsidc.colorado.edu
E-mail: nsidc@kyros.colorado.edu

The National Snow and Ice Data Center provides a national and international focus for snow and ice data information services. The Center provides: broad user access to snow and ice data through specialized data reports and inventories in Glaciological Data; through special data sets maintained in the Center; through tailored bibliographies; and through access to the Snow and Ice Library. There is a small fee for some services. They can answer such questions as:

1) How does exhaust from jet aircraft affect cloud cover?

2) Where can data be accessed on glacier fluctuations?

3) How has snow cover varied over time in North America?

4) What current research is being undertaken regarding avalanches?

5) What is the difference between fresh water ice and sea ice?

Solid Waste Information Clearinghouse

P.O. Box 7219
1100 Wayne Ave., Suite 700
Silver Spring, MD 20907-7219
800-67-SWICH
Fax: 301-589-7068

www: http://www.swana.org
E-mail: swana@millkern.com

The Solid Waste Information Clearinghouse (SWICH) is concerned with how state and local offices and industries get rid of solid waste. The general public is also welcome to request information. SWICH can show how to economically and ecologically get rid of waste by source reduction, recycling, composting, planning, education, public training, public participation, legislation and regulation, waste combustion, and collection. They can answer such questions as:

1) How can I implement a recycling program in my community?

2) What is the most economical way to dispose of a waste product?

3) How have other communities started and benefited from recycling?

4) What types of disposal is available to my community or business?

National Space Science Data Center

National Aeronautics and Space Administration
Goddard Space Flight Center
Greenbelt, MD 20771
301-286-7354
Data Request: 301-286-6695
Fax: 301-286-1771

www: http://nssdc.gsfc.nasa.gov/
E-mail: request@nssdca.gsfca.nasa.gov

The National Space Science Data Center (NSSDC) is an organization that provides a variety of valuable services for scientists throughout the world. The Center furthers the use of data obtained from space and earth science investigations, maintains an active data repository, and supports scientific research. The data are contained on more than 120,000 magnetic tapes, tens of thousands of film products, and optical, video, and magnetic disks. NSSDC works with individual users to address their specific requirements. There is a charge for most data, but it is only on a cost recovery basis. They can answer such questions as:

1) What satellites are currently operating in space and which ones are planned for future launch?

2) What data from space can provide estimates of marine phytoplankton in the ocean?

3) Where can photographs taken from APOLLO be located?

4) What data is available to researchers studying the ozone?

5) What information exists on a particular rocket launch?

Technology Transfer Competitiveness

Administrator
Federal Laboratory Consortium
P.O. Box 545
Sequim, WA 98382
360-683-1005
Fax: 360-683-6654

www: http://www.zyn.com/slc/

The mission of the Federal Laboratory Consortium is to facilitate technology transfer among government, business, and academic entities in order to promote American economic and technological competitiveness. It sponsors conferences and seminars and publishes a free monthly newsletter. For very specific questions from researchers who find themselves at an impasse, the Consortium will conduct a database search to refer the inquirer to an appropriate lab. Write or call for a free general information packet explaining the organization, how to access its services, facilities available for testing, and examples of technology transfers. They can answer such questions as:

1) How can the heat pipes used to cool satellites be converted for use in a business?

2) How can toothpaste used by astronauts benefit those that are used on Earth?

3) What research is being conducted on electric cars?

4) Where can a business locate information on humidity control for a warehouse?

Technology Transfer Program

NASA Scientific and Technical Information Facility
Technology Transfer Office
NASA-CASI
800 Elkridge Landing Rd.
Linthicum Heights, MD 21090-2934
410-859-5300, ext. 242
Fax: 301-621-0134

 www: http://www.nasa.gov

Technology Transfer is an ideal way to apply the National Aeronautics and Space Administration's (NASA) experience and discoveries to your research or business. The transfer of aerospace technology which embraces virtually every scientific and technical discipline is paying off in a broad spectrum of practical applications in industry. The Technology Transfer System is a network of specialized organizations dedicated to helping industry access, apply, and utilize NASA's pool of innovations and technical resources. This allows you to access a wide range of information, products, services and technical expertise. A staff of experts assists you in pinpointing problems, identifying needs, and exchanging ideas. They can answer such questions as:

1) How can ultra-sensitive measuring devices used to measure space dust be put to use measuring environmental pollutants?

2) How can standard doorknobs be replaced with electronic openers?

3) Is it possible to convert spacesuits for use by firefighters or workers in industrial situations?

4) What lunar tool technology can be used in designing cordless power tools?

Toxic Substance Control Act

U.S. Environmental Protection Agency (EPA)
Environmental Assistance Division
401 M St., SW
Washington, DC 20460
202-554-1404
Fax: 202-554-5603

E-mail: tsca_hotline@epamail.epa.gov

The Toxic Substance Control Act (TSCA) regulates the storage and removal of toxic substances and spills. They are concerned with safely containing toxic substances that may be harmful to our environment. TSCA is open to the general public as well as to industries and environmental groups. They can answer such questions as:

1) What chemicals can a manufacturer produce, and are they on the toxic inventory list?

2) What can I do if a toxic substance was spilled or contained on my property?

3) What are the latest regulations regarding production and handling of toxic substances?

4) How can I get a listing of places where toxic waste is stored?

Undersea Research

National Undersea Research Program
National Oceanic and Atmospheric Administration (NOAA)
U.S. Department of Commerce
R/OR2, Room 11853
Building SSMC-3
1315 East-West Highway
Silver Spring, MD 20910
301-713-2427
Fax: 301-713-0799

The National Undersea Research Program (NURP) develops programs and provides support to scientists and engineers to accomplish research underwater for the study of biological, chemical, geological, and physical processes in the world's oceans and lakes. NURP provides investigators with modern undersea facilities including submersibles, habitats, air and mixed gas SCUBA, and remotely operated vehicles. They can answer such questions as:

1) How do I get a grant from NURP?

2) What is the appropriate undersea center for me to contact in my region?

3) How deep in the sea does NURP support scientists work?

4) What kind of research expenses will be covered under a NURP grant?

5) Does NURP support coral reef research?

EPA National
Small Flows Clearinghouse (Wastewater)

West Virginia University
P.O. Box 6064
Morgantown, WV 26506
800-624-8301
Fax: 304-293-3161

The National Small Flows Clearinghouse is the center for small systems wastewater technology transfer. The Clearinghouse provides training resources and expertise in management and maintenance of small wastewater systems. It assists small communities in meeting environmental goals and water quality requirements. The Clearinghouse offers products and services to aid consultants, local officials, and developers in designing, constructing, operating, and managing small wastewater systems. Its products and services include databases, publications, video programs, workshops, and seminars. The staff can answer such questions as:

1) How can I find out more about the use of constructed wetlands that are used to treat domestic wastewater?

2) How can I find out more about sequencing batch reactors? How do they compare with conventional continuous waste treatment systems?

3) What should I look for when hiring qualified wastewater personnel?

4) How can our community get the most out of our existing wastewater resources and facilities?

5) What are some current technologies for cleansing polluted water?

Watershed Resource Information System

U.S. Environmental Protection Agency (EPA)
1717 K St., NW
Suite 801
Washington, DC 20006
800-726-LAKE (5253)

www: http://www.epa.gov

The Watershed Resource Information System is an information resource on lake restoration, protection, and management. Its Watershed Information Resource Database contains abstracts and citations of technical materials and information and bibliographies. A specialist will conduct a database search for you for a fee of $25, plus $.10 per page per reference. You may purchase the system for $250 or a demo disk for $20. The staff can answer such questions as:

1) What information exists on different methods for restoring polluted lakes?

2) How can I find out about a particular lake's water quality?

3) What are some effective watershed management techniques?

4) What techniques can be used to reduce the incidence of acidification in lakes?

5) What are some effective methods of reducing toxic substances in lakes?

National Weather Service

National Oceanic and Atmospheric Administration
1325 East-West Highway
Silver Spring, MD 20910
301-713-0622

 www: http://www.nws.noaa.gov

The National Weather Service, through a network of field offices, predicts the nation's weather and issues storm and flood warnings. They also publish a weekly series of daily weather maps which include the highest and lowest temperatures chart and the precipitation areas. They can send anyone interested a sample copy or subscription information on this material. They also have publications on a variety of weather conditions, as well as films, videos, and slides. They can answer such questions as:

1) What should be done in the event of a hurricane?

2) What is a tornado?

3) How are severe storms forecast and where can more information be obtained about them?

4) Is there information available on monthly and seasonal predictions of temperature and precipitation?

5) What is a flash flood?

Wetlands Protection Hotline

Labat-Anderson, Inc.
401 M St.
MC4502F
Washington, DC 20460
800-832-7828
Fax: 703-525-0201

www: http://www.epa.gov

The Wetlands Protection Hotline is a toll-free telephone service that responds to questions about the value and function of wetlands in our world. The staff is interested in protecting our wetlands and showing how wetlands play an important role in our changing environment. They have free publications and fact sheets available. They can answer such questions as:

1) Where can I get the *1987 Corps of Engineers Wetlands Delineation Manual?*

2) Is there any information available on constructed wetlands?

3) Is it legal to dig out a wetlands area?

4) What is the White House's policy on the protection of wetlands?

5) What regulations must farmers comply with when they have wetlands on their property?

Other

Boating Safety Hotline

Consumer and Regulatory Affairs Branch
Auxiliary, Boating, and Consumer Affairs Division
Office of Navigation Safety and Waterways Services
U.S. Coast Guard
U.S. Department of Transportation
2100 2nd St., SW
Washington, DC 20593
800-368-5647
Fax: 202-267-4285

 www: http://www.navcen.uscg.mil

The Boating Safety Hotline can provide you with information on such topics of interest to boaters as safety recalls, publications, Coast Guard department contacts and addresses, public education courses, and free Coast Guard Services. They have a wealth of free information and publications to share. They can answer such questions as:

1) What statistics exist on boating accidents?

2) How can parents teach children about water safety?

3) What things do people need to consider regarding floatation devices?

4) What licenses or regulations should boaters be aware of?

5) Where can people receive information on water charts and other navigational aids?

Children's Literature Center

Library of Congress
National Programs
Washington, DC 20540
202-707-5535
Fax: 202-707-4632

The Children's Center prepares lists and scholarly bibliographies and provides other reference services for individuals and organizations who study, produce, collect, interpret, and disseminate children's books, films, television programs, or other forms of materials destined for children's information and recreational use, usually outside of the classroom. The Library holds approximately 180,000 children's books and related items, such as boxed and board games, sound recordings, maps, and illustrations. The Center also provides many publisher's catalogues that list titles to be published in the upcoming year, a wide range of periodicals about children's literature, and lists from rare and used book sellers. They can answer such questions as:

1) How can literature be used in the classroom to teach history to 7th graders?

2) What information sources exist for Japanese children's books published after World War II?

3) How can children learn about people with disabilities through literature?

4) Are there books specific to helping children deal with the issues of death and dying?

5) Where could a writer locate materials to help with a book on teaching children to be aware of strangers?

Congressional Research Service

Library of Congress
Washington, DC 20540
202-707-5700
Fax: 202-707-6745

The Congressional Research Service (CRS) at the Library of Congress prepares hundreds of non-partisan background reports each year on current issues large and small, domestic and foreign, social and political. CRS also publishes hundreds of major Issue Briefs each year designed to keep members of Congress informed on timely issues. Written in simple and direct language, these briefs provide background information and are updated daily. These studies generated by CRS cover almost any topic imaginable and are a fantastic resource for students, researchers, and anyone else who needs statistics or an analysis of a subject. You must request free copies of these reports through your U.S. Representative or Senator (202-224-3121 Congress Switchboard). The CRS Reports can answer such questions as:

1) What is the history of abortion rights in the U.S. and what legislation is currently before Congress regarding abortion?

2) What information exists on the protection of endangered sea turtles?

3) What is the current status of nuclear missile proliferation in the world?

4) What reports have been done on obscenity on television and radio?

5) What programs are there for working in a foreign country?

Federal Assistance Programs Retrieval System

Federal Domestic Assistance Catalog Staff
General Services Administration
300 7th St., SW
Ground Floor
Reporters Building
Washington, DC 20407
202-708-5126
800-669-8331

 www: http://www.gsa.gov/

The Federal Assistance Programs Retrieval System (FAPRS) is your online link to the Catalog of Federal Domestic Assistance. It contains federal domestic assistance programs, including federal grants, loans, loan guarantees, and technical assistance. Their database contains more than 1,000 assistance programs administered by 51 federal agencies, with summaries of agency functions, descriptions of assistance programs, eligibility criteria, and contact information. Users include state and local governments, small businesses, researchers, and libraries. Fees are on a cost-recovery basis, with no initiation or monthly fees. Contact FAPRS for telephone and data processing charges. They can answer such questions as:

1) What assistance programs would help a rural hospital obtain needed medical equipment?

2) How can a student obtain a doctorate in housing policy at no cost?

3) How can schools obtain science equipment from the government?

4) How can a choreographer receive funds to create a dance?

5) Where can a business turn for assistance in the field of energy?

American Folklife Center

Library of Congress
Washington, DC 20540
202-707-6590
Fax: 202-707-2076

The American Folklife Center at the Library of Congress has been a national advocate for the preservation and presentation of American folklife. The Center serves a varied constituency (state and local organizations, scholars, researchers, students, and the general public), maintains relations and coordinates programs with other federal agencies, and offers a wide range of programs and services. The Folklife Center has conducted or assisted with surveys or major field projects in many states. It conducts research projects based on the documentary collections of the Library of Congress. It sponsors a variety of conferences, workshops, concerts, and other events at the Library and elsewhere. The Archive houses more that 35,000 hours of audio recordings, controls more than 100,000 pages of manuscript materials, and maintains over 4,000 books, directories, and periodicals dealing with folk music and folklore. They can answer such questions as:

1) What information or recordings exist regarding early jazz?

2) Where can someone locate information on Native American architecture?

3) Where are recordings on Australian folk songs?

4) What data is there on the native crafts of Hawaii?

5) Are there videos available to educate students about various cultures?

Forest Service

U.S. Department of Agriculture
Public Affairs
201 14th and Independence Ave., SW
Washington, DC 20250
202-205-1760
Fax: 202-205-0885

 www: http://www.fs.fed.us

The nation's National Forests offer more than 114,300 miles of trails, a Scenic Byway System consisting of nearly 5,000 miles of highways in 32 states, 70 wild and scenic rivers covering nearly 3,500 miles and much more. *A Guide to Your National Forest* lists regional offices, several private and one Forest Service Interpretative Association, and a list of State Boards of Tourism where camping information may be obtained. They can answer such questions as:

1) What state forests in Maryland offer good sailing opportunities?

2) How far in advance must I reserve a campsite?

3) What is the best time of year to plan a camping trip in Tennessee?

4) Which rivers in North Carolina are recommended for canoeing or rafting?

5) How do I receive a listing of national scenic and historic trails?

Genealogy Research

Reference Services Branch
8th St. and Pennsylvania Ave., NW
Washington, DC 20408
202-501-5400
Fax: 202-501-7154

www: http://www.nara.gov
E-mail: inquire@nara.gov

The National Archives maintains the historically valuable records of the U.S. Government dating from the Revolutionary War era to the recent past. They preserve records and prepare finding aids to facilitate their use and makes records available for use in research rooms. They can provide assistance and training aids to help you with your research. They can answer such questions as:

1) Where can information be located regarding ship passenger arrival records?

2) What ship plans are available on World War II navy vessels?

3) How can military service and pension records be accessed?

4) How can people most easily trace their family history?

5) Where are prisoner-of-war records of the Civil War maintained?

Geographic Names Information

Branch of Geographic Names
U.S. Geological Survey (USGS)
National Center, MS 523
Reston, VA 22092
703-648-4544
Fax: 703-648-5644

www: http://www.usgs.gov/

The USGS Branch of Geographic Names maintains a national research, coordinating, and information center to which all problems and inquiries concerning domestic geographic names can be directed. This office compiles name information, manages a names data repository, maintains information files, and publishes materials on domestic geographic names. The Branch works on standardizing names within the Federal government by keeping track of all the names put on maps that the various government agencies publish. They also assist the Board of Geographic Names in resolving name problems, such as if a name is derogatory or the usage is conflicting. The USGS, in cooperation with the Board of Geographic Names, maintains the National Geographic Names Data Base and compiles The National Gazetteer of the United States of American on a state-by-state basis. They can answer such questions as:

1) Where are islands located referred to as "No Man's Island"?

2) Where can a researcher find the location of a town that no longer exists?

3) What background information exists on the name of a town?

4) What is a variant name for the town of Rocky Gap, Colorado?

5) What are the geographic coordinates for a particular location?

Geography and Map Division

Library of Congress
Washington, DC 20540
202-707-6277
Fax: 202-707-8531

E-mail: maps@loc.gov

The Geography and Map Division of the Library of Congress provides cartographic and geographic information for all parts of the world to the Congress, federal and local governments, the scholarly community, and to the general public. It is the largest and most comprehensive cartographic collection in the world, numbering almost 4 million maps, 51,000 atlases, and 8,000 reference works. The Division also has custody of over 350 globes, 2,000 three-dimensional plastic relief models, and a large number of cartographic materials in other formats. They can answer such questions as:

1) What maps are available for genealogists tracing a family history in Virginia?

2) What maps exist on colonial America?

3) Where can aerial photos be located in order to assess erosion and flood damage in a particular area?

4) Are there maps of old railroad lines available?

5) Where can information be located on Revolutionary War battlefields?

Bureau of Indian Affairs

Office of Public Affairs
U.S. Department of the Interior
18th and C Sts., NW
Mailstop 1340
Washington, DC 20240
202-208-3710
Fax: 202-501-1516

www: http://www.usgs.gov/doi/bureau'indian'affairs.html

The Bureau of Indian Affairs principal objectives are to encourage and assist Indian and Alaska Native people to manage their own affairs under the trust relationship with the federal government; to facilitate the full development of their human and natural resource potential; and to mobilize all aids for their advancement. The Bureau can provide you with a wide variety of information on Native Americans, the history of the Bureau and more. They have publications and fact sheets, and can refer you to other resources for more information. They can answer such questions as:

1) What tribes are currently recognized by the U.S.?

2) What are the demographics of American Indians?

3) Which state has the largest percentage of American Indians?

4) What are the labor force estimates by states for Native Americans?

5) How do Indian Tribes govern themselves?

Library of Congress

101 Independence Ave., SE
Washington, DC 20540
202-707-5522

 www: http://www.loc.gov

The Library of Congress is the national library of the United States, offering diverse materials for research including the world's most extensive collections in many areas such as American history, music, and law. They not only have books and periodicals, but also prints, photographs, films, music, and more. This office can direct you to the correct division within the Library. If your question requires extensive research and you cannot come to the Library, they have lists of freelance researchers to assist you for a fee. Many Divisions have their own databases to search citations or bibliographies or literature guides to help readers locate published materials on a particular subject. There may be a charge involved for some services, although many are free. To begin a search, researchers should first contact their local library, and then, proceed to the Library of Congress if they are unable to find adequate information. The Library can answer such questions as:

1) Where can one find information about medicinal plants?

2) What are some good reference sources for children's literature?

3) Where can information be found on medieval law?

4) How can books in braille be accessed?

5) Where can literature guides on a variety of science topics be found?

Manuscript Division

Library of Congress
Washington, DC 20540
202-287-5387

www: http://www.loc.gov

The Manuscript Division holds nearly 40 million items, including some of the greatest manuscript treasures of American history and culture. Among these are Jefferson's rough draft of the Declaration of Independence, James Madison's notes on the Federal Convention, George Washington's first inaugural address, the paper tape of the first telegraphic message, Abraham Lincoln's Gettysburg Address and second inaugural address, Alexander Graham Bell's first drawing of the telephone, and many more. The holdings encompass approximately 10,000 separate collections. The Reading Room is open only to qualified researchers. Only under exceptional circumstances are undergraduates permitted to consult manuscripts. The staff at the Division can answer such questions as:

1) Where can copies of George Washington's speeches be located for a biography of Washington?

2) Are records kept of nongovernmental organizations which have significantly affected American life, such as the NAACP?

3) Where is information held on the first Supreme Court justices?

4) How did the Declaration of Independence change from the rough draft version to the final copy?

5) What resources exist for a researcher studying the generals active in World War II?

Motion Picture Broadcasting and Recorded Sound Division

Library of Congress
Washington, DC 20540
202-707-5840
Fax: 202-707-2371

www: http://www.loc.gov

The Motion Picture Broadcasting and Recorded Sound Division has responsibility for the acquisition, cataloging, preservation, and service of the motion picture and television collections, including items on film, videotape, and videodisc. The Division has similar responsibilities for the Library's collections of sound recordings and radio programs. Viewing facilities are provided for those doing research of a specific nature, and must be scheduled well in advance. The reference staff answers written and telephone inquiries about its holdings. They can answer such questions as:

1) What World War II newsreels were produced in Germany?

2) What collections exist for films produced prior to 1915?

3) Where can a researcher look for information on silent films and their music?

4) Where can Afro-American folk music be found?

5) Are their recordings of authors, poets, and other artists reading their own works, such as Robert Frost?

National Park Service

Office of Public Inquiries
U.S. Department of the Interior
P.O. Box 37127
Washington, DC 20013-7127
202-208-4747

www: http://www.nps.gov

Along with other responsibilities, the Park Service administers 350 maintained areas in the National Park System, collects the National Register of Historic Places and a registry of natural sites, and manages the Urban Park and Recreation Recovery Program. It provides technical assistance in planning, acquisition and development of recreation resources, conducts surveys of historic buildings and engineering works, has available programs and resources for teachers, and administers a program in interagency archeological services. Information including brochures, maps, and a publications catalogue listing items ranging in price from $1 to $30 can be ordered from the Government Printing Office. The Office of Public Inquiries can refer you to other Park Service offices and can answer such questions as:

1) What archeological digs are currently in progress and where are they located?

2) What statistics are available on Park Service use, such as: total visits, visits by region and state, and overnight stays?

3) Where can I locate videos on historic people or national landmarks?

4) How do I find out whether or not my home is eligible for listing on the National Historic Register?

5) How can I receive a listing of the lesser known National Parks?

John F. Kennedy Center for the Performing Arts

Performing Arts Library
2700 F St., NW
Washington, DC 20566
202-416-8780

The Performing Arts Library is a joint project of the Library of Congress and the Kennedy Center, and offers information and reference assistance on dance, theater, opera, music, film, and broadcasting. The Performing Arts Library serves the research and information needs of the public, artists, and staff of the Center. The Library also identifies and locates the creative and resource materials necessary to develop new works and productions in the performing arts. Reference service is available by phone, in person, or by mail. They can answer such questions as:

1) How can an orchestral program of Irish composers be tailored for a young audience?

2) What information exists on different dance companies based in New York?

3) Is there information on what is required to start a record company?

4) Are there recordings of interviews or videotapes of famous actresses discussing their works?

5) Where can recordings of poetry readings be located?

Prints and Photographs Division

Library of Congress
James Madison Memorial Building, Room 337
First St. and Independence Ave., SW
Washington, DC 20540
202-707-6394
Fax: 202-707-6647

www: http://lcweb.loc.gov/rr/print/

The visual collections of the Library of Congress provide a record of people, places, and events in the United States and throughout the world. The Prints and Photographs Division has custody of more than 10 million images in a variety of forms and media: Architecture, Design, and Engineering collections, Documentary Photographs, Fine Prints, Master Photographs, Popular and Applied Graphic Art, and Posters. Researchers may consult the collections in the Prints and Photographs Reading Room. The Reading Room houses the general and special card catalogues, files of photoprint reference copies, and a limited collection of reference books. Reference specialists are available for assistance. The division will accept limited requests by letter, but the staff cannot make lengthy searches. They can answer such questions as:

1) How can someone obtain a print of the Wright Brothers first flight?

2) What photos taken by Brady exist on the Civil War?

3) Where can someone locate photos of various housing projects undertaken by the Work Projects Administration under President Roosevelt?

4) What material is available to study the architecture of Frank Lloyd Wright?

5) What references are there chronicling the history of political cartooning?

Rare Books and Special Collections

Library of Congress
Washington, DC 20540
202-707-5434

www: http://www.loc.gov

The Rare Book and Special Collections Division contains more than 300,000 volumes and 200,000 broadsides, pamphlets, theater playbills, title pages, prints, manuscripts, posters, and photographs acquired with various collections. The materials the Division houses have come into its custody for a variety of reasons: monetary value, importance in the history of printing, binding, association interest, or fragility. Reference assistance is offered by telephone, in person, and by mail. They can answer such questions as:

1) What information exists on the history of ballooning?

2) What books do you have that contain the Confederate States imprint?

3) What references do you have on the history of print making?

4) Do you have information researchers can study regarding Columbus' discovery of America?

5) Do you have 15th century illuminated manuscripts for art history research?

Rural Information Center

National Agricultural Library
U.S. Department of Agriculture (USDA)
10301 Baltimore Blvd.
Beltsville, MD 20705
301-504-5372
800-633-7701
Fax: 301-504-5181

www: http://www.nal.usda.gov/answers/answers.html
E-mail: ric@nal.usda.gov

The Rural Information Center is designed to provide information and referral services to local government officials, businesses, community organizations, and rural citizens working to maintain the vitality of America's rural areas. The Center provides customized information products to specific inquiries, refers users to organizations or experts in the field, performs database searches, furnishes bibliographies, identifies current USDA research and Cooperative Extension System programs, and assists users in accessing the National Agricultural Libraries' extensive collection.

There is a cost recovery fee for photocopying articles and searches. They can answer such questions as:

1) Which organizations focus on rural health issues?

2) What resources for the historic preservation of farmland are available in rural areas?

3) How can tourism be promoted in small towns?

4) What are some examples of the more innovative economic development projects in rural communities?

5) What rural organizations focus specifically on research and development?

Science and Technology Division

Library of Congress
Washington, DC 20540
202-707-5639

www: http://www.loc.gov

The Science and Technology Division's collection contains 3.5 million books, nearly 60,000 journals, and 3.7 million technical reports. The collections include such treasures as first editions of Copernicus and Newton and the personal papers of the Wright Brothers and Alexander Graham Bell. The Division has primary responsibility for providing reference and bibliographic services and for recommending acquisitions in the broad areas of science and technology. Reference services are provided to users in person, by telephone, and by mail. Indirect reference service is provided through bibliographic guides (Tracer Bullets) and research reports prepared by Division subject specialists and reference librarians. Copies of reference guides are available at no charge. They can answer such questions as:

1) Where can one begin looking for information on lasers and their applications?

2) What are some good sources of information on volcanoes?

3) What resources exist on extraterrestrial life?

4) Where could someone find sources for information on medicinal plants?

5) How would one go about creating a hologram?

Women's Bureau Clearinghouse

U.S. Department of Labor
200 Constitution Ave., NW
Room S3306
Washington, DC 20210
800-827-5335
202-219-6631
Fax: 202-219-5529

www: http://www.dol.gov/dolwb/dol
E-mail: wb_wwc@dol.gov

The Women's Bureau Clearinghouse was designed and established to assist employers in identifying the most appropriate policies for responding to the dependent care needs of employees seeking to balance their dual responsibilities. They can also provide information on women's issues, as well as work force issues that affect women. They can offer information and guidance in areas such as women-owned businesses, women workers, alternative work schedules, dependent care issues, and much more. They also have publications and other information available, much of which is free. They can answer such questions as:

1) What are some elder care program options?

2) What is the earning difference between men and women?

3) How does flex time work in companies similar to mine?

4) What are some alternate work schedules and how do they work?

5) What literature and other resources are available on employer-supported child care?

Statistics

National Agricultural Statistics Service

USDA South Bldg.
U.S. Department of Agriculture (USDA)
Washington, DC 20250
202-720-3896
Fax: 202-690-1311

www: http://www.usda.gov/nass/

The National Agricultural Statistics Service collects data on crops, livestock, poultry, dairy, chemical use, prices, and labor, and publishes the official USDA state and national estimates through its Agricultural Statistics Board. There are nearly 400 reports annually covering domestic agriculture, such as estimates of production, stocks, inventories, prices, disposition, utilization, farm numbers and land, and other factors. They provide national profiles gathered from regular surveys of thousands of farmers, ranchers, and agribusinesses that voluntarily provide data on a confidential basis. Publications are available and range from free to $12. They can answer such questions as:

1) How has the use of a specific chemical for crop growth changed over the past five years?

2) Has the size of farms increased or decreased over the past ten years?

3) What statistics exist on wildlife damage to crops?

4) How has the weekly crop weather affected crop growth?

5) What data is there on livestock slaughter?

Federal Aviation Administration

Office of Public Affairs
800 Independence Ave., SW
Washington, DC 20591
202-366-4000

www: http://www.dot.gov
E-mail: gramick@postmaster2.dot.gov

The Federal Aviation Administration (FAA) is the starting place for any information on airlines, airports, and aircraft. The FAA regulates air commerce, develops civil aeronautics, installs and operates airports, conducts aeronautic research, and provides guidance and policy on accident prevention in general aviation. They keep statistics on air travel, accidents, and more. There are free publications on airline careers, aviation, and airplanes, as well as videos and curriculum guides. They can answer such questions as:

1) Which airlines had the worst on time rate for a given month?

2) What videos are available on aviation?

3) What is some historical information on women in aviation?

4) What are some statistics on air traffic accidents?

5) What methods are used to reduce the noise level of new aircraft?

National Clearinghouse for Census Data Services

Administrative Customer Service Division
Bureau of the Census
Washington, DC 20233
301-457-4100
Fax: 301-457-4714

www: http://www.census.gov

The National Clearinghouse for Census Data Services provides a referral service for persons who need assistance in obtaining

Census Bureau data or in using Census Bureau products. This assistance ranges from market research using census data to tape copying or microcomputer services. The Clearinghouse includes organizations that provide services for accessing and using economic data and information from the Census Bureau's 1990 Census TIGER geographic database. They can answer such questions as:

1) How can I update my business's mailing list using 1990 census statistics?

2) How can the census help me trace my genealogical history?

3) What is the TIGER geographic database, and how can I use it?

4) Which products are available on CD-ROM?

5) Does the Bureau have an on-line data service?

Census Information on Business

Bureau of the Census
U.S. Department of Commerce
Washington, DC 20233
301-457-4100
Fax: 301-457-4714

www: http://www.census.gov

The Bureau of the Census is a statistical agency that collects, tabulates, and publishes a wide variety of statistical data about the people and the economy of our nation. The Bureau makes available statistical results of its censuses, surveys, and other programs to the public through printed reports, computer tape, CD-ROMs, microfiche, and more. It also produces statistical compendia, catalogues, guides, and directories that are useful in locating information on specific subjects. A fee is charged for some of the information and searches. They can answer such questions as:

1) What is the percentage of people who have a bachelor's degree in a particular state?

2) What percent of women in the U.S. had a child last year?

3) What is the total amount of water area in a given state?

4) What are some statistics available on city government expenditures?

5) What are the 10 fastest growing occupations?

Crime Statistics

Law Enforcement Support Section
Federal Bureau of Investigation
Gallery Row Bldg.
Washington, DC 20535
202-324-5015

 www: http://www.fbi.gov

The Law Enforcement Support Section of the Federal Bureau of Investigation collects statistics for many towns with over 10,000 people, and can provide you with information such as the number of murders, robberies, assaults, burglaries, auto thefts, and more, although they do not rank cities. Many libraries carry their annual report, *Crime In The U.S.*, for which there is a cost. They can run a search on their database for specific information, although there is a fee assessed for this service. They can answer questions such as:

1) When weapons are involved in a crime, which ones are most frequently used?

2) How has the rate of auto theft in the U.S. changed over the past five years?

3) Is Washington, DC still the murder capitol of the U.S.?

4) Have the number of murders committed changed since the death penalty was reinstituted?

5) What is the difference in the rate of burglaries from small towns to major metropolitan areas?

Economics: National and Regional

Bureau of Economic Analysis
U.S. Department of Commerce
1441 L St., NW
Washington, DC 20230
202-606-9900
Fax: 202-606-5310

www: http://bea.doc.gov

The Bureau of Economic Analysis (BEA) provides information on national and regional economics. BEA collects basic information on such key issues as economic growth, inflation, regional development, and the nation's role in the world economy. It distributes a number of publications that measure, analyze, and forecast economic trends, which are available on recorded messages, online through the Economic Bulletin Board, and in BEA reports. They can answer such questions as:

1) What is the average per capita income in the United States?

2) Will the rate of inflation increase or decrease over the next five years, and by what percent?

3) What percentage of the Gross National Product (GNP) does the government spend on health care?

4) How does the United States' national unemployment rate compare to that of other industrialized countries?

5) What was the unemployment rate in Pennsylvania from 1989 to 1993?

Educational Research

Office of Educational Research and Improvement's
  Information Service
U.S. Department of Education
Education Information Branch
555 New Jersey Ave., NW
Washington, DC 20208-5641
800-424-1616
Fax: 202-219-1694

www: http://www.ed.gov

The Education Information Branch staff specialists can provide information on topics such as early childhood education, elementary and secondary education, higher education, adult and vocational education, education finance, longitudinal statistical studies, and special education. They have publications and reports, many of which are free. They can answer such questions as:

1) What statistics are there on the number of students who receive loans, grants, and work/study assistance from state sources?

2) What are the statistics on private postsecondary education, such as enrollment, earned degrees conferred, and full and part-time faculty members and their salaries?

3) What information is available on how to choose a school for a child and what factors make a school a good one?

4) How can parents help their children become better readers?

5) What are the enrollment outcomes for recent master's and bachelor's degree recipients?

Fishery Statistics Division

Office of Research and Environmental Information
National Marine Fisheries Service
National Oceanic and Atmospheric Administration
U.S. Department of Commerce
1335 East-West Highway, Room 12362
Silver Spring, MD 20910
301-713-2328
Fax: 301-713-4137

www: http://remora.ssp.nips.gov/mrfss

The Fisheries Statistics Division publishes statistical bulletins on marine recreational fishing and commercial fishing, and on the manufacture and commerce of fishery products. This Division has several annual and biannual reports available. They can answer such questions as:

1) How many fish were imported in a year, and what kind?

2) What is the most popular fish to export?

3) What kinds of fish are frozen?

4) What statistics exist on processed fish?

5) How many fish were caught by weekend fishermen?

Clearinghouse on Health Indexes

National Center for Health Statistics
U.S. Department of Health and Human Services
Public Health Service
6525 Belcrest Rd.
Hyattsville, MD 20782
301-436-8500

www: http://www.cdc.gov/nchswww/nchshome.htm

The National Center for Health Statistics provides information assistance in the development of health measures to health researchers, administrators, and planners. The Clearinghouse's definition of a health index is a measure that summarizes data from two or more components and purports to reflect the health status of an individual or defined group. Services provided to users include annotated bibliographies and reference and referral service. A publications catalogue is available, with items ranging in price from free to $20. They can answer such questions as:

1) What are the characteristics of persons with and without health care coverage?

2) What type of health care is generally provided to adolescents?

3) What method of contraception is used most frequently in the U.S.?

4) What data exists on the current living arrangements of women of childbearing ages in the U.S.?

5) What survey data exists on the firearm mortality rate among children?

United States International Trade Commission

Office of Industries
500 E St., SW
Washington, DC 20436
202-205-3296
Fax: 202-205-3161

 www: http://www.usitc.gov/

The Office of Industries at the U.S. International Trade Commission has experts assigned to every commodity imported into the U.S. These experts are responsible for investigation of the customs laws of the United States and foreign countries, the volume of imports in comparison with domestic production, the effects relating to competition of foreign industries, and all other factors affecting competition between articles of the U.S. and imported articles. They are knowledgeable about the domestic and foreign industry, and have statistical and factual information. They also have information regarding the tariff schedules. There is no charge for this information. They can answer such questions as:

1) What is the rate of duty for a product from a particular country?

2) What is the rate of import-export, the size of the market, and the major producers of women's sweaters?

3) How much of a product is exported and what is the size of the potential market for that product?

4) What happens if someone suspects an imported article is being subsidized or sold at less then fair value?

5) What can a company do if they feel they are being unfairly affected by import trade?

Justice Statistics Clearinghouse

Bureau of Justice Statistics
U.S. Department of Justice
Box 6000
Rockville, MD 20850
800-732-3277
Fax: 301-251-5212

www: http://ncjrs.aspensys.com:81/ncjrshome.html
E-mail: askncjrs@aspensys.com

The Bureau of Justice Statistics (BJS) supports this Clearing-house for those seeking crime and criminal justice data. In addition to distributing BJS publications, the Clearinghouse responds to statistics requests by offering document database searches, statistics information packages, referrals, and other related products and services. They can answer such questions as:

1) What is the annual national estimate of crime against persons and households?

2) What are the characteristics of victims?

3) In what ways are juveniles handled differently from adults in the criminal justice system?

4) How prevalent is organized crime?

5) What is the recidivism rate, and when criminals are rearrested, with what crimes are they normally charged?

Labor Statistics Clearinghouse

Office of Publications
Bureau of Labor Statistics
U.S. Department of Labor
2 Massachusetts Ave., NE, Room 2863
Washington, DC 20212

202-606-7828
Fax: 202-606-7890

www: http://stats.bls.gov
E-mail: labstat.helpdesk@bls.gov

The Bureau of Labor Statistics (BLS) is the principal data-gathering agency of the federal government in the field of labor economics. The Bureau collects, processes, analyzes, and disseminates data relating to employment, unemployment, and other characteristics of the labor force; prices and consumer expenditures; wages, other worker compensation, and industrial relations; productivity; economic growth and employment projections; and occupational safety and health. This office can also provide you with a release schedule for BLS major economic indicators and the recorded message number. BLS can refer you to experts within the Bureau who can answer your specific question, provide you with historical information, and refer you to tables and charts for data. The BLS has publications, periodicals, magnetic tapes, diskettes, and more for sale. They can answer questions such as:

1) What are the employment statistics and the outlook for a particular occupation?

2) What is the unemployment rate for a state?

3) What is the current wage for a word processor in Seattle, and what benefits are normally offered with such a position?

4) What is the employment projection for a specific job?

5) What is the consumer/producer price index, and how has it changed over time?

Current Events and Homework (Guide to CRS Products)

Whether you are struggling with a school term paper or are eager to impress your boss by obtaining the latest statistics and analysis on practically any subject, help is right at hand. Few people, even those of us living in Washington, DC, are aware of all the studies generated around the clock by a division of the Library of Congress. Approximately 500 PhDs working at the Congressional Research Service (CRS) grind out these reports on almost any topic imaginable and these studies are constantly made available to all 525 members of Congress.

Your U.S. Representative and Senators have immediate access to over 10,000 reports on current events through a computerized online network. And a phone call or letter to one of your legislators is all it takes for you to tap into this rich information resource. To get copies of these reports, you must go through the office of your U.S. Representative or Senator. There is no charge for these concise reports which are unquestionably the "best information value" because the material is prepared by other experts in federal government agencies as well as from the private sector. Researchers, students of all ages, marketing reps, entrepreneurs, and ordinary citizens should take advantage of this information gold mine.

The Reason Why These Reports Are Constantly Updated

If a congressional committee plans an investigation, for example, on the home health care situation, the CRS specialists will complete a background study and their findings will be available to anyone in the public domain. If a lawmaker is concerned about the situation in Poland, these experts will prepare a complete analysis of the situation and when warranted, will update it daily as events change. If a Congressman is going to address an industry group on a subject like "The Economics of Export Promotion," most likely his staff is going to rely on the information generated by CRS. They can tap into this database and find a 10 to 30-page report written by an expert who spends much of his or her career doing nothing but studying this subject.

CRS Reports Are Easy to Understand ... They're Written for Congressmen

Although these studies are prepared by PhDs, you don't have to worry about understanding them. These reports summarize historical context as well as fast breaking developments and are presented in layman's language. Also, the CRS adheres to its non-partisan mission to serve all members of Congress. One rationale for getting CRS studies is to see what material legislators and their staff are using as background information, whether it be for speeches or policy decisions. In addition to covering most business or student subject areas, these reports are an easy way to stay current on complex world events and issues of peripheral concern.

How to Get a Report

Getting your hands on a half a dozen reports can be easy. Just remember you cannot get studies directly from CRS but only by contacting a Member's Washington or district office. It is important to have the proper title or product number of the CRS report that you are requesting. If you don't receive copies in a week or two, a follow-up phone call may be necessary. Keep in mind that helping constituents in this way is a welcome task for an elected official, especially when a legislator's reelection is close at hand. If you find one office uncooperative, try another. Remember we each have two Senators and one Representative. You can contact all legislators in Washington, DC by calling the Capitol Hill Switchboard at 202-224-3121.

Although these reports are available through your U.S. Representative or Senator, you may be able to contact the author of the report directly at: Congressional Research Service, Library of Congress, Washington, DC 20540, 202-707-5700. Also, after reading the reports or issue briefs, you may want to follow up and check with the CRS specialist to track down any of his or her articles which have been published in trade publications. Since the Congressional Research Service is only in the habit of responding to requests from Congress, it is especially important to treat CRS experts with respect.

Federal Government Directory Assistance

Do you know help is out there but you don't know where to turn? Contact your Federal Information Center. They can give you phone numbers and information to get you started in your search. They have a database of programs which they can access to direct you to resources and services to answer all of your questions. They cover topics such as:

- camping
- passports
- travel
- job training
- college assistance
- legal help
- health issues
- discrimination
- diet and nutrition

Contact the Federal Information Center at 800-688-9889.

Your State Can Help

The federal government has thousands of programs to help people, and so does your state. All states have housing programs to help people become homeowners; financial assistance programs to pay for college; business information or services to help small businesses get started. This is just the tip of the iceberg. How do you tap into these services? Contact your state government information operator (see list below). They will be able to give you phone numbers of various offices to get you started on your search. Remember, you have a Representative in the State Government, who should also be able to help you maneuver through the various state programs.

State Information Operators

Alabama
334-242-8000

Alaska
907-465-2111

Arizona
602-542-4900

Arkansas
501-682-3000

California
916-657-9900

Colorado
303-866-5000

Connecticut
203-240-0222

Delaware
302-739-4000

Florida
904-488-1234

Georgia
404-656-2000

Hawaii
808-586-2211

Idaho
208-334-2411

Illinois
217-782-2000

Indiana
317-232-1000

Iowa
515-281-5011

Kansas
913-296-0111

Kentucky
502-564-3130

Louisiana
504-342-6600

Maine
207-582-9500

Maryland
410-555-1212

Massachusetts
617-722-2000

Michigan
517-373-1837

Minnesota
612-296-6013

Mississippi
601-359-1000

Missouri
314-751-2000

Montana
406-444-2511

Nebraska
402-471-2311

Nevada
702-687-5000

New Hampshire
603-271-1110

New Jersey
609-292-2121

New Mexico
505-827-4011

New York
518-474-2121

North Carolina
919-733-1110

North Dakota
701-328-2000

Ohio
614-466-2000

Oklahoma
405-521-2011

Oregon
503-378-3111

Pennsylvania
800-932-0784

Rhode Island
401-277-2000

South Carolina
803-734-1000

South Dakota
605-773-3011

Tennessee
615-741-3011

Texas
512-463-4630

Utah
801-538-3000

Vermont
802-828-1110

Virginia
804-786-0000

Washington
360-753-5000

West Virginia
304-558-3456

Wisconsin
608-266-2211

Wyoming
307-777-7011

Help is as Close as your County

Are you having trouble in your garden? Trying to figure out your finances? Is learning to sew or cook better a goal for you? Teaching your kids how to care for a pet? County Cooperative Extension Service is located in almost every county across the United States, and can answer all of these questions and more. Many have special hotlines that can help you with all your gardening needs. Programs and services vary from county to county, but most Cooperative Extension offices provide services such as:

- financial counseling
- nutrition information
- pest control
- business services
- cooking and sewing classes
- information on how to choose a day care
- household hints
- consumer issues

Contact your nearest Cooperative Extension Service office by looking in the blue pages of your phone directory, or by contacting the main state office from the list below.

County Cooperative Extension Offices

Alabama

Dr. Gaines Smith, Director
Alabama Cooperative Extension Service
109 A Duncan Hall
Auburn University
Auburn, AL 36849-5612
334-844-4444

Dr. Thomas Harris, Director
Cooperative Extension Program
U.S. Department of Agriculture
Tuskegee University
Marson and Mayberry Hall
Tuskegee, AL 36088-1731
334-727-8806

Alaska
Hollis D. Hall, Director
Alaska Cooperative Extension
University of Alaska Fairbanks
P.O. Box 756180
Fairbanks, AK 99775-6180
907-474-7246

Arizona
Jim Christenson, Director
Cooperative Extension Office
University of Arizona
Forbes 301
Tucson, AZ 85721
602-621-7205

Arkansas
David Foster, Director
Cooperative Extension Service
P.O. Box 391
Little Rock, AR 72203
501-671-2000

Dr. Mazo Price, Director
Cooperative Extension Service
1200 N. University
Box 4005
University of Arkansas at Pine Bluff
Pine Bluff, AR 71601
501-543-8131

California
Dr. W.R. Gomes, Vice President
University of California
Division of Agriculture and Natural Resources
300 Lakeside Drive, 6th Floor
Oakland, CA 94612-3560
510-987-0060

Colorado
Milan Rewets, Director
Colorado State University
Cooperative Extension
1 Administration Building
Fort Collins, CO 80523
970-491-6281

Connecticut
Associate Director
Cooperative Extension System
University of Connecticut
1376 Storrs Road
Storrs, CT 06269-4036
203-486-4125

Delaware
Dr. Richard E. Fowler, Director
Cooperative Extension
131 Townsend Hall
University of Delaware
Newark, DE 19717-1303
302-831-2504

Dr. Starlene Taylor
Assistant Administrator
Delaware State College
Cooperative Extension Service
1200 N. DuPont Highway
Dover, DE 19901
302-739-5157

District of Columbia
Clinton Turner, Acting Director
Cooperative Extension Service
University of the District of Columbia
901 Newton Street, NE
Washington, DC 20017
202-274-6900

Florida
John T. Woeste, Director
Florida Cooperative Extension Service
P.O. Box 110210
University of Florida
Gainesville, FL 32611-0210
904-392-1761

Lawrence Carter, Director
Cooperative Extension Service
215 Perry Paige Building
Florida A&M University
Tallahassee, FL 32307
904-599-3546

Georgia
Wayne Jordon, Director
Cooperative Extension Service
University of Georgia
1111 Conner Hall
Athens, GA 30602
706-542-3824

Dr. Fred Harrison, Jr., Director
Cooperative Extension Service
P.O. Box 4061
Fort Valley State College
Fort Valley, GA 31030
912-825-6269

Hawaii
Dr. Po'Yung Lai, Assistant Director
Cooperative Extension Service

3050 Maile Way
Honolulu, HI 96822
808-956-8397

Idaho

Dr. LeRoy D. Luft, Director
Cooperative Extension System
College of Agriculture
University of Idaho
Moscow, ID 83844-2338
208-885-6639

Illinois

Donald Uchtmann, Director
University of Illinois
Cooperative Extension Service
122 Mumford Hall
1301 W. Gregory Drive
Urbana, IL 61801
217-333-2660

Indiana

Dr. Wadsworth, Director
1140 AGAD
CES Administration
Purdue University
West Lafayette, IN 47907-1140
317-494-8489

Iowa

Dr. Nolan R. Hartwig, Director
Cooperative Extension Service
315 Boardshear
Iowa State University
Ames, IA 50011
515-294-9434

Kansas

Mark Johnson, Director
Cooperative Extension Service
Kansas State University

114 Waters Hall
Manhattan, KS 66506
913-532-7137

Kentucky
Dr. Absher, Director
Cooperative Extension Service
310 W.P. Garrigus Building
University of Kentucky
Lexington, KY 40546
606-257-1846

Dr. Harold Benson, Director
Kentucky State University
Cooperative Extension Program
Frankfort, KY 40601
502-227-5905

Louisiana
Dr. Jack Bagent, Director
Cooperative Extension Service
Louisiana State University
P.O. Box 25100
Baton Rouge, LA 70894-5100
504-388-4141

Dr. Adell Brown, Assistant Administrator
Cooperative Extension Program
Southern University and A&M College
P.O. Box 10010
Baton Rouge, LA 70813
504-771-2242

Maine
Vaughn Holyoke, Director
Cooperative Extension Service
University of Maine
5741 Libby Hall, Room 102
Orono, ME 04469-5741
207-581-3188

Maryland

Dr. James Wade
Regional Directors Office
Cooperative Extension Service
Room 1200, Simons Hall
University of Maryland
College Park, MD 20742
301-405-2907

Dr. Henry Brookes, Administrator
Cooperative Extension Service
UMES
Princess Anne, MD 21853
410-651-6206

Massachusetts

Dr. John Gerber, Associate Director
212C Stockbridge Hall
University of Massachusetts
Amherst, MA 01003
413-545-4800

Michigan

Gail Emig, Director
Michigan State University Extension
Room 108, Agriculture Hall
Michigan State University
East Lansing, MI 48824
517-355-2308

Minnesota

Katherine Fennelly
Minnesota Extension Service
University of Minnesota
240 Coffey Hall
1420 Eckles Avenue
St. Paul, MN 55108
612-624-1222

Mississippi
Danny Cheatham, Director
Cooperative Extension Service
Mississippi State University
Box 9601
Mississippi State, MS 39762
601-325-3034

LeRoy Davis, Dean
P.O. Box 690
Alcorn Cooperative Extension Program
Lorman, MS 39096
601-877-6128

Missouri
Ronald J. Turner, Director
Cooperative Extension Service
University of Missouri
309 University Hall
Columbia, MO 65211
314-882-7754

Dr. Dyremple Marsh, Director
Cooperative Extension Service
Lincoln University
110A Allen Hall
P.O. Box 29
Jefferson City, MO 65102-0029
314-681-5550

Montana
Andrea Pagenkopf
Vice Probost for Outreach and Director of Extension
212 Montana Hall
Montana State University
Bozeman, MT 59717
406-994-4371

Nebraska
Randall Cantrell, Director
University of Nebraska

S.E. Research and Extension Center
211 Mussehl Hall, East Campus
Lincoln, NE 68583
402-472-3674

Nevada
Bernard M. Jones, Director
Nevada Cooperative Extension
University of Nevada, Reno
Mail Stop 189
Reno, NV 89557-0106
702-784-1614

New Hampshire
Peter J. Horne
Dean and Director
UNH Cooperative Extension
59 College Road
Taylor Hall
Durham, NH 03824
603-862-1520

New Jersey
Mr. Helsel, Director
Rutgers Cooperative Extension
P.O. Box 231
New Brunswick, NJ 08903
908-932-9306

New Mexico
William Lacy, Director
Cornell Cooperative Extension
276 Roberts Hall
Ithaca, NY 14853
607-255-2237

North Carolina
Dr. Jon F. Ort, Director
Cooperative Extension Service
North Carolina State University
Box 7602

Raleigh, NC 27695
919-515-2811

Dr. Daniel Godfrey, Director
Cooperative Extension Program
North Carolina A&T State University
P.O. Box 21928
Greensboro, NC 27420-1928
910-334-7956

North Dakota
Sharon Anderson, Director
Cooperative Extension Service
North Dakota State University
Morrill Hall, Room 315
Box 5437
Fargo, ND 58105
701-231-8944

Ohio
Keith Smith, Director
OSU Extension
2120 Fiffe Road
Agriculture Administration Building
Columbus, OH 43210
614-292-6181

Oklahoma
Dr. Ray Campbell
Associate Director
Oklahoma Cooperative Extension Service
Oklahoma State University
139 Agriculture Hall
Stillwater, OK 74078
405-744-5398

Dr. Ocleris Simpston, Director
Cooperative Research and Extension
P.O. Box 730
Langston University

Langston, OK 73050
405-466-3836

Oregon
Lyla Houglum, Director
Oregon State Extension Service Administration
Oregon State University
Ballard Extension Hall #101
Corvallis, OR 97331-3606
503-737-2711

Pennsylvania
James Starling, Director
Pennsylvania State University
Room 201, A.G. Administration
University Park, PA 16802
814-863-3438

Rhode Island
Kathleen Mallon, Director
Cooperative Extension Education Center
University of Rhode Island
East Alumni Avenue
Kingston, RI 02881-0804
401-874-2900

South Carolina
Carol Culbertson, Director
Clemson University
Cooperative Extension Service
P.O. Box 995
Pickens, SC 29671
803-868-2810

Director
Cooperative Extension Service
P.O. Box 8103
South Carolina State University
Orangeburg, SC 29117
803-536-8928

South Dakota
Mylo Hellickson, Director
SDSU
Box 2207D
AG Hall 154
Brookings, SD 57007
605-688-4792

Tennessee
Billy G. Hicks, Dean
Agricultural Extension Service
University of Tennessee
P.O. Box 1071
Knoxville, TN 37901-1071
423-974-7114

Cherry Lane Zon Schmittou, Extension Leader
Davidson County Agricultural Service
Tennessee State University
800 Second Avenue N., Suite 3
Nashville, TN 37201-1084
615-254-8734

Texas
Dr. Zerle Carpenter, Director
Texas Agricultural Extension Service
Texas A&M University
Administration Building, Room 106
College Station, TX 77843-7101
409-845-7967

Dr. Linda Willis, Director
Cooperative Extension Program
P.O. Box 3059
Prairie View, TX 77446-2867
409-857-2023

Utah
Dr. Robert Gilliland
Vice President for Extension and Continuing Education
Utah State University Extension

Logan, UT 84322-4900
801-797-2200

Vermont
Larry Forchier, Dean
Division of Agriculture, Natural Resources,
and Extension
University of Vermont
601 Main
Burlington, VT 05401-3439
802-656-2990

Virginia
Dr. Clark Jones, Interim Director
Virginia Cooperative Extension
Virginia Tech
Blacksburg, VA 24061-0402
540-231-5299

Lorenza Lyons, Director
Cooperative Extension
Virginia State University
Petersburg, VA 23806
804-524-5961

Washington
Harry Burcalow, Director
Cooperative Extension
411 Hulbert
Washington State University
Pullman, WA 99164-6230
509-335-2811

West Virginia
Bob Maxwell, Director
Cooperative Extension
305 Stewart Hall
P.O. Box 6201
West Virginia University
Morgantown, WV 26506-6201
304-293-5691

Wisconsin
Aeyse Somersan, Director
432 North Lake Street, Room 601
Madison, WI 53706
608-262-7966

Wyoming
Edna McBreen, Director
CES
University of Wyoming
Box 3354
Laramie, WY 82071
307-766-3567

Index

A

B

D

E

F

G

H

J

K

L

M

N

O

P

U

V

W